NETWORKING EUROPE AND NEW COMMUNITIES OF
INTERPRETATION (1400–1600)

NEW COMMUNITIES OF INTERPRETATION
CONTEXTS, STRATEGIES, AND PROCESSES OF RELIGIOUS
TRANSFORMATION IN LATE MEDIEVAL AND EARLY MODERN EUROPE

VOLUME 4

General Editors
Sabrina Corbellini, *Rijksuniversiteit Groningen*
John Thompson, *Queen's University Belfast*

Editorial Board
Pavlína Rychterová, *Österreichischen Akademie der Wissenschaften*
Ian Johnson, *University of St Andrews*
Géraldine Veysseyre, *Institut de recherche et d'histoire des textes*
Chiara Lastraioli, *Centre d'Études Supérieures de la Renaissance*
Pawel Kras, *John Paul II Catholic University of Lublin*
Marina Gazzini, *Universita degli Studi di Milano Statale*
Marco Mostert, *Universiteit Utrecht*
Rafael M. Pérez García, *Universidad de Sevilla*

Networking Europe and New Communities of Interpretation (1400–1600)

Edited by
MARGRIET HOOGVLIET,
MANUEL F. FERNÁNDEZ CHAVES, *AND*
RAFAEL M. PÉREZ GARCÍA

BREPOLS

© 2023, Brepols Publishers n.v., Turnhout, Belgium.

All rights reserved. No part of this publication may be reproduced, stored in a retrieval system, or transmitted, in any form or by any means, electronic, mechanical, photocopying, recording, or otherwise without the prior permission of the publisher.

D/2023/0095/110
ISBN 978-2-503-60621-7
eISBN 978-2-503-60622-4
DOI 10.1484/M.NCI-EB.5.133694

Printed in the EU on acid-free paper.

Table of Contents

List of Illustrations   7

Introduction. Networking Europe and New Communities of Interpretation
Margriet Hoogvliet, Manuel F. Fernández Chaves, and Rafael M. Pérez García   9

Transnational History and Social Network Theory. A Brief Introduction to Theory and Terminology
Suzan Folkerts and Margriet Hoogvliet   19

European Connections

Francisco de Osuna's *Tercer Abecedario Espiritual* and the Medieval Mystical Tradition in Western Europe
Rafael M. Pérez García   39

The Sixteenth-Century Polish Protestant Martyrology and its Latin Sources
Mirosława Hanusiewicz-Lavallee   53

(Re-)Constructing a Community of Readers. The Image of the Laity in Books Printed in Delft (1477–1500)
Marcin Polkowski   71

Exiles, Diasporas, and Migrants

Spanish Merchants and Dissidents outside Spain in the Sixteenth Century
Ignacio García Pinilla   101

The Library of the Pious House and Chapel of Saint Andrew of the Flemish Nation in Seville under Philip V
Manuel F. Fernández Chaves   119

Mobility and Merchants

Business is Business. Book Merchants, Printers, and the Spanish Inquisition during the Sixteenth Century
Natalia Maillard Álvarez   171

The Colony of the Republic of Ragusa Merchants in Belgrade in the Sixteenth Century and their Printing Press
Vladimir Abramović   201

The Spiritual Road. European Networks and Pilgrim Travels from Northern France and the Low Countries to Rome, Venice, and Santiago (Late Fifteenth–Early Sixteenth Century)
Margriet Hoogvliet   215

List of Illustrations

Manuel F. Fernández Chaves

Figure 7.1. Number of books by religious authors (%). Source: Seville, Arch. Hist. Prov. Prot. de Sev., Notarial Protocols of Seville, file 14674, fols 662ʳ–64ᵛ. 129

Figure 7.2. Origin of the religious authors (%). Source: Seville, Arch. Hist. Prov. Prot. de Sev., Notarial Protocols of Seville, file 14674, fols 662ʳ–664ᵛ. 130

Figure 7.3. Classification by subject (%). Source: Seville, Arch. Hist. Prov. Prot. de Sev., Notarial Protocols of Seville, file 14674, fols 662ʳ–64ᵛ. 134

Vladimir Abramović

Figure 9.1. Hortulus animae — Ортус аниме (Belgrade, 1567). Archive HAZU, Zbirka kodeksa, sig. III a 25. Image taken from *Istorija Beograda*, I, p. 457, with permission from IP Prosveta AD. All rights reserved. 207

Figure 9.2. Tetraevangelion (Belgrade: Trojan Gundulić, 1552), the beginning of the Gospel of Matthew (frontispiece). Belgrade City Museum, inv. num. I1 1196. With permission from Belgrade City Museum. All rights reserved. 209

Figure 9.3. Tetraevangelion (Belgrade: Trojan Gundulić, 1552), afterword and colophon. Belgrade City Museum, inv. num. I1 1196. With permission from Belgrade City Museum. All rights reserved. 210

Margriet Hoogvliet

Map 10.1. Jean de Tournai's itinerary from Valenciennes to Venice (1488–1489): Valenciennes — Brussels — Antwerp — 's-Hertogenbosch — Cleves — Cologne — on board a river barge up the river Rhine to Mainz — Worms — Speyer — Ulm — Kempten — Landeck [probably taking the old Roman *Via Claudia Augusta*] — Trento — Verona — Bologna — Florence 223

	— Siena — Rome — Spoleto — Ancona — over sea to Cesenatico — Ravenna — Venice. Credit: Geodienst, University of Groningen.	
Map 10.2.	The itinerary of Jehan de Zeilbeke's 1512 pilgrimage to Santiago de Compostela: Comines (Komen) — Nieuwpoort — Portsmouth — Dartsmouth — Ribadeo (*Rimerres*) — Santiago de Compostela — A Coruña — Nieuwpoort — Comines. Credit: Geodienst, University of Groningen.	225
Map 10.3.	Canon Pierre Mesenge and his party's itinerary to Venice (1508): Rouen — Évreux — Orléans — probably using a part of the *Via Agrippa* to Lyon — the *Via francigena* to Val di Susa — Turin or Genoa — Pavia — aboard a river barge over the river Po to Venice. Credit: Geodienst, University of Groningen.	228

MARGRIET HOOGVLIET, MANUEL F.
FERNÁNDEZ CHAVES, AND RAFAEL M.
PÉREZ GARCÍA

Introduction

*Networking Europe and New Communities of Interpretation**

> Hoc tibi nunc quoque affirmare ausim, si huc uenias, fore, ut, quicquid propter hanc rem opere sumpseris, magnis te premiis uberrimaque mercede redemisse dicas.
>
> (I have no hesitation in assuring you that if you come here, whatever effort you had to make to do so, you will say that it has well been worth the expense and it has brought you valuable rewards.)[1]

These words were hastily penned in Pavia in the summer or autumn of 1472 by the Dutch humanist Rudolph Agricola, born in the small hamlet of Baflo near Groningen, in a letter to his friend Johannes Vredewold, who was at that point still living in the city of Groningen. Agricola was studying

---

* The editors would like to express their gratitude to Susanne de Jong and Marco Mostert for their invaluable corrections and assistance in preparing this book for publication.

1 Agricola, *Letters*, 66–67.

> **Margriet Hoogvliet** • is a specialist in the field of biblical and religious reading cultures of lay people living and working in the towns of late medieval France.
>
> **Manuel F. Fernández Chaves** • is Associate Professor in the Early Modern History Department at the Universidad de Sevilla.
>
> **Rafael M. Pérez García** • is currently Associate Professor at the Department of Early Modern History at the Universidad de Sevilla.

Networking Europe and New Communities of Interpretation (1400–1600), ed. by Margriet Hoogvliet, Manuel F. Fernández Chaves, *and* Rafael M. Pérez García, New Communities of Interpretation, 4 (Turnhout: Brepols, 2023), pp. 9–18
BREPOLS ❧ PUBLISHERS   10.1484/M.NCI-EB.5.134307

classical Latin and Greek in Italy, and in this letter he tried to persuade his friend through phrases written in elegant humanist Latin to come to Italy as well, in order to absorb its culture and learning.

Nearly a century later, Juan de Ovando, president of the *Consejo de Indias* in Madrid, wrote to the Spanish humanist Benito Arias Montano, resident in Antwerp, informing him that he had received the Flemish books and objects that Montano had sent:

> He recibido el astrolabio que ... es la mejor pieça que e visto en my vida ... Y ansí mismo e recibido el breviario y la Biblia que vuestra merced me enbió con don Pedro de Luna, y la Biblia me a contentado ynfinito, y no la dexo de las manos. Vuestra merced diga al Plantino que le soy aficionadíssimo ... Recibí el ánulo astronómico que vuestra merced me envió ... y ansí mesmo recibí el báculo astronómico ... estímolo en mucho, porque cierto está eçelentemente labrado. Tanbién recibí del dicho Francisco de Palma dos catálogos ynpresos de los libros que an venido del nuevo ynpresor que an venido a las dos últimas ferias de Francaforte.[2]

> (I have received the astrolabe ... which is the best piece I have seen in my life ... and I have also received the breviary and the Bible which your Grace sent me with don Pedro de Luna, and the Bible has pleased me so much, and I never put it down. Tell Plantin that I am very fond of his person ... I received also the astronomical *annulus* that your Grace sent me ... and the astronomical rod [Jacob's Staff]... I esteem it very much, because it is extremely well carved. I also received from Francisco de Palma two printed catalogues of the books of the new printer that came from the last two Frankfurt fairs.)

In the sixteenth century Montano used an extensive network of Spanish and Flemish merchants and travellers between Flanders and the Iberian Peninsula to send astronomical artefacts, books, Bibles, and also printed catalogues of books presented at the Frankfurt book fair. This information shows us how the cultural influence of the northern European printing press, together with the arts and crafts related to the fabrication of scientific objects, was channelled through mercantile and official networks with Spain, from north to south, paralleling the journey from Groningen to Pavia proposed by Agricola at the end of the fifteenth century.

A network of more than 120 researchers from twenty-five countries in the European Union and from associated countries had similarly enriching

---

2 Macías Rosendo, *La correspondencia de Benito Arias Montano con el presidente de Indias Juan de Ovando*, 206. Letter of Juan de Ovando to Benito Arias Montano, Madrid, 31 March 1570.

experiences during their Europe-wide travels in order to participate in the meetings and other activities of COST Action IS-1304, 'New Communities of Interpretation: Contexts, Strategies and Processes of Religious Transformation in Late Medieval and Early Modern Europe', that was active between 2013 and 2017. Just like Agricola, Bredewoldt, and Montano, modern researchers and students, all of them scholars and historians specializing in the fifteenth and sixteenth centuries, travelled from their institutions to a great variety of European countries participating in the COST Action for meetings, where they found 'valuable rewards' in the exchange of ideas and research results.

This book is the outcome of the meetings of the Action's Working Group 3: 'European Networks of Knowledge Exchange'. The COST Action in itself already being an important opportunity for scholarly exchange and networking, one of the approaches uniting the participants' research activities is 'Networking Europe', with which we refer to the long-distance social ties connecting Europeans from all geographical corners of the continent during the long fifteenth century and allowing the sharing of religious texts, books, iconography, ideas, and practices. In the theoretical Introduction to this volume, Suzan Folkerts and Margriet Hoogvliet will provide further details about our approach to 'connectivity' and 'social networks', as well as a further development of our understanding of this terminology.

As set out in the official Memorandum of Understanding of the Action, the goal of our Working Group is to study late medieval and early modern processes of religious transformation by means of:

> reconstructing European networks of knowledge exchange, exploring how religious ideas and strategies of transformation 'travelled' and were shared in European cultural space (e.g. mobility of 'readers', printers, authors and groups of believers; dialogues and discussions within literary associations and institutions; organisation of and participation in Church Councils). As a matter of fact, a better-calibrated reconstruction of intellectual and mercantile networks, clusters of literary associations and institutions, networks of collaboration with religious communities and religious orders, mobility of people, texts and ideas is essential for the reconstruction of the circulation, the appropriation and the transformation of religious knowledge and the essential challenging of national paradigms.

In order to come to a better understanding of Europe-wide processes of religious culture and religious change in the late medieval and early modern periods, we intend to focus on the agency of the laity instead of that of the intellectual elites, the aristocracy, and religious institutions. This focus on the laity and their active involvement in religious life has also resulted in a renewed interest in texts in the European vernaculars instead of in Latin, or the vernacular texts that existed alongside those in Latin. In reality, and as often observed before, the traditional coupling of the terminology professional religious–Latin and layperson–vernacular became more fluid during this period, with some laypeople reading and writing in Latin and some professional religious reading and writing in their mother tongue. Nevertheless, the agency of religious literature in the European vernaculars in processes of religious purification, reform, and innovation during the long fifteenth century is still largely underestimated. In our view, the development of new religious and cultural identities can be best studied from the perspective of 'new communities of interpretation'. To quote again the Memorandum of Understanding:

> These new 'communities of interpretation' were often formed by an urban laity active in politics, finance and commerce. Over time, this *respublica laicorum* took a growing interest in the organisation of cultural and religious activities and in the production of literary, religious and scientific texts — and most interestingly recognised the opportunities offered by reading and writing in the vernacular to further their interests.

In addition to studying 'new communities of interpretation' through the lenses of the laity with special attention paid to the European vernacular languages, the contributions to this volume also aim to step away from studying 'national' textual production and consumption, by approaching these topics instead from a European and interconnected perspective. Just as Latin functioned as a supranational language in the European later Middle Ages, most vernacular languages were not tied to a specific political or geographical area, because a) several linguistic communities were larger than political territories — the 'cosmopolitan vernacular' Middle French being a case in point; b) medieval vernacular languages usually consisted of a patchwork of variants (dialects is not the correct term here); c) many people were multilingual and could communicate in several vernacular languages, even if in only a very basic form; and d) during the later Middle Ages people were mobile and they spent often time 'abroad' for reasons of commerce, education, pilgrimage, or exile.

Following the mobility of people and objects during the long fifteenth century, religious texts and material books should also be studied from a supranational or transnational perspective: many religious texts were translated into several vernacular languages, thus becoming 'international bestsellers', and this justifies the necessity of studying religious texts from a Europe-wide or even global perspective. In addition, books were transportable commodities, and these were exported via commercial networks in order to be sold and read in all corners of the European area, and sometimes even across the seas in the new territories of the European monarchies. As a consequence of human and textual mobility, not only were religious texts shared within communities, but they also contributed to the creation of international and multilingual communities of interpretation.

The contributions to this book explore late medieval and early modern networks connecting people and transporting texts, in some cases including the transatlantic New World, following three main axes of investigation. Firstly, the chapters in the section, 'European connections', focus on religious texts that were connecting local and European communities of readers; the following section, 'Exiles, diasporas, and migrants', will address textual networks created by early modern people living far away from their homelands; and, thirdly, the section, 'Mobility and dissemination', will ask how late medieval and early modern mobility and travel networks enabled the transportation of texts, books, and ideas.

European Connections

In the chapter discussing 'Francisco de Osuna's 'Tercer Abecedario Espiritual' and the Medieval Mystical Tradition in Western Europe', Rafael M. Pérez García proposes to move beyond national and nationalistic approaches to spiritual literature from the sixteenth century and to investigate this textual culture instead as the expression of a shared European and Christian culture. Starting from the *Third Spiritual Alphabet* (1527), written in the Spanish vernacular by the Franciscan Friar Francisco de Osuna, the chapter retraces the medieval and European textual network of sources that converged in his text. Even if most of these works were originally intended exclusively for monastic and clerical practices of mysticism, Francisco de Osuna, by means of a new elaboration of Pseudo-Dionysian exegesis of the *Song of Songs*, opened up to lay readers the search for a mystical union with the divine.

European textual connections are also addressed in Mirosława Hanusiewicz-Lavallee's chapter 'The Sixteenth-Century Polish Protestant Martyrology and Its Latin Sources'. The Polish vernacular compendium collecting stories of the sufferings of European proto-Reformation and Reformation martyrs, *History of Harsh Persecution of God's Church*, was printed in 1567 in Brest, then situated in the Grand Duchy of Lithuania, and translated and adapted by Cyprian Bazylik. Hanusiewicz-Lavallee retraces Bazylik's European sources, most notably Latin treatises of Protestant martyrs, such as John Foxe's *Rerum in Ecclesia gestarum [...] commentarii* (1559), Jean Crespin's Latin martyrology (1560), Jan van Utenhove's *Simplex et fidelis narratio* (1560), and Heinrich Pantaleon's *Martyrum historia* (1563). Through Bazylik's Polish martyrology, historical, textual, and religious connections were created between the Polish Protestants and the Reformed communities elsewhere in Europe, thus establishing 'textual communities' and connected histories of Protestant martyrs.

A geographically smaller, but socially more diverse community reading biblical and religious texts in Middle Dutch, often translated from Latin and other European vernaculars, is studied by Marcin Polkowski in his chapter '(Re-)Constructing a Community of Readers: The Image of the Laity in Books Printed in Delft (1477–1500)'. Polkowski addresses the conceptualization of laypeople (*laici*) as 'virtual' textual actors (after Bruno Latour's 'Actor–Network' model) and their representation as 'ideal readers' by authors and printers from the Dutch city of Delft during the 'long sixteenth century'. In Delft, the output of authors and printers was received in an urban society which was characterized by the existence of a myriad of social networks, often connecting laity and clergy, which were all supportive of religious textual culture. The vernacular textual output of the Delft printing presses suggests that these contributed to specific religious reading practices including to the creation of a religious identity for the laity, but one which could also include clerical readers.

Exiles, Diasporas, and Migrants

In the chapter 'Spanish Merchants and Dissidents outside Spain in the Sixteenth Century', Ignacio García Pinilla shows the important role of merchant colonies of businessmen from Burgos, Seville, and Valencia that were established in the Low Countries in the sixteenth century (especially in Bruges and Antwerp) in the circulation of ideas and the dissemination of Protestantism within the mercantile networks that connected the main economic centres in Western Europe (from London and the Low Countries to Burgos, Seville, Florence, and Rome). This article shows how, besides the economic functions of these networks, we can approach the processes of cultural change that those networks made possible, shaking the same familiar and mercantile structures over which they were built. Among others, the case of the Valencian humanist Luis Vives and the well-known cases of the families San Román and Encinas from Burgos are studied.

Manuel Fernández Chaves, in the chapter entitled 'The Library of the Pious House and Chapel of Saint Andrew of the Flemish Nation in Seville under Philip V', studies the type of books that were part of the library that the Flemish Nation in Seville had in its confraternity and pious chapel. Working with an inventory from 1734, the author analyses the main topics and authors that were important to the Flemish community in the city, such as history, classical authors, theology, and religious controversies, among others. The library comprised books dating to between the sixteenth and the eighteenth centuries, with most from the seventeenth century. Their study allows us to identify the religious and cultural profile that the Flemish community developed in the city, using books in Latin, Spanish, French, and Flemish. These were not only intended for the use of their chaplain but also for their members, which is a very telling fact about the self-representation of a community of readers during almost three centuries.

Mobility and Dissemination

In the chapter 'Business is Business: Book Merchants, Printers, and the Spanish Inquisition during the Sixteenth Century', Natalia Maillard-Alvarez studies the interrelations between mercantile interests, the printing press, and the boundaries of religious orthodoxy. She analyses the different strategies developed by book professionals to avoid the mechanisms of supervision and Inquisitorial control, focusing on the ways they used to adapt their business and activity as printers and book importers to the shifting situation concerning the religious and cultural changes in the sixteenth century. Maillard-Alvarez shows that we can find the printers in situations that vary from persecution to a certain tolerance from, and even cooperation with, the Holy Office — not only as *familiares* or informers on other printers suspected of being Protestants, but also as publishers or suppliers of paper and other materials. In other words, we can see how the Inquisition showed indulgence with regard to some crimes or complaints against printers, or preferred some booksellers and printers more than others, being pragmatic in many cases, mainly to avoid the suffocation of the printing press business. Moreover, some members of the Inquisition permitted the introduction of forbidden authors or titles into the peninsula in exchange for money. The article also discusses cases in Spain and Mexico, bringing out the connections between the main European centres of the printing press with those in New Spain.

In the chapter 'The Colony of the Republic of Ragusa Merchants in Belgrade in the Sixteenth Century and their Printing Press', Vladimir Abramović explores the activities of the Ragusan merchant community established in Belgrade during the sixteenth century, showing the merchants' role as economic and cultural connectors between the Ottoman Empire and Western Europe. The activities of these merchants reveal a world where Serbian, Italian, and Latin coexisted in different oral and written registers. Among other businesses, they were very active in the book trade, importing to Belgrade Cyrillic liturgical books printed in Serbian in Venice or Ancona. In this mercantile network we can find the figure of Trojan Gundulić. He established the first printing press in Belgrade, which issued the first book printed in the Balkans. In this way, the Ragusan merchants contributed to the expansion of the Republic of Letters in south eastern Europe.

The closing chapter of the book, written by Margriet Hoogvliet, addresses roads, means of transportation, and lodgings as the 'hardware' of European connections in the late Middle Ages and the early sixteenth century. In the chapter 'The Spiritual Road: European Networks and Pilgrim Travels from Northern France and the Low Countries to Rome, Venice, and Santiago (Late Fifteenth–early Sixteenth Century)', three pilgrims' accounts in Middle French are scrutinized for the information they contain concerning the daily practice of travel around the year 1500, including roads and other provisions for travellers. The accounts are very informative about the well-functioning infrastructure that was in place for long-distance travel and about social networks that connected people living huge distances apart from each other. The pilgrims' accounts also show how these networks were crucial in the transportation of information about religious and spiritual topics.

Taken together, the chapters in this book cover a huge geographical network that stretches from Poland to Spain and the New World, and from the Low Countries to the Balkan Peninsula. It is, of course, not possible to cover in detail in one collective book all the particularities of these European and transatlantic areas. It is our conviction, however, that the study of 'connections' and 'networks' will be a fruitful approach for future research, by re-connecting people and ideas that were actually connected in the late Middle Ages and early modern period. Ideally this will lead to more inclusive approaches and an opening up of historiographies of national exceptionalism.

Works Cited

Agricola, Rudolph, *Letters*, ed. and trans., with notes by Adrie van de Laan and Fokke Akkerman (Assen: Koninklijke Van Gorcum, 2002)

Macías Rosendo, Baldomero, *La correspondencia de Benito Arias Montano con el presidente de Indias Juan de Ovando* (Huelva: Universidad de Huelva, 2008)

SUZAN FOLKERTS AND
MARGRIET HOOGVLIET

Transnational History and Social Network Theory

A Brief Introduction to Theory and Terminology

To provide an outline of the theoretical foundations uniting the articles in this volume, as well as to streamline a shared vocabulary, this chapter will give a brief (and certainly not exhaustive) overview of recent ideas on Transnational History and Network Theory, together with their theoretical backgrounds. It is our intention to show how these models can be used to approach the flow of religious texts among individuals, groups, networks, and spaces, as well as through connecting links, during the late Middle Ages and the early modern period. This overview will also ask how we may arrive at a better understanding of connectivity and the functioning of networks, especially in the case of the Europe-wide and in some cases transatlantic dissemination of religious texts and the creation of widely shared values concerning lay communities of interpretation.

Suzan Folkerts • is curator of manuscripts and early printed books at the Athenaeumbibliotheek Deventer. Previously she was a postdoctoral researcher at the University of Groningen. She specializes in the medieval transmission and readership of hagiography and Bible translations, as well as in Deventer book production.

Margriet Hoogvliet • is a specialist in the field of biblical and religious reading cultures of lay people living and working in the towns of late medieval France. Her research is concerned with the social, material, and spatial aspects of the reception of religious texts in French and their dissemination amongst the population.

Transnational History

For a long time, history in Europe, as well as the history of those parts of the world Europe influenced, has been national history.[1] Even nowadays, to a non-negligible extent history still is national history, based on the political borders of the European nation states as they had become established by the nineteenth century, or in some cases only after the end of the Cold War in the 1990s. National histories tend to perceive nation states above all as discrete entities united by a commonly shared national language of identity and a collective ancestry (which is sometimes even thought to be genetically retraceable), while overemphasizing arguments for national exceptionality and (often perceived) differences with other countries. It is well known that these approaches grew out of Romanticism and from a Western anthropology dating from the nineteenth and twentieth centuries, which was mainly focused on searching for timeless 'national characters'. These perspectives are still with us, even though their focus clearly generates limited visions of the historical past.[2]

For researchers working on the medieval and early modern periods, the model of the nation inhabiting its own nation state quickly becomes uncomfortable, because the ever-shifting political borders and the mobility of people in the past differ in many cases from modern ideas of territorial and political delimitations. Moreover, the historical variants of national languages do not fit neatly into the imagined linguistic unity of modern nation states: linguistic variety and multilingualism seem to have been the common rule rather than the exception — and often they still are nowadays.[3]

As a consequence of recent migratory movements, resulting in the development of multicultural societies, and in combination with processes of decolonization and globalization, the idea of exceptional European nation states, supposedly characterized by cultural, genetic, and linguistic purity, has been rendered highly questionable. One of the critical approaches proposed by cultural analysis is Transnational History. While transnational approaches have their roots in the 1960s and 1970s, this notion has gained momentum in the early twenty-first century, due to the specific social context of globalization, as Patricia Seed observes: 'Transnational history [...] implies a comparison between the contemporary movement

---

1 This paragraph is in part based on Suzan Folkerts's keynote lecture '"A World of Communities": Transnational, Regional, and Entangled Approaches to the Circulation and Transformation of Religious Knowledge in Late Medieval Europe', plenary meeting of COST Action IS1301 'Going Transnational', University of Groningen, 3–5 November 2016.
2 Caro Baroja, *El mito del carácter nacional*.
3 See for instance: Hsy, *Trading Tongues*; Morato and Schoenaers, eds, *Medieval Francophone Literary Culture*; Selig and Ehrich, eds, *Mittelalterliche Stadtsprachen*.

of groups, goods, technology, or people across national borders and the transit of similar or related objects or people in an earlier time'.[4]

One of the most important critics of nationalistic and ethnocentric approaches to history is Sanjay Subrahmanyam, who argues:

> Nationalism has blinded us to the possibility of connection, and historical ethnography, whether in one of its western variants of high Orientalism, or whether practised in the East, has aided and abetted this unfortunate process. The thrust of such ethnography has always been to emphasize difference.[5]

And, moreover:

> For the historian who is willing to scratch below the surface of his sources, nothing turns out to be quite what it seems to be in terms of fixity and local rootedness.[6]

If we turn to the borders that are thought to separate nations, cultures, ethnicities, and languages neatly from each other, these, too, turn out to be highly problematic, variable, and permeable. Borders and margins are, in fact, sites of contact, of exchange, of sharing, and of integration, as Noel Parker has made clear in a groundbreaking publication:

> To examine how margins are articulated, we need to see the identities of selves and their others engaged in a continuous interactive asserting, claiming, (r)ejecting, sharing, and sharing-out of features that become integrated in their own and/or the others' identities.[7]

If borders are increasingly perceived as permeable and national identities as subject to change, as a consequence comparative approaches become highly problematic, because the terms of comparison cannot be delimited clearly. Among others, Jürgen Kocka and Heinz-Gerhard Haupt have observed that comparative history often disregards interactions and connections:

> While the comparative approach separates the units of comparison, entanglement-oriented approaches stress the connections, the

---

4 Patricia Seed in Bayly and others, 'AHR Conversation', p. 1442. Other publications that address globalization and history include: Irie, *Global and Transnational History*; Gruzinski, 'Les Mondes mêlés de la monarchie catholique'; Douki and Minard, 'Global History, Connected Histories'.
5 Subrahmanyam, 'Connected Histories', p. 761.
6 Subrahmanyam, 'Connected Histories', p. 745.
7 Parker, 'From Borders to Margins'. For an excellent discussion of border studies and transregional approaches, see: Soen and others, 'How to do Transregional History'.

continuity, the belonging-together, the hybridity of observable spaces or analytical units, and reject distinguishing them clearly.[8]

Sanjay Subrahmanyam, too, opposes the idea of separate and thus comparable cultures, and proposes to replace it with connected history:

> But ideas and mental constructs, too, flowed across political boundaries in that world, and — even if they found specific local expression — enable us to see that what we are dealing with are not separate and comparable, but connected histories.[9]

The actual study of connections could take the approach of *l'histoire croisée*, as developed by Michael Werner and Bénédicte Zimmermann in an often quoted, but less well understood article. They note the fact that the process of decolonization and globalization have, as a consequence, reorientated and reconfigured the social sciences and the humanities. *L'histoire croisée* is a relational, interactive, and process-oriented approach that examines intersections, because objects and practices will change as a consequence of cultural contacts. Consequently, 'the objects of research should not only be investigated in their relation to one another, but also through each other in terms of relations, interactions, and circulation'.[10] This is especially important for transnational studies because these should:

> make visible a network of dynamic interrelations, of which the constituent parts are partially defined through the links they maintain and the connections that structure their positions. Seen from this perspective, *l'histoire croisée* can open promising roads for writing a history of Europe that is not limited to the sum of the history of its member states or their mutual political relations, but instead takes into account the diversity of transactions, negotiations and new interpretations that take place in different places and around a great variety of objects. The combination of these different perspectives will contribute to the creation of a multi-level European history.[11]

Likewise, in recent thinking about approaches to connectivity and exchanges in the history of the late medieval and early modern period,

---

8 Kocka and Haupt, 'Comparison and Beyond'.
9 Subrahmanyam, 'Connected Histories', p. 745.
10 Translation Margriet Hoogvliet of Werner and Zimmermann, 'Penser l'histoire croisée', p. 15. See also: Werner and Zimmermann, eds, *De la comparaison*; Werner and Zimmermann, 'Beyond Comparison'; Schilling and Tóth, eds, *Cultural Exchange*. A key publication concerning the origin and development of the theory of decolonization is Vega, *Imperios de papel*.
11 Werner and Zimmermann, 'Penser l'histoire croisée', p. 17. Translation Margriet Hoogvliet.

'places and processes of exchange'[12] and 'contact zones'[13] take an increasingly central place.

Although most chapters in this book engage most notably with European history, it is important to bear in mind that another consequence of globalization and postcolonial emancipation is the 'decentring of the West' by studying its connectivity to the wider world. Subrahmanyam argues that the writing of history should move from the incommensurability of different empires to the lens of commensurability and hybridity: 'what usually happened was approximation, improvisation, and eventually a shift in the relative positions of all concerned'.[14] As Timothy Brook has shown in his study of Vermeer's paintings, during the early modern period locally made objects, with primarily local functions, were often connected in some way to broader and even global forces.[15] In part as a result of these developments in recent thinking about history, historians of the medieval period are also shifting their outlook towards the 'Global Middle Ages'.[16]

These broader horizons and textual connections, stretching out over long geographical and cultural distances (in some cases intercontinental and transatlantic connections), will be addressed in all the chapters of this book.[17] The approach uniting these chapters is the focus on connections, exchanges of texts, interactions, and intersections, as well as infrastructures and their practices, in order to uncover shared European patterns of religious reading cultures in the European vernaculars and the emergence of new religious identities of the laity. Together they produce an approach to European history that is thought-provoking and potentially leading to new insights — with a necessarily flexible delimitation of Europe and European Christian cultures.

---

12 Hackett, 'Introduction', p. 12.
13 Greenblatt, 'A Mobility Studies Manifesto', p. 251.
14 Subrahmanyam, *Courtly Encounters*, pp. 24–30. For similar approaches, see: Hillerbrand, 'Was there a Reformation'; Arnzen and Thielmann, eds, *Words, Texts and Concepts*.
15 Brook, *Vermeer's Hat*; Gerritsen and Riello, eds, *The Global Lives of Things*; Fennetaux and others, eds, *Objets nomades*; Christian and Clark, eds, *European Art and the Wider World*; Boucheron, eds, *Histoire mondiale de la France*; Heerma van Voss, ed., *Wereldgeschiedenis van Nederland*. See also Italian 'microstoria', that perceives small-scale historical events and objects primarily in their relation with the wider historical contexts at large: Ginzburg, 'Microhistory'; and 'glocalisation', the interplay between the local and the global: Roudometof, *Glocalization*.
16 Holmes and Standen, 'Introduction: Towards a Global Middle Ages'.
17 For the study of the contact zones and cultural exchange in colonial and transatlantic spaces during the early modern period, see Hespanha, *Filhos da Terra*. Talking about the cultural exchanges in the Ibero-American world, Paiva, *Dar nome ao novo*. About the Atlantic exchange of books and culture in the Iberian Atlantic, Maillard Álvarez and Fernández Chaves, eds, *Bibliotecas de la Monarquía Hispánica en la primera globalización*.

Networks

As discussed in the previous paragraph, transnational history and connectivity are concerned with contact zones and connecting links. These links, connecting two or more entities, can also be studied through the lens of the network model.

Even though the later Middle Ages have sometimes been heralded as having produced the birth of individualism as a result of the growth of private devotions,[18] the same period also witnessed the flowering of many formal and informal social networks connecting individuals to each other and to larger social groups.[19] The formal networks included, for instance, the urban communal movements, knightly orders, parishes, confraternities, guilds, beguinages, and Third Order communities. Towns all over late medieval Europe included very similar social network structures, and some networks even stretched out supra-locally. Among the latter were not only the religious orders, but also lay organizations, such as international banker's firms, entrepreneurial *compagnie*, and Hansa trading networks.[20] Moreover, during the early modern period, the mercantile colonies and the members of the religious diasporas (Huguenots, Quakers, Mennonites, Jews, *Moriscos*), alongside Catholics,[21] acted as connectors involved in wider networks that made possible cultural exchanges and the creation of new communities of interpretation in Europe as well as in the colonial Atlantic world.[22]

Social Network Theory (SNT) has emerged as one of the major theories guiding social studies and social history. It is in part inspired by the development of modern communication networks and the interhuman

---

18 See, for instance: Smith, *Art, Identity, and Devotion*, p. 4; Fuchs and others, eds, *Religious Individualisation*; Arlinghaus, 'Conceptualising Pre-Modern and Modern Individuality'.
19 This paragraph is indebted to Margriet Hoogvliet's collaboration with Christina Williamson and Megan Williams for the module 'Mediterranean III: The Blue Web', University of Groningen (2013); as well as to the presentations by Megan Williams and Arie van Steensel during the plenary meeting of COST Action IS1301 in Groningen, 2–5 November 2016. Medieval networks were also addressed during the international virtual conference 'Communities and Networks in Late Medieval Europe (c. 1300–1500)', University of Cambridge, 9–10 September 2021: https://communitiesandnetworks21.wordpress.com; and the International Medieval Congress in Leeds will have as central theme 'Networks and Entanglements' in 2023.
20 For recent publications on medieval trading networks, see: Parker, 'Entrepreneurs, Families, and Companies'; Lugli, 'Linking the Mediterranean'; Blockmans and others, 'Maritime Trade Around Europe'; Caracausi and Jeggle, 'Introduction'; Ewert and Selzer, 'Social Networks'; Nagy and others, eds, *The Medieval Networks in East Central Europe*.
21 Freist and Lachenicht, eds, *Connecting Worlds and People*; Herrero Sánchez and Kaps, eds, *Merchants and Trade Networks in the Atlantic and the Mediterranean*.
22 Maillard Álvarez, *Books in the Catholic World*; Hampe Martínez, *Bibliotecas privadas*; González Sánchez, *New World Literacy*.

connectivity created by online social media. It has led historians working on the late Middle Ages and the early modern period to realize that these twenty-first-century theoretical models may also be used to describe very well social connections as found in 500- to 600-year-old historical sources, in some cases even dating from still earlier ages, and that networks can be used as a productive analytical tool for historical processes.

Until the 1960s and 1970s organizations and societies, both modern and historical, have often been understood as being constructed following the centre-periphery model: a command centre in the middle that gives directions to subordinated entities surrounding it. Another often used metaphor for describing social relations is the tree: a hierarchical and genealogical structure where dependent entities branch out from a common ancestral stem. In the 1980s the inequalities inherent in these conceptualizations were criticized by Gilles Deleuze and Félix Guattari, who proposed instead the idea of a web-like, horizontally growing root structure of rhizome plants (such as bamboo, certain grasses, and orchids) to represent the non-hierarchical connectivity and heterogeneity of phenomena such as knowledge, power structures, and cultures.[23] More recently, the German philosopher Peter Sloterdijk has proposed the model of foams for describing the non-centrally directed masses and ever-changing connectivity of modern societies.[24]

The development of computer networks, Internet, and mobile communication has provided one of the most widely used models, that of the Network Society as proposed by Manuel Castells in his seminal study with the same title.[25] Yet, already as early as the 1930s Jacob Moreno proposed to represent social structures as networks and to use network graphs for quantitative analysis.[26] Next to Castells's work, the basic network model generally used for Social Network Theory is based on Paul Baran's ideas concerning the Distributed Network as a resilient system for technology-based communication, first published in 1964.[27] Baran distinguished three types of networks: centralized, decentralized, and distributed. The distributed network is a non-centralized network, with multiple connections between each of its points, not unlike the rhizome model of societies. When a part of the distributed communication network is destroyed, the remaining parts will take over its activities, allowing the network to remain functional.

---

[23] Deleuze and Guattari, *Capitalisme et schizophrénie*.
[24] Sloterdijk, *Sphären*.
[25] Castells, *The Rise of the Network Society*.
[26] Freeman, *The Development of Social Network Analysis*; Prell, *Social Network Analysis*, pp. 19–58.
[27] Baran, 'On Distributed Communication Networks'.

As a consequence of their origins, the central terms commonly used in Social Network Analysis are often borrowed from the terminology developed for computer-based communication networks:

Network: a collection of interlinked nodes that exchange information.
Node: the most basic part of the network; for example, a user or computer.
Tie (or Link): the connection between two nodes.
Hub (or Server): a node that has connections to a relatively large number of other nodes.[28]

An important point of departure for the articles in this book is the idea that social networks are not inactive entities, but are understood as having functions and agency, most notably their instrumentality in the transportation of objects, ideas, information, and texts.[29] Moreover, the nodes in the network are not only thought of as human beings, but objects, environments, texts, books, and ideas can also be represented as nodes with agency in the network.[30]

Network-based data models were first conceived for quantitative analyses of social phenomena,[31] and scholars such as Manuel Vásquez have argued against the 'positivist and reductive tendencies in network analysis'.[32] However, the network model can also be used in a more general way for understanding the fundamental interconnectedness of past individual and collective social entities, as famously argued by Barry Wellman and S. D. Berkowitz:

We suggest that network analysis is neither a method nor a metaphor, but a fundamental intellectual tool for the study of social structures. In our view, an important key to understanding structural analysis is recognising that social structures can be represented as *networks* — as sets of *nodes* (or social system members) and sets of *ties* depicting their interconnections.

---

28 'Beyond Distributed and Decentralized': What is a Federated Network?', <https://networkcultures.org/unlikeus/resources/articles/what-is-a-federated-network/>, accessed 7 January 2022.
29 For studies of connected places that receive and transmit goods, information, and ideas, see: Burghartz and others, eds, *Sites of Mediation*.
30 Vásquez, 'Studying Religion in Motion', p. 169, quoting White: 'As temporal and spatialized forms of relationality, networks are also negotiated "phenomenological realities" consisting of narratives, practices, cognitive maps, and microhistories. In other words, meaning, orientation, and intentionality are not just commodities that circulate but are constitutive of the networks themselves'. See also the 'Actor–Network' model, in Latour, *Reassembling the Social*.
31 For historical studies, see: Jullien, 'Netzwerkanalyse in der Mediävistik'; Lemercier, 'Formal Network Methods in History'.
32 Vásquez, 'Studying Religion in Motion', p. 171.

This is a marvellously liberating idea. It immediately directs analysts to look at linked social relations and frees them from thinking of social systems as collections of individuals, two-person dyads, bounded groups, or simple categories. Usually, structural analysts have associated 'nodes' with individual people, but they can just as easily represent groups, corporations, households, nation-states, or other collectives in this way. 'Ties' are used to represent flows of resources, symmetrical friendships, transfers, or structured relationships between nodes.[33]

Network Theory, in a great variety of formats and methods, is increasingly used for the study of historical societies. For instance, the notion of connectivity, proposed in Peregrine Horden and Nicholas Purcell's study of Mediterranean history, is often used as a model for the analysis of historical social networks, including those of the Middle Ages and the early modern period.[34] For Horden and Purcell, however, connectivity functions primarily within and between the microecologies that are typical for the Mediterranean marine milieu. In their view, long-distance shipping lanes crossing the sea that were used for commerce were not as important as often thought, but rather the 'shifting webs of casual, local, small-scale contacts' were the connections primarily used throughout the area.[35]

In a more recent article, Peregrine Horden stresses that the notion of connectivity as used in *The Corrupting Sea* was primarily developed for the particularities of the Mediterranean landscapes and their microecologies.[36] Horden strongly disapproves singling out connectivity while disregarding its original context and using it as a 'fig leaf' for the study of other cultures in different geographical areas. On the other hand, small-scale exchanges in any form between different areas, together with 'global links with other big areas', as Horden puts it, point towards a potentially fruitful approach for this collection of essays as well.[37] More recently, pre-modern networks and networking behaviour operating at a larger scale, such as 'long-range networks criss-crossing Eurasia and parts of Africa', are emerging as a lens for research into the 'global' Middle Ages and the 'global' early modern period.[38]

---

33 Wellmann and Berkowitz, 'Introduction: Studying Social Structures', p. 4. See also the excellent contribution to this book by Wellmann, 'Structural Analysis from Method and Metaphor'.
34 Horden and Purcell, *The Corrupting Sea*, esp. pp. 123–43.
35 Horden and Purcell, *The Corrupting Sea*, p. 144.
36 Horden, 'The Maritime, the Ecological, the Cultural'.
37 Horden, 'The Maritime, the Ecological, the Cultural', p. 71. For the use of the concept of 'connectivity' in cultural history, see also: Folkerts, 'Introduction', pp. 14–15.
38 Shepard, 'Networks', p. 149.

The usefulness of relational concepts and relational thinking for historical studies and archaeology is presented in an excellent way by Tom Brughmans, Anna Collar, and Fiona Susan Coward in their introductory chapter to the collection of essays entitled *The Connected Past*:[39]

> First, taking a network perspective means that the individual entities of research interest, such as technological innovations, objects, individual humans or communities, archaeological sites, and islands, are never studied in isolation. Instead, it is assumed that these entities are engaged in relationships that are fundamental to understanding their behaviour in the past. The physical size or materiality of the entities under study is largely irrelevant: almost anything can be usefully considered a node depending on the research question, potentially allowing network perspectives to bridge different spatial, social, and conceptual scales of analysis.
> Second, the relationships between entities can be equally diverse: a recorded action of information transmission, spatial proximity; a physical connection such as a road, friendship; political alliance; membership of an institution; presence of similar structures on different sites; the morphological similarity of objects.[40]

Next to the social interconnectedness of people and objects, in their view networks from the past can take many forms:

> Archaeologists and historians aim to understand past phenomena, whether they are past networks of some sort that are hypothesized to have existed (e.g. a road network) or aspects of human behaviour that translate less straightforwardly into network concepts (e.g. trade).[41]

In the essays of this book, various international travel networks and commercial networks from the late Middle Ages and early modern period are not only hypothesized, but also well documented as existing and retraceable entities.

Roads, waterways, and other travel infrastructure are yet another interesting category of subjects for social network analysis, because they are physical and often surviving 'hardware' that makes visible the networks connecting people. The frequency of contacts is sometimes measurable, for instance in business administration and toll registers. The importance of commercial networks, diasporas, and medieval travel infrastructure is

---

39 Brughmans and others, 'Network Perspectives on the Past'. See also: Collar, ed., *Networks and the Spread of Ideas in the Past*. Useful examples from archaeological research can be found in: Knappett, ed., *Network Analysis in Archaeology*; Knappett, *An Archaeology of Interaction*.
40 Brughmans and others, eds, *The Connected Past*, p. 7.
41 Brughmans and others, eds, *The Connected Past*, p. 8.

a key feature connecting the contributions to this volume, most notably historical networks in the book trade, a subject taken up earlier by John Hinks. In the introductory chapter on Social Network Theory, Hinks suggest that people, places, events, ideas and books are interconnected:

> Networks help to demonstrate how things fit together: people, places, events and ideas. [...] Written or printed texts are key connectors within networks, virtual networks perhaps, but still networks. So a solitary scholar is connected to a network of ideas by the books he or she reads — and perhaps by the books he or she publishes. [...] The book trade historically depended on networks of various kinds, for both the production and distribution of books and other related goods.[42]

The contributions to this book take up the idea of social networks as facilitators of the dissemination of religious ideas and religious books, but Hinks refers here to another network brought about by the act of reading: a 'textual community',[43] or, in the terminology of COST Action IS1301, the creation of 'new communities of interpretation'.[44]

The essays that follow use the lens of connectivity and networks on a trans-European and in some cases a transatlantic scale, in order to analyse processes of the transfer of religious knowledge and religious texts shared by different communities. All the contributions focus on networks of religious texts and networks of readers, meanwhile uncovering shared European patterns of religious reading. This has resulted in a richer documentation and a more calibrated understanding of late medieval and sixteenth-century textual communities.

---

42 Hinks, 'Beyond Metaphor', p. 1.
43 Scase, 'Reading Communities'; Hoogvliet, '"Pour faire laies personnes entendre"'; Irvine, *The Making of Textual Culture*, pp. 272–98, 405–60; Campbell, *The Call to Read*; Rehberg Sedo, *Reading Communities*; Hexter, 'Location, Location, Location'; Van Dussen and Soukup, eds, *Religious Controversy in Europe*. For an overview and a critical discussion of theoretical aspects of "textual communities" (most useful when presented as a question rather than a solution), see: Heath, 'Textual Communities'; Korhonen, 'Textual Communities'.
44 See the general introduction to this book.

Works Cited

Secondary Studies

Arlinghaus, Franz-Josef, 'Conceptualising Pre-Modern and Modern Individuality: Some Theoretical Considerations', in *Forms of Individuality and Literacy in the Medieval and Early Modern Periods*, ed. by Franz-Josef Arlinghaus (Turnhout: Brepols, 2015), pp. 1–45

Arnzen, Rüdiger, and Jörn Thielmann, eds, *Words, Texts and Concepts Cruising the Mediterranean Sea: Studies on the Sources, Contents and Influences of Islamic Civilization and Arabic Philosophy and Science* (Leuven: Peeters, 2004)

Baran, Paul, 'On Distributed Communication Networks', *IEEE Transactions on Communications*, 12 (1964), 1–9

Bayly, Christopher A., Sven Beckert, Matthew Connelly, Isabel Hofmeyr, Wendy Kozol, and Patricia Seed, 'AHR Conversation: On Transnational History', *American Historical Review*, 111.5 (2006), 1441–64

'Beyond Distributed and Decentralized': What is a Federated Network?', <https://networkcultures.org/unlikeus/resources/articles/what-is-a-federated-network/> [accessed 7 January 2022]

Blockmans, Wim, Mikhail Krom, and Justyna Wubs-Mrozewicz, 'Maritime Trade Around Europe 1300–1600: Commerical Networks and Urban Autonomy', in *The Routledge Handbook of Maritime Trade Around Europe 1300–1600*, ed. by Wim Blockmans, Mikhail Krom, and Justyna Wubs-Mrozewicz (Abingdon: Routledge, 2017), pp. 1–14

Boucheron, Patrick, eds, *Histoire mondiale de la France* (Paris: Seuil, 2017)

Brook, Timothy, *Vermeer's Hat: The Seventeenth Century and the Dawn of the Global World* (New York: Bloomsbury, 2008)

Brughmans, Tom, Anna Collar, and Fiona Susan Coward, 'Network Perspectives on the Past: Tackling the Challenges', in *The Connected Past: Challenges to Network Studies in Archaeology and History*, ed. by Tom Brughmans, Anna Collar, and Fiona Susan Coward (Oxford: Oxford University Press, 2016), pp. 3–20

——, ——, and ——, eds, *The Connected Past: Challenges to Network Studies in Archaeology and History* (Oxford: Oxford University Press, 2016),

Burghartz, Susanna, Lucas Burkart, and Christine Göttler, eds, *Sites of Mediation: Connected Histories of Places, Processes, and Objects in Europe and Beyond, 1450–1650* (Leiden: Brill, 2016)

Campbell, Kirsty, *The Call to Read: Reginald Pecock's Books and Textual Communities* (Notre Dame: University of Notre Dame Press, 2010)

Caracausi, Andrea, and Christof Jeggle, 'Introduction', in *Commercial Networks and European Cities, 1400–1800*, ed. by Andrea Caracausi and Christof Jeggle (London: Pickering & Chatto, 2014), pp. 1–12

Caro Baroja, Julio, *El mito del carácter nacional* (Madrid: Caro Raggio, 2004)

Castells, Manuel, *The Rise of the Network Society* (Oxford: Wiley-Blackwell, 1996)

Christian, Kathleen, and Leah R. Clark, eds, *European Art and the Wider World, 1350–1550* (Manchester: Manchester University Press, 2017)

Collar, Anna, ed., *Networks and the Spread of Ideas in the Past: Strong Ties, Innovation and Knowledge Exchange* (Milton: Taylor & Francis, 2022)

Deleuze, Gilles, and Félix Guattari, *Capitalisme et schizophrénie*, II: *Mille plateaux* (Paris: Minuit, 1980)

Douki, Caroline, and Philippe Minard, 'Global History, Connected Histories: A Shift of Historiographic Scale?', *Revue d'histoire moderne et contemporaine*, 54.4 (2007), 7–21

Ewert, Ulf Christian, and Stephan Selzer, 'Social Networks', in *A Companion to the Hanseatic League*, ed. by Donald J. Harreld (Leiden: Brill, 2015), pp. 162–93

Fennetaux, Ariane, Anne-Marie Miller-Blaise, and Nancy Oddo, eds, *Objets nomades. Circulations matérielles, appropriations et formation des identités à l'ère de la première mondialisation, XVIe–XVIIIe siècles* (Turnhout: Brepols, 2018)

Fernández Chaves, Manuel F., Rafael M. Perez García, and Béatrice Perez, eds, *Mercaderes y redes mercantiles en la Península Ibérica. Siglos XV–XVIII* (Seville: Universidad de Sevilla, 2019)

Folkerts, Suzan, 'Introduction: Religious Connectivity as a Holistic Approach to Urban Society', in *Religious Connectivity in Urban Communities: Reading, Worshipping, and Connecting through the Continuum of Sacred and Secular (1400–1550)*, ed. by Suzan Folkerts, New Communities of Interpretation, 1 (Turnhout: Brepols, 2021), pp. 11–20

Freeman, Linton C., *The Development of Social Network Analysis: A Study in the Sociology of Science* (Vancouver: Empirical Press, 2004)

Freist, Dagmar, and Susanne Lachenicht, eds, *Connecting Worlds and People: Early Modern Diasporas* (London: Routledge, 2017)

Fuchs, Martin, Antje Linkenbach, Martin Mulsow, Bernd-Christian Otto, Rahul Bjørn Parson, and Jörge Rüpke, eds, *Religious Individualisation: Historical Dimensions and Comparative Perspectives* (Berlin: De Gruyter, 2019)

Gerritsen, Anne, and Giorgio Riello, eds, *The Global Lives of Things: The Material Culture of Connections in the Early Modern World* (London: Routledge, 2016)

Ginzburg, Carlo, 'Microhistory, Two or Three Things That I Know about It', *Critical Inquiry*, 20.1 (1993), 10–34

González Sánchez, Carlos A., *New World Literacy: Writing and Culture across the Atlantic, 1500–1700* (Lewisburg: Bucknell University Press, 2011)

Greenblatt, Stephen, 'A Mobility Studies Manifesto', in *Cultural Mobility: A Manifesto*, ed. by Stephen Greenblatt (Cambridge: Cambridge University Press, 2010), pp. 250–53

Gruzinski, Serge, 'Les Mondes mêlés de la monarchie catholique et autres "connected histories"', *Annales. Histoire, Sciences Sociales*, 56 (2001), 88–89

Hackett, Helen, 'Introduction', in *Early Modern Exchanges: Dialogues Between Nations and Cultures, 1550–1750*, ed. by Helen Hackett (Farnham: Ashgate, 2015), pp. 1–26

Hampe Martínez, Teodoro, *Bibliotecas privadas en el mundo colonial. La difusión de libros e ideas en el virreinato del Perú (siglos XVI–XVII)* (Frankfurt: Vervuert, 1996)

Heath, Jane, 'Textual Communities: Brian Stock's Concept and Recent Scholarship on Antiquity', in *Scriptural Interpretation at the Interface between Education and Religion: In Memory of Hans Conzelmann*, ed. by Florian Wilk (Leiden: Brill, 2018), pp. 5–35

Heerma van Voss, Lex, ed., *Wereldgeschiedenis van Nederland* (Amsterdam: Ambo-Anthos, 2018)

Herrero Sánchez, Manuel, and Klemens Kaps, eds, *Merchants and Trade Networks in the Atlantic and the Mediterranean, 1550–1800: Connectors of Commercial Maritime Systems* (London: Routledge, 2017)

Hespanha, António Manuel, *Filhos da terra: identidades mestiças nos confins da expansão portuguesa* (Lisbon: Tinta da China, 2019)

Hexter, Ralph, 'Location, Location, Location: Geography, Knowledge, and the Creation of Medieval Latin Textual Communities', in *The Oxford Handbook of Medieval Latin Literature*, ed. by Ralph J. Hexter and David Townsend (Oxford: Oxford University Press, 2012), pp. 192–214

Hillerbrand, Hans J., 'Was there a Reformation in the Sixteenth Century?', *Church History*, 72 (2003), 525–52

Hinks, John, 'Beyond Metaphor: A Personal View of Historical Networks in the Book Trade', in *Historical Networks in the Book Trade*, ed. by Catherine Feely and John Hinks (Abingdon: Routledge, 2017), pp. 1–13

Holmes, Catherine, and Naomi Standen, 'Introduction: Towards a Global Middle Ages', *Past & Present*, 238.13 (2018), 1–44

Hoogvliet, Margriet, '"Pour faire laies personnes entendre les hystoires des escriptures anciennes": Theoretical Approaches to a Social History of Religious Reading in the French Vernaculars During the Late Middle Ages', in *Cultures of Religious Reading in the Later Middle Ages: Instructing the Soul, Feeding the Spirit and Awakening the Passion*, ed. by Sabrina Corbellini (Turnhout: Brepols, 2013), pp. 247–74

Horden, Peregrine, and Nicholas Purcell, *The Corrupting Sea: A Study of Mediterranean History* (Oxford: Blackwell, 2000)

——, 'The Maritime, the Ecological, the Cultural — and the Fig Leaf: Prospects for Medieval Mediterranean Studies', in *Can we Talk Mediterranean? Conversations on an Emerging Field in Medieval and Early Modern Studies*, ed. by Brian A. Catlos and Sharon Kinoshita (Cham: Palgrave MacMillan, 2017), pp. 65–79

Hsy, Jonathan, *Trading Tongues: Merchants, Multilingualism, and Medieval Literature* (Columbus: The Ohio State University Press, 2013)

Irie, Akira, *Global and Transnational History: The Past, Present, and Future* (Basingstoke: Palgrave MacMillan, 2013)

Irvine, Martin, *The Making of Textual Culture: 'Grammatica' and Literary Theory, 350–1100* (Cambridge: Cambridge University Press, 1994)

Jullien, Eva, 'Netzwerkanalyse in der Mediävistik. Probleme und Perspektiven im Umgang mit mittelalterlichen Quellen', *Vierteljahrschrift für Sozial- und Wirtschaftsgeschichte*, 100.2 (2013), 135–53

Knappett, Carl, ed., *Network Analysis in Archaeology: New Approaches to Regional Interaction* (Oxford: Oxford University Press, 2013)

——, *An Archaeology of Interaction: Network Perspectives on Material Culture and Society* (Oxford: Oxford University Press, 2015)

Kocka, Jürgen, and Heinz-Gerhard Haupt, 'Comparison and Beyond: Traditions, Scope, and Perspectives of Comparative History', in *Comparative and Transnational History: Central European Approaches and New Perspectives*, ed. by Heinz-Gerhard Haupt and Jürgen Kocka (New York: Berghahn, 2009), pp. 1–30

Korhonen, Kuisma, 'Textual Communities: Nancy, Blanchot, Derrida', *Culture Machine*, 8 (2006), unpaginated; <https://culturemachine.net/community/textual-communities/> [accessed 7 January 2022]

Latour, Bruno, *Reassembling the Social: An Introduction to Actor–Network–Theory* (Oxford: Oxford University Press, 2005)

Lemercier, Claire, 'Formal Network Methods in History: Why and how?', in *Social Networks, Political Institutions, and Rural Societies*, ed. by Georg Fertig (Turnhout: Brepols, 2015), pp. 281–310

Lugli, Emmanuele, 'Linking the Mediterranean: The Construction of Trading Networks in 14th and 15th-Century Italy', in *The Globalization of Renaissance Art: A Critical Review*, ed. by Daniel Savoy (Leiden: Brill, 2017), pp. 158–85

Maillard Álvarez, Natalia, ed., *Books in the Catholic World during the Early Modern Period* (Leiden: Brill, 2014)

Maillard Álvarez, Natalia, and Manuel F. Fernández Chaves, eds, *Bibliotecas de la Monarquía Hispánica en la primera globalización (siglos XVI–XVIII)* (Zaragoza: Prensas de la Universidad de Zaragoza, 2021)

'Memorandum of Understanding', COST Action IS1301, Brussels, 24 May 2013, <https://www.cost.eu/actions/IS1301/> [accessed 7 January 2022]

Morato, Nicola, and Dirk Schoenaers, eds, *Medieval Francophone Literary Culture Outside France: The Moving Word* (Turnhout: Brepols, 2017)

Nagy, Balázs, Felicitas Schmieder, and András Vadas, eds, *The Medieval Networks in East Central Europe: Commerce, Contacts, Communication* (London: Routledge, 2019)

Paiva, Eduardo França, *Dar nome ao novo. Uma história lexical da Ibero-América entre os séculos XVI e XVII (as dinâmicas de mestiçagens e o mundo do trabalho)* (Belo Horizonte: Autêntica, 2015)

Parker, Charles H., 'Entrepreneurs, Families, and Companies', in *The Cambridge World History*, VI: *The Construction of a Global World, 1400–1800*, ed. by Jerry H. Bentley, Sanjay Subrahmanyam, and Merry Wiesner-Hanks (Cambridge: Cambridge University Press, 2015), pp. 190–212

Parker, Noel, 'From Borders to Margins: A Deleuzian Ontology for Identities in the Postinternational Environment', *Alternatives*, 34 (2009), 17–39

Prell, Christina, *Social Network Analysis: History, Theory, and Methodology* (Los Angeles: Sage, 2012)

Rehberg Sedo, DeNel, ed., *Reading Communities from Salons to Cyberspace* (Basingstoke: Palgrave Macmillan, 2011)

Roudometof, Victor, *Glocalization: A Critical Introduction* (New York: Routledge, 2016)

Scase, Wendy, 'Reading Communities', in *The Oxford Handbook of Medieval Literature in English*, ed. by Greg Walker and Elaine Treharne (Oxford: Oxford University Press, 2010), pp. 557–73

Schilling, Heinz, and István György Tóth, eds, *Cultural Exchange in Early Modern Europe*, I: *Religion and Cultural Exchange in Europe, 1400–1700* (Cambridge: Cambridge University Press, 2006)

Selig, Maria, and Susanne Ehrich, eds, *Mittelalterliche Stadtsprachen* (Regensburg: Schnell & Steiner, 2016)

Shepard, Jonathan, 'Networks', *Past & Present, Supplement*, 13 (2018), 116–57

Sloterdijk, Peter, *Sphären*, III: *Schäume* (Frankfurt am Main: Suhrkamp, 2004)

Smith, Kathryn Ann, *Art, Identity, and Devotion in Fourteenth-Century England: Three Women and Their Books of Hours* (London: British Library, 2003)

Soen, Violet, Bram De Ridder, Alexander Soetaert, Werner Thomas, Johan Verberckmoes, and Sophie Verreyken, 'How to do Transregional History: A Concept, Method and Tool for Early Modern Border Research', *Journal of Early Modern History*, 21.4 (2017), 343–64

Subrahmanyam, Sanjay, 'Connected Histories: Notes towards a Reconfiguration of Early Modern Eurasia', *Modern Asian Studies*, 31.3, Special Issue: *The Eurasian Context of the Early Modern History of Mainland South East Asia, 1400–1800* (1997), 735–62

——, *Courtly Encounters: Translating Courtliness and Violence in Early Modern Eurasia* (Cambridge, MA: Harvard University Press, 2012)

Trivellato, Francesca, *The Familiarity of Strangers: The Sephardic Diaspora, Livorno and Cross-Cultural Trade in the Early Modern Period* (New Haven: Yale University Press, 2009)

Van Dussen, Michael, and Pavel Soukup, eds, *Religious Controversy in Europe, 1378–1536: Textual Transmission and Networks of Readership* (Turnhout: Brepols, 2013)

Vásquez, Manuel A., 'Studying Religion in Motion: A Networks Approach', *Method and Theory in the Study of Religion*, 20 (2008), 151–84

Vega, María José, *Imperios de papel. La crítica literaria postcolonial* (Barcelona: Crítica, 2003)

Wellmann, Barry, and S. D. Berkowitz, 'Introduction: Studying Social Structures', in *Social Structures: A Network Approach*, ed. by Barry Wellmann and S. D. Berkowitz (Cambridge: Cambridge University Press, 1988), pp. 1–14

——, 'Structural Analysis from Method and Metaphor to Theory and Substance', in *Social Structures: A Network Approach*, ed. by Barry Wellmann and S. D. Berkowitz (Cambridge: Cambridge University Press, 1988), pp. 19–61

Werner, Michael, and Bénédicte Zimmermann, 'Penser l'histoire croisée: entre empirie et réflexivité', *Annales. Histoire, Sciences Sociales*, 57 (2003), 7–34

——, ed., *De la comparaison à l'histoire croisée* (Paris: Seuil, 2004)

——, 'Beyond Comparison: Histoire croisée and the Challenge of Reflexivity', *History and Theory: Studies in the Philosophy of History*, 45.1 (2006), 30–50

European Connections

RAFAEL M. PÉREZ GARCÍA

Francisco de Osuna's *Tercer Abecedario Espiritual* and the Medieval Mystical Tradition in Western Europe

Introduction

From the late nineteenth century, researchers working on Spanish sixteenth-century spiritual literature have explored its literary sources and the influences it absorbed from other European spiritual traditions.[1] Connections have been drawn with the Low Countries,[2] Germany,[3] and Italy,[4] as well as with Sufi mystics,[5] and there has also been interest in the role played by converts. The latter are regarded as a privileged niche for the reception of Erasmist ideas.[6] The arguments proffered were based on romantic and nationalistic perceptions of European culture, which tended to divide literary analysis according to political, linguistic, and ideological borders. The relationships between works written in different countries and languages were perceived in terms of 'influences' that were only possible when the national characters in which they were rooted were deemed to be compatible. We know today that this is an inadequate way to explore the history of spiritual literature,[7] which was, in reality, the

---

1 Andrés Martín, *Historia de la mística*, pp. 203–21; Pérez García, 'Communitas Christiana'.
2 Groult, *Los místicos de los Países Bajos*.
3 Sanchís Alventosa, *La escuela mística alemana*; Orcibal, *San Juan de la Cruz*.
4 Sáinz Rodríguez, *Espiritualidad española*, pp. 73–118.
5 Asín Palacios, *Sadilíes y alumbrados*.
6 Castro, *Aspectos del vivir hispánico*; Bataillon, *Erasmo y España*; Pérez García, 'El tema de la crítica al clero'; Pérez García, 'Judeoconversos y espiritualidad cristiana'.
7 Pérez García, 'Francisco de Osuna y Santa Teresa de Jesús'.

> **Rafael M. Pérez García** is currently Associate Professor at the Department of Early Modern History at the Universidad de Sevilla. His research interests include cultural and religious history in sixteenth-century Spain, and social history, with a special focus on social minorities (Moriscos, slaves).

expression of a shared European and Christian culture.[8] Questions remain concerning how this literature was produced and how different spiritual traditions that were neither identical nor synchronic converged. I shall use the Franciscan Francisco de Osuna's *Tercer Abecedario Espiritual* (*Third Spiritual Alphabet*), published in Toledo in 1527, to answer this question. This was, without a doubt, the key mystical work in Spain in the first half of the sixteenth century, and the last major exponent of the European medieval mystical tradition.

So, this article intends to analyse mystical literature in Spain in the first third of the sixteenth century through the examination of Francisco de Osuna's *Tercer Abecedario Espiritual*. In particular, I will try to explain how different spiritual traditions (mostly those of the Cistercians, Carthusians, Victorines, and Franciscans) converged in this text, which deliberately joined the ecclesiastical tradition while advocating a radical transformation in the relationship between society and mystical literature. Finally, the nuptial exegesis of the *Song of Songs*, applied to the mystical writings of Pseudo-Dionysius the Areopagite, will be presented as a key for the understanding of the processes involved in the production of Christian mystical literature.

The Medieval Spiritual Sources of the *Tercer Abecedario*

Thanks to Pierre Groult's and especially to Fidèle de Ros' pioneering studies, we have a fairly accurate understanding of the sources consulted by Osuna for his *Tercer Abecedario*. De Ros did not hesitate to argue that 'Osuna est avant tout un disciple du Moyen Age. C'est là qu'il faut chercher ses maîtres' (Osuna is first and foremost a disciple of the Middle Ages. His teachers can be found there), especially Saint Bernard, Richard of Saint Victor, and Jean Gerson.[9] Behind the many explicit references to Saint Bernard, De Ros could identify some of his authentic works (*Epistolae*, *Sermones in Cantica canticorum*, and *Sermones varii*), but also a large number of texts in the monastic tradition that were, in fact, not the work of the founder of the Cistercian Order, namely *Epistola seu tractatus ad fratres de monte Dei* by Abbot Guillaume de Saint-Thierry, *Scala claustralium* by the Carthusian Guigo II, *Formula honestae vitae*, *Tractatus de conscientia*, *Octo puncta perfectionis assequendae*, *Meditationes de cognitione humanae conditionis*, and *Tractatus de interiori domo* (the last two having sometimes been attributed to Hugh of Saint Victor).[10] A series of treatises by Richard

---

8 Pérez García, 'Communitas Christiana'.
9 De Ros, *Un maître de Sainte Thérèse*, p. 353.
10 De Ros, *Un maître de Sainte Thérèse*, pp. 354–57.

of Saint Victor (*Benjamin minor*, *Benjamin major*, and *Tractatus de gradibus charitatis*) form the second pillar on which *Tercer Abecedario* is based.[11] Bernard's and Richard's works, written in the twelfth century, and the monastic works that followed, are the cornerstone of Osuna's mystic of withdrawal (*recogimiento*), which was to be highly influential in sixteenth-century Spain. Osuna also repeatedly made use of the works by the French Jean Gerson to deal with tricky matters of spirituality (diabolical lures, extraordinary gifts, temptations, the role of the spiritual guide, etc.), and this author can be considered the third main influence in *Tercer Abecedario*. Gerson's presence is explained by his mystical authority and by the context of *Tercer Abecedario*, written in the midst of intense theological controversies and in a period during which Castile's Franciscans were in the sights of the Inquisition.[12]

According to Fidèle de Ros, few authors other than Bernard, Richard, and Gerson can be considered to have had a significant influence on *Tercer Abecedario*. Surprisingly, references to the Franciscan Saint Bonaventure are few, and some are, in fact, mistaken references to the Carthusian Hugh of Balma's *Mystica theologia*,[13] written in the late thirteenth century. In the same way, the abundant references to Saint Cyprian often hide the work of another twelfth-century Cistercian, Arnaud de Bonneval, one of Saint Bernard's companions.[14] The sources of *Tercer Abecedario* are not limited to these works, but include many others, some of which are not cited at all, such as *Tratado de la vida espiritual*, by the Valencian Dominican Saint Vincente Ferrer, who died in 1419 and was canonized a few decades later.[15] The number of Christian theological authors cited is large, with no fewer than 274 mentions in 280 folios in quarto, including twenty-four authors who span the ecclesiastical literature between the third and the sixteenth centuries.[16] De Ros adds that '[l]e Frère Mineur complète ses lectures par les traditions franciscaines, par les confidences de ses amis et dirigés, par son expérience personnelle' (the Friar Minor supplements his readings with the Franciscan traditions, with the confessions made by his friends and those under his spiritual direction, with his personal experience).[17]

---

11 De Ros, *Un maître de Sainte Thérèse*, pp. 357–58.
12 Pérez García, 'Tradición espiritual y autoridad'; De Ros, *Un maître de Sainte Thérèse*, pp. 358–61.
13 'dice San Buenaventura en su *Mística teología*, declarando a San Dionisio' (according to Saint Bonaventure in his *Mística teología*, quoting Dionysius), Francisco de Osuna, *Tercer Abecedario Espiritual*, p. 149.
14 De Ros, *Un maître de Sainte Thérèse*, pp. 361–63.
15 De Ros, *Un maître de Sainte Thérèse*, p. 363; Francisco de Osuna, *Tercer Abecedario Espiritual*, p. 255, where he simply refers to 'un santo' (a saint).
16 Pérez García, 'Tradición espiritual y autoridad'.
17 De Ros, *Un maître de Sainte Thérèse*, p. 363.

Tercer Abecedario: From the Medieval Mystical Tradition to Dissemination in the Early Modern Age

The weight of monastic, especially Cistercian, literature in *Tercer Abecedario* may sound strange, but the fact is that, from the twelfth century onwards, this genre had become a major source of Christian spirituality. Franciscan reformism, which proliferated in Castile from the late fourteenth century onwards and continued, through the periods of the *Observancia* (Franciscan Observance) and the *Descalcez* (Discalced Franciscans), until Osuna's time, and it never ceased to draw inspiration from the monastic orders.[18] The successful process of reform led by the Benedictine congregation in Valladolid ended,[19] as far as spiritual literature is concerned, with the publication in 1500 in the monastery of Montserrat of *Exercitatorio de la vida spiritual* by Abbot García Jiménez de Cisneros. This work, published in both Latin and Spanish,[20] drew heavily on the rich tradition of medieval monastic spiritual literature as well as on Franciscan spiritual authors.[21]

It seems clear that no obvious difference existed between monks and mendicant friars, especially Franciscans, in their approach to spirituality; within the Franciscan Order, hermit-like groups which wished to withdraw from the world proliferated constantly.[22] Saint Bernard and Richard of Saint Victor, alongside a host of other authors, monastic or otherwise, such as Hugh of Saint Victor (whose works Osuna was also familiar with), coined the main concepts and the specific vocabulary to explain the relationship and mystical union of the soul with God. Especially important was the contribution made by the Victorines, who carefully undertook the task of systematizing mysticism (especially contemplation and ecstasy) in detail, laying the foundations for a systematic way to present the topic in the following centuries.[23] For this reason, they became inevitable references for all authors who, as part of this monastic tradition, wrote about mystical theology in the centuries that followed. Jean Gerson's (1363–1429) commentary on Dionysius the Areopagite was also built on the technical foundations laid out by Saint Bernard and Richard of Saint Victor, as well as, to a lesser extent, by Hugh of Saint Victor, Guillaume de Saint-Thierry, Hugh of Balma, and Saint Bonaventure.[24] This spiritual current reacted against new trends, such as that led by Ruysbroeck, whom

---

18 Pérez García, '*Communitas Christiana*'.
19 Colombás, *Un reformador benedictino*.
20 Pérez García, *La imprenta y la literatura espiritual castellana*, p. 304.
21 Baraut Obiols, 'La bibliothèque ascétique'; Baraut Obiols, 'Les fonts franciscanes'.
22 De Lejarza, 'Orígenes de la descalcez franciscana'; Meseguer Fernández, 'Programa de gobierno del P. Francisco de Quiñones'.
23 Healey, 'The Mysticism of the School of Saint Victor'.
24 Combes, *Jean Gerson commentateur dionysien*, pp. 58–61, 106–07.

Gerson criticized systematically[25] and whom Osuna seems not to have known[26] or at least followed.

In *Tercer Abecedario*, Franciscan sources and authors play a greater role than the few references to Saint Francis of Assisi[27] and Saint Bonaventure[28] might suggest. Although some of the writings of the founder of the order are cited explicitly,[29] and some references to the Creation[30] and other topics[31] are clearly Franciscan in tone or are directly dependent on Franciscan sources, the fact is that the Franciscan footprint on *Tercer Abecedario* is much more important than it looks at first sight.

However, we need to ask the following question: how was mystical literature, which is generally regarded as a continuous line, rooted in the past and projected into the future, produced on the basis of such apparently miscellaneous materials? The answer is not an easy one. In my opinion, some of the explanation lies in the following factors: firstly, Christian authors, including Osuna, regardless of the order to which they belonged or the country they came from, agreed that the works listed above were the main foundations of mystical theology; secondly, the practice of spirituality and its transmission within the religious orders ensured the continuity of a set of perfectly constructed texts from generation to generation;[32] thirdly, there is the key role played by the *Corpus Dionisianum* and the *Song of Songs*, as well as their medieval commentators. In the remainder of this chapter, I shall only consider the third of these factors.

---

25 Combes, *Essai sur la critique de Ruysbroek par Gerson*.
26 De Ros, *Un maître de Sainte Thérèse*, pp. 204–05, 219.
27 Francisco de Osuna, *Tercer Abecedario Espiritual*, pp. 127, 153, 185, 360–61, 382, 488.
28 Francisco de Osuna, *Tercer Abecedario Espiritual*, pp. 149, 186, 268, 348, 478, 543, 565.
29 Osuna copied the whole of Chapter 2 of Treatise 13 of Saint Francis's *Paraphrase*, about the Lord's Prayer (Francisco de Osuna, *Tercer Abecedario Espiritual*, pp. 360–61; cf. Saint Francis of Assisi, *Escritos. Biografías*, pp. 31–33). He also cited *Regola Bullata* (Francisco de Osuna, *Tercer Abecedario Espiritual*, p. 382; cf. Saint Francis of Assisi, *Escritos. Biografías*, pp. 133–34).
30 Francisco de Osuna, *Tercer Abecedario Espiritual*, pp. 114–16.
31 Such as the insistence on having but few books (Francisco de Osuna, *Tercer Abecedario Espiritual*, pp. 339 or 255; cf. Tomás de Celano, *Vida segunda*, in Saint Francis of Assisi, *Escritos. Biografías*, p. 285) or the notion of humility as the foundation of spiritual life (Francisco de Osuna, *Tercer Abecedario Espiritual*, p. 498; cf. Tomás de Celano, *Vida segunda*, in Saint Francis of Assisi, *Escritos. Biografías*, p. 328).
32 For the issue of creation and transmission of meaning among communities of readers in the Middle Ages and the sixteenth century, see Illich, *En el viñedo del texto*; Pérez García, *Sociología y lectura espiritual*; Freitas Carvalho, *Lectura espiritual en la Península Ibérica*.

Dionysian Exegesis of the *Song of Songs* and Connecting Mysticism to Lay Readers

Talking about mystical theology in Europe from the twelfth to the sixteenth centuries implies that we need to refer to Pseudo-Dionysius the Areopagite, whose *Mystical Theology* sought the mysteries of God in 'the blackest darkness', renouncing the sensitive and intellectual faculties of knowledge to ascend to the 'mysterious darkness of not-knowing': by renouncing knowledge, the 'union with Him who is unknowable becomes possible'.[33] Although the doctrinal relationship between Dionysius and Saint Bernard is controversial,[34] Hugh of Saint Victor's *Expositio super angelicam hierarchiam* is open to few doubts.[35] Saint Bonaventure cites Dionysius constantly, as well as regarding him as a disciple of Saint Paul, following Albertus Magnus, Alexander of Hales, and Thomas Aquinas,[36] even if he never produced a commentary on him, like other Franciscans such as Robert Grosseteste, Pietro Olivi, and Francesco of Mayronnes.[37] The alleged transmission of secret lore from Saint Paul to Dionysius and from him to his disciples was, in Balma's opinion, a bulwark for mystical theology against its critics.[38]

For Osuna, Dionysius is first and foremost the indisputable master of the *vía negativa* towards knowledge, the very definition of mystical theology.[39] Osuna's *Tercer Abecedario* used the *vía negativa* to define withdrawal (*recogimiento*),[40] the art of knowing God through love and beyond the understanding and the senses,[41] which is the recurrent theme that runs through the whole of *Tercer Abecedario*. Osuna makes it explicit:

---

33 Pseudo-Dionysius the Areopagite, *Teología mística*, pp. 371–73.
34 Boissard, 'Saint Bernard et le Pseudo-Aréopagite'; Faes de Mottoni, *Il 'Corpus Dionysianum' nel Medioevo*, p. 31.
35 Faes de Mottoni, *Il 'Corpus Dionysianum' nel Medioevo*, pp. 37–39.
36 Bougerol, 'Saint Bonaventure et le Pseudo-Denys l'Aréopagite', p. 33.
37 Bougerol, 'Saint Bonaventure et le Pseudo-Denys l'Aréopagite', pp. 34–35; Faes de Mottoni, *Il 'Corpus Dionysianum' nel Medioevo*, pp. 14–15.
38 Pérez García, 'El argumento histórico'.
39 Francisco de Osuna, *Tercer Abecedario Espiritual*, p. 144. Osuna is obviously referring to Chapter III of Dionysius the Areopagite's *Mystical Theology* (cf. Pseudo-Dionysius the Areopagite, *Teología mística*, pp. 375–77).
40 Francisco de Osuna, *Tercer Abecedario Espiritual*, pp. 199–203.
41 'Esta arte se llama de amor [...]. Llámase también este ejercicio profundidad, la cual contiene oscuridad y hondura; porque este ejercicio se funda en la hondura y profundo corazón del hombre, el cual debe estar oscuro; esto es, privado de humano conocimiento, para que de esta manera estando [en] tinieblas, sobre él venga el espíritu de Dios sobre las aguas de sus deseos a decir que se haga luz divina' (This art is called love [...] This exercise is also called profundity, and is full of darkness and depth; because the exercise is based on the depth of man's heart, which must be dark; that is, devoid of all human knowledge, so the spirit of God can come over the water of his wishes as the bearer of divine light), Francisco de Osuna, *Tercer Abecedario Espiritual*, pp. 202–03.

Y San Dionisio dice: Deja con fuerte lucha los sentidos y las intelectivas operaciones y todas las cosas sensibles y inteligibles, y todas las cosas que permanecen y no permanecen; y así como fuere posible, levántate, no sabiendo, a la unión de aquel que es sobre toda sustancia y conocimiento.[42]

(And Saint Dionysius says: Leave your senses and your intellectual operations and all things sensible and intelligible, and all things permanent and impermanent; and as far as possible, step up not knowing to be one with Him who is above all substance and knowledge.)

Given the role assigned to Dionysius by Osuna, it is not strange that five of the seven citations in *Tercer Abecedario* are found in Treatise 21, in which Osuna explains the act of silencing the intellect and justifies the validity of the *vía negativa* by citing a selection of ecclesiastical writers, which he refers to as 'los doctores auténticos que hablaron de esta materia' (the true doctors who have sustained this matter):[43] Anthony the Great, Abbot Isaac of Nineveh, Saint Augustine, Hugh of Saint Victor, Gregory of Nazianzus, Saint Bonaventure, and Saint Bernard. Among these, Dionysius stands out for his authority, and Jean Gerson as his interpreter.[44] The two remaining

---

42 Francisco de Osuna, *Tercer Abecedario Espiritual*, p. 565.
43 'Para favor de aquesta letra presente y de todo este tercer libro quiero poner aquí una autoridad de cada uno de los doctores auténticos que hablaron de esta materia, dejando otros muchos autores de aquesto, cuyas escrituras no son en poco tenidas de los que saben; y dejando también los testimonios que dan cada día del recogimiento los que tienen de él experiencia y lo siguen por el bien que conocen venir a sus ánimas con él; y estos testimonios, aunque los incrédulos no hagan fe, ni se deban decir a ellos, como manda San Dionisio, no por eso pierden su vigor y fuerza ni carecen de culpa los impugnadores' (In support of this passage, and of all this third book, I want to refer to the authority of all the true doctors who spoke thus; they wrote much about this, and their opinions are appreciated not a little by those who know about these things; and we shall hear about the experience on withdrawal from some of those who have experienced it; the disbelief of sceptics, as Saint Dionysius makes clear, makes these arguments not false or their accusers guiltless), Francisco de Osuna, *Tercer Abecedario Espiritual*, p. 563.
44 'Si tú no entiendes a San Dionisio, no por eso está por entender, ca Gerson está ahí y otros doctores santos que lo entendieron' (If you do not understand Saint Dionysius, that does not mean that he is not understood, because there are Gerson and other saintly doctors who understood him), Francisco de Osuna, *Tercer Abecedario Espiritual*, p. 558; 'Empero, entretanto hácese algunas veces aquello que, conforme a San Dionisio, dice Gerson: Juntarse el ánima a las cosas inefables y no conocidas inefable y no conocidamente' (Sometimes what Gerson says, based on Saint Dionysius, is done: to join the soul with ineffable and unknown things, ineffably and unknowingly), Francisco de Osuna, *Tercer Abecedario Espiritual*, p. 564. And he concludes 'De innumerables testimonios muy creíbles que ha de santos y aprobados doctores en favor de la presente letra, no he querido traer sino los menos; y creo que bastan para los no ejercitados, que los otros en cada parte de la Escritura leen espiritualmente aqueste ejercicio; y más de verdad en sus corazones, donde Dios con su gracia se lo escribe tan de verdad, que, aunque lo tengan muchos por loco, no deja él, como dice San Dionisio,

references to Dionysius in the *Tercer Abecedario* are supplementary to Osuna's argument.[45] Therefore, the Dionysius of *Tercer Abecedario* stands for nothing less than a radical reduction of the fundamental idea of the unity of the soul with God, which is achieved through love, in the absence of knowledge. It was thus easy to link Dionysius's ideas with the lexicon deployed by Saint Bernard and Richard of Saint Victor and with Guigo II's *Scala claustralium*'s description of the ecstatic union.[46]

The substantial number of Franciscan commentaries on Dionysius's works clearly illustrates the interest that this author aroused among the order's theologians during the Middle Ages. In addition, the fact that the Carthusian Hugh of Balma's *Mystica theologia* (written in the late thirteenth century) was often attributed to Saint Bonaventure must have increased the prestige of the work among the members of the order. It is also possible that this wrong attribution was only a subterfuge to increase

---

de estar muy seguro con el testimonio de su conciencia' (Trustworthy testimonies from many saints and doctors support this writing, and I have mentioned but a few; I think this is enough for beginners, the others will see this spiritual exercise written all over the Scriptures; and more truly still in their hearts, on which God graciously writes so true that, even if they are taken for fools, they shall never, as Dionysius says, doubt their testimony), Francisco de Osuna, *Tercer Abecedario Espiritual*, p. 567.

45 'Porque, según dice San Dionisio, todas las cosas que hace nuestro Señor Dios, así con los buenos como con los malos, las convierte al amor de Su Majestad; y nosotros hemos de hacer lo mismo en cuanto fuere posible, contemplando en todas las cosas, como nuestra letra dice, el amor' (Because, as Saint Dionysius says, all things done by Our Lord, both good and bad, he turns into love for His Majesty; and we must do likewise whenever possible, seeing love in all things), Francisco de Osuna, *Tercer Abecedario Espiritual*, p. 436; 'Porque la inflamación del amor, según San Dionisio, se atribuye a los serafines, de la cual dice que está lleno su corazón' (Because the swell of love, according to saint Dionysius, is attributed to the Seraphs of which his heart is said to be full), Francisco de Osuna, *Tercer Abecedario Espiritual*, p. 512.

46 For instance, when he claims: 'Debes saber que cuando la inteligencia del ánima, que es la más alta fuerza entre las que conocen, pasa en afección o amor de las cosas que contempla, casi es dicha levantarse sobre sí misma, y la tal obra se llama exceso de ánima o levantamiento sobre sí mismo o sobre el espíritu suyo, según hallarás en muchos libros escrito' (You must know that when the intelligence of the soul, which is the strongest force known to man, loves the things that it contemplates, is almost a joy when it stands on itself, and this is called an excess of soul, or of lifting itself on its own spirit, as you will find in many books), Francisco de Osuna, *Tercer Abecedario Espiritual*, p. 201. The basic elements of Richard of Saint Victor's *Beniamin maior* and *Beniamin minor* run through the whole of *Tercer Abecedario* (cf. Francisco de Osuna, *Tercer Abecedario Espiritual*, pp. 196, 278, 294, 437–38, 556–57), and something similar happens with Saint Bernard (for instance, Francisco de Osuna, *Tercer Abecedario Espiritual*, pp. 566 or 231–32 which refers to Sermon 32 on *Song of Songs*, cf. Saint Bernard, *Sermones sobre el Cantar de los Cantares*, pp. 412–15, on 'la guarda del corazón' (guard of the heart), a key topic for Osuna); for the term *excessus* in Saint Bernard to refer to ecstasy see Boissard, 'Saint Bernard et le Pseudo-Aréopagite', pp. 223–24. Again, with Chapter V of *Scala claustralium* which Osuna copies in full and attributes to Saint Bernard (Francisco de Osuna, *Tercer Abecedario Espiritual*, pp. 305–06; cf. Guigo II, *Scala claustralium*, cols 479–80).

the 'Franciscanism' of Balma's work, which was nothing but an explanation of Dionysius's mystical arguments. In Castile, where Osuna lived and wrote, the fact that Balma's work had been translated into Spanish by Father Antonio de Ciudad Real, the vicar of the Franciscan convent of San Juan de los Reyes in Toledo (it was published in this city in 1514 under the title *Sol de contemplativos*), increased the apparent veracity of this attribution even more. The prologue to the translation claimed that 'it was written by Hugh of Balma or, according to some, the seraphic and devout Saint Bonaventure'.[47] The colophon insisted on this, claiming a direct link with Saint Dionysius: 'This ends the book, called the mystic theology of Saint Dionysius, written by Hugh of Balma or, according to others, by Saint Bonaventure'.[48] Accepting this attribution, Osuna's *Tercer Abecedario* erroneously cites Balma as Saint Bonaventure.[49] The prologue of *Sol de contemplativos* also drew a link between an exegesis of *Song of Songs* and Dionysius's mystical theology, by interpreting the wife as the devout soul that joins and embraces her beloved God,[50] and by associating the lover's bed from which the longed-for lover is absent (*Song of Songs* 3. 1) with the night of knowledge which makes the contemplation of love possible:

> De este sueño hablaba la esposa en los *Cantares*: En mi cama por las noches busqué aquel que ama mi ánima. En la cama y por las noches busca el ánima a su esposo cuando en el reposo de la contemplación duerme a las cosas temporales y vela a las eternas. Y entonces, cuanto más oscuridad y menos conocimiento tiene de lo temporal tanto más es alumbrada de la claridad soberana según bien largamente trata el divino Dionisio hablando de aquella santa oscuridad en la cual los devotos contemplan a Dios.[51]

> (The wife in the *Song* referred to the dream [of knowledge] in the *Song of Songs*: at night in my bed I sought him who loves my soul. In the bed, at night, the soul searches for her husband when contemplation is asleep for the things of the world and awake for the eternal. And then, the darker and more unknown the world, the more the sovereign light will shine, as rightly argued by Saint Dionysius when he referred to that saintly darkness in which the devout contemplates God.)

In this way, the reduction of Dionysius's thought to a single fundamental idea, as well as its identification with the union between the soul and

---

47 Hugo de Balma, *Sol de contemplativos*, pp. 29–30.
48 Hugo de Balma, *Sol de contemplativos*, p. 194.
49 Francisco de Osuna, *Tercer Abecedario Espiritual*, p. 149: 'Saint Bonaventure's *Mystical Theology* argues, citing Saint Dionysius'.
50 After Song of Songs 8. 5; cf. Hugo de Balma, *Sol de contemplativos*, p. 29.
51 Hugo de Balma, *Sol de contemplativos*, p. 30.

God through the exegetic tradition that interpreted the *Song of Songs* in spiritual terms, played a key role in unifying the sense of a wide array of literary traditions, monastic in origin or otherwise. Osuna cites the *Song of Songs* often in his *Tercer Abecedario* (no less than twenty-six citations, involving twenty-two verses in total),[52] and he sometimes uses these nuptial metaphors to describe the passionate and loving union between the soul and God.[53]

For Henri de Lubac Francisco de Osuna was the culmination of medieval spiritual traditions,[54] and, based on the way Osuna constructed his major work on mystical theology, I too have few doubts that he should be regarded as the last major medieval mystic.[55] It is also true that he played a key role in radically reorienting mysticism; this makes him the first major early modern mystic. As De Lubac argues, this way of writing about spirituality had for centuries been directed towards the inhabitants of conventual cloisters,[56] while Osuna tried tenaciously to bring it into the outside world. Dionysius's *Mystical Theology*, in a passage that Osuna cites but interprets in a biased way,[57] warned against the dissemination of a form of knowledge that he considered secret and only fit for initiates;[58] in the Middle Ages this was tantamount to saying it was fit only for members of the clergy. Osuna expressed in no uncertain terms that he wished to bring mystic theology to all social groups, letting it abandon the seclusion of the convents and monasteries within which it had been transmitted throughout the Middle Ages.[59] By so doing, Osuna consolidated the avenue opened in 1500 by Gómez García's *Carro de dos vidas* (which included a full Spanish translation of the *Scala claustralium* and was

---

52 Cf. Francisco de Osuna, *Tercer Abecedario Espiritual*, pp. 602–03.
53 Francisco de Osuna, *Tercer Abecedario Espiritual*, pp. 202, 342–43.
54 De Lubac, *Éxégèse médiévale*, IV, pp. 497–98.
55 Pérez García, 'Tradición espiritual y autoridad'.
56 De Lubac, *Éxégèse médiévale*, IV, p. 500.
57 'Y estos testimonios, aunque los incrédulos no hagan fe, ni se deban decir a ellos, como manda San Dionisio, no por eso pierden su vigor y fuerza ni carecen de culpa los impugnadores' (The disbelief of sceptics, as Saint Dionysius makes clear, makes these arguments not false nor their accusers guiltless), Francisco de Osuna, *Tercer Abecedario Espiritual*, p. 563.
58 'Pero ten cuidado de que nada de esto llegue a oídos de ignorantes: los que son esclavos de las cosas mundanas. Se imaginan que no hay nada más allá de lo que existe en la naturaleza física, individual. Piensan, además, que con su razón pueden conocer a aquel que "puso su tienda en las tinieblas"', cf. Psalm 18. 12 (But beware, and do not let this reach the ears of ignorant people: they are slaves of the world. They imagine that there is nothing beyond what has a physical and individual nature. They also think that their reason will allow them to know Him who pitched "His tent in the darkness"'), Pseudo-Dionysius the Areopagite, *Teología mística*, pp. 371–72.
59 Pérez García, *La imprenta y la literatura espiritual castellana*, pp. 73–101.

clearly inspired by Richard of Saint Victor's work),[60] and in 1514 by *Sol de contemplativos*. The prologue of the Toledo edition clearly advocated the universal dissemination of mystic theology: 'all the faithful should try to reach a high state of contemplation'.[61]

---

[60] Pérez García, *Sociología y lectura espiritual*, pp. 371–84.
[61] Hugo de Balma, *Sol de contemplativos*, p. 29.

Works Cited

Primary Sources

Saint Francis of Assisi, *Escritos. Biografías. Documentos de la época*, ed. by José Antonio Guerra (Madrid: Biblioteca de Autores Cristianos, 2003)

Francisco de Osuna, *Primer Abecedario Espiritual*, ed. by José Juan Morcillo Pérez, Místicos Franciscanos Españoles, 3 (Madrid: Editorial Cisneros, 2004)

——, *Segundo Abecedario Espiritual*, ed. by José Juan Morcillo Pérez, Místicos Franciscanos Españoles, 4 (Madrid: Editorial Cisneros, 2004)

——, *Tercer Abecedario Espiritual*, ed. by Saturnino López-Santidrián, Místicos Franciscanos Españoles, 2 (Madrid: Biblioteca de Autores Cristianos, 1998)

Guigo II, *Scala Claustralium. Sive Tractatus de modo orandi*, ed. by Jacques Paul Migne, Patrologiae cursus completus: series latina, 184 (Paris: Garnier, 1854), cols 475–84

Hugo de Balma, *Sol de contemplativos*, ed. by Teodoro H. Martín, Ichtys, 14 (Salamanca: Ediciones Sígueme, 1992)

Pseudo-Dionysius the Areopagite, *Teología mística*, in *Obras Completas del Pseudo Dionisio Areopagita*, ed. by Teodoro H. Martín (Madrid: Biblioteca de Autores Cristianos, 1990)

Saint Bernard, *Sermones sobre el Cantar de los Cantares*, in *Obras Completas de San Bernardo*, v: *El Cantar de los Cantares*, ed. by Iñaki Aranguren and Mariano Ballano (Madrid: Biblioteca de Autores Cristianos, 2014)

Secondary Studies

Andrés Martín, Melquiades, *Historia de la mística de la Edad de Oro en España y América* (Madrid: Biblioteca de Autores Cristianos, 1994)

Asín Palacios, Miguel, *Sadilíes y alumbrados* (Madrid: Hiperión, 1990)

Baraut Obiols, Cebrià, 'Les fonts franciscanes dels escrits de Garsias de Cisneros', *Analecta montserratensia*, 9 (1962), 65–78

——, 'La bibliothèque ascétique de García de Cisneros abbé de Montserrat (1493–1510)', *Studia monastica*, 9 (1967), 327–39

Bataillon, Marcel, *Erasmo y España. Estudios sobre la historia espiritual del siglo xvi* (México: Fondo de Cultura Económica, 1966)

Boissard, Edmond, 'Saint Bernard et le Pseudo–Aréopagite', *Recherches de Théologie ancienne et médiévale*, 26 (1959), 214–63

Bougerol, Jacques Guy, 'Saint Bonaventure et le Pseudo-Denys l'Aréopagite', *Études franciscaines*, 28 (1968), 33–123

Castro, Américo, *Aspectos del vivir hispánico* (Madrid: Alianza Editorial, 1987)

Colombás, García M., *Un reformador benedictino en tiempo de los Reyes Católicos. García Jiménez de Cisneros, abad de Montserrat* (Montserrat: Abadía de Montserrat, 1955)

Combes, André, *Essai sur la critique de Ruysbroek par Gerson*, Études de Théologie et d'Histoire de la Spiritualité, 6, 4 vols (Paris: Vrin, 1945–1972)

——, *Jean Gerson commentateur dionysien. Pour l'histoire des courants doctrinaux a l'université de Paris a la fin du XIVe siècle*, Études de Philosophie Médiévale, 30 (Paris: Vrin, 1973)

Faes de Mottoni, Barbara, *Il 'Corpus Dionysianum' nel Medioevo. Rassegna di studi: 1900–1972* (Bologna: Il Mulino, 1977)

Freitas Carvalho, José Adriano, *Lectura espiritual en la Península Ibérica (siglos XVI–XVII)* (Salamanca: SEMYR, 2007)

Groult, Pierre, *Los místicos de los Países Bajos y la literatura espiritual española del siglo XVI*, Biblioteca de Hispanismo, 1, 2 vols (Madrid: Fundación Universitaria Española, 1976)

Healey, Patrick Joseph, 'The Mysticism of the School of Saint Victor', *Church History*, 1 (1932), 211–21

Illich, Ivan, *En el viñedo del texto. Etología de la lectura: un comentario al Didascalicon de Hugo de San Víctor* (México: Fondo de Cultura Económica, 2002)

Krynen, Jean, 'La pratique et la theorie de l'amour sans connaissance dans le *Viae Sion lugent* d'Hughes de Balma', *Revue d'Ascétique et de Mystique*, 40 (1964), 161–83

Lejarza, Fidel de, 'Orígenes de la descalcez franciscana', *Archivo Ibero-Americano*, 22 (1962), 15–131

Lubac, Henri de, *Éxégèse médiévale. Les quatre sens de l'Écriture*, 4 vols (Paris: Ed. Desclée de Brouwer, 1993)

Meseguer Fernández, Juan, 'Programa de gobierno del P. Francisco de Quiñones, Ministro General O.F.M.', *Archivo Ibero-Americano*, 21 (1961), 5–51

Orcibal, Jean, *San Juan de la Cruz y los místicos renano–flamencos* (Salamanca: Universidad Pontificia de Salamanca & Fundación Universitaria Española, 1987)

Pérez García, Rafael M., *Sociología y lectura espiritual en la Castilla del Renacimiento, 1470–1560*, Serie Teología, 4 (Madrid: Fundación Universitaria Española, 2005)

——, *La imprenta y la literatura espiritual castellana en la España del Renacimiento, 1470–1560. Historia y estructura de una emisión cultural*, Biblioteconomía y Administración Cultural, 156 (Gijón: Trea, 2006)

——, 'La Biblia en la construcción del texto espiritual del Renacimiento: la historia de José, hijo de Jacob, en la obra de Francisco de Osuna', in *Franciscanos, místicos, herejes y alumbrados*, ed. by Álvaro Castro Sánchez, Juan A. Egea Aranda, Rosa M. García Naranjo, Óscar Morales Pérez, and Emilio J. Navarro Martínez (Córdoba: Universidad de Córdoba & Editorial Séneca, 2010), pp. 153–76

———, 'El tema de la crítica al clero en la obra de Francisco de Osuna en el contexto del pensamiento católico reformista pretridentino', in *Iglesia, poder y fortuna. Clero y movilidad social en la España moderna*, ed. by Enrique Soria Mesa and Antonio José Díaz Rodríguez (Granada: Comares, 2012), pp. 139–89

———, '*Communitas Christiana*: The Sources of Christian Tradition in the Construction of Early Castilian Spiritual Literature, ca. 1400–1540', in *Books in the Catholic World during the Early Modern Period*, ed. by Natalia Maillard Álvarez (Leiden: Brill, 2014), pp. 71–113

———, 'Francisco de Osuna y Santa Teresa de Jesús. Algunas notas sobre la historia de la mística cristiana en la España del siglo XVI', *eHumanista Conversos*, 6 (2018), 159–77 <https://www.ehumanista.ucsb.edu/conversos/6> [accessed 17 August 2021]

———, 'El argumento histórico acerca de la transmisión de la Teología Mística y la autoridad de Dionisio Areopagita en la España del siglo XVI', in *Memoria de los orígenes. El discurso histórico-eclesiástico en el mundo moderno*, ed. by José Jaime García Bernal and Clara Bejarano Pellicer (Sevilla: Editorial Universidad de Sevilla, 2019), pp. 24–47

———, 'Judeoconversos y espiritualidad cristiana en la España de los siglos XV y XVI. El proceso formativo', in *Los judeoconversos en el mundo ibérico*, ed. by Enrique Soria Mesa and Antonio José Díaz Rodríguez (Córdoba: Ediciones Universidad de Córdoba, 2019), pp. 13–31

———, 'Tradición espiritual y autoridad en el *Libro llamado Abecedario Espiritual* de Francisco de Osuna', *Hispania Sacra*, 73 (2021), 389–402

Ros, Fidèle de, *Un maître de Sainte Thérèse. Le Père François d'Osuna. Sa vie, son oeuvre, sa doctrine spirituelle* (Paris: Gabriel Beauchesne Éditeur, 1936)

Sáinz Rodríguez, Pedro, *Espiritualidad española* (Madrid: Rialp, 1961)

Sanchís Alventosa, Joaquín, *La escuela mística alemana y sus relaciones con nuestros místicos del Siglo de Oro* (Madrid: Verdad y Vida, 1946)

MIROSŁAWA HANUSIEWICZ-LAVALLEE

The Sixteenth-Century Polish Protestant Martyrology and its Latin Sources

Authorship and European Sources of the Polish *History of Harsh Persecution*

In 1567, the printing press in Brest (Grand Duchy of Lithuania) published a monumental book of 842 pages *in folio* entitled *Historyja o srogim prześladowaniu Kościoła Bożego* (History of Harsh Persecution of God's Church).[1] It presented a comprehensive account of proto-Reformation and Reformation martyrs in Europe, beginning with Wycliff and the Lollards until the year 1563. Its author, Cyprian of Sieradz (Ciprianus Siradiensis), known at the time already as Cyprian Bazylik (*c.* 1535–after 1591), was running the Brest publishing house himself. Born into a burgher family and educated in the Cracow Academy, he had made his previous career as a composer and a poet. In 1557, Cyprian had been knighted by Jacob Heraclides Basilikos who — in recognition of his talents — included the young man into his own (shady) kinship and coats of arms, shortly before he himself had ventured to become a wretched prince of Moldavia.[2]

The Brest press was established by Prince Mikołaj Radziwiłł 'the Black' (1515–1565) and served the needs of the Calvinist Church in Poland–Lithuania. Only four years earlier it had published the Brest Bible, the first full Protestant translation of the Bible into Polish. Bazylik, as it seems,

---

1 Cyprian Bazylik, *Historyja o srogim prześladowaniu Kościoła Bożego*.
2 Stoy, 'Jacob Basilikos Heraclides (Despot Vodă)'; Czamańska, 'Jakub Bazylikos Heraklides'.

Mirosława Hanusiewicz-Lavallee is a professor at the John Paul II Catholic University of Lublin, and a member of the Polish Academy of Arts and Sciences. She has published extensively on Polish Baroque poetry and its European context, Renaissance humanism in Poland–Lithuania, and early modern Polish–British literary links. Her current research focuses on early modern Jesuit translations.

Networking Europe and New Communities of Interpretation (1400–1600), ed. by Margriet Hoogvliet, Manuel F. Fernández Chaves, *and* Rafael M. Pérez García, New Communities of Interpretation, 4 (Turnhout: Brepols, 2023), pp. 53–70
BREPOLS PUBLISHERS   10.1484/M.NCI-EB.5.134310

was involved in this endeavour and some other projects, so in the preface to his *History of Harsh Persecution* he confesses to some difficulties in the course of writing the martyrology. With no attempts to hide that the work is compiled from Latin sources, Bazylik explains that in 1564, three years prior to the printing, he started translating them in order to 'comply with the orders of certain persons of high estate as well as with the requests of other godly people',[3] after which he abandoned his work, 'busy with other things, because it was decided that someone else would complete the translation of these books'.[4] However, it turned out that the would-be translator failed to do his job, so when the press had already started printing the first parts of the book, Bazylik had to step in to complete the translation and supervise the publishing.

Interestingly enough, something similar happened to Bazylik two years later, when he had to complete Andreas Volanus's rendition of Marin Barleti's work (this time he decided to mention in the preface the unreliable translator's name).[5] It is entirely possible that Volanus, who was at the time the most distinguished Calvinist theologian in Vilnius, had previously been charged with the duty to work on the *History of Harsh Persecution*. Both writers were cooperating on different projects, which could be confirmed by the fact that in 1577 Volanus wrote a preface to Bazylik's Polish translation of Frycz Modrzewski's *De republica emendanda*.

However, it is also possible that in the passage quoted above the author of the *History* referred to his predecessor in the office of Brest printing press's manager, Stanisław Murmelius. The surviving inventory of the latter's library mentions books that provided the material for the martyrology.[6] In a dedicatory letter to Olbrycht Łaski Bazylik openly declares them as his sources:

> Though many learned people used to write such histories both in old ages and in our lifetime, those who wrote them in the most comprehensive way, collecting from different sources, were: John Foxe the Englishman, Heinrich Pantaleon, and Jean Crispin. I made one book of those three, picking from each of them stories according to the

---

3 Cyprian Bazylik, *Historyja o srogim prześladowaniu Kościoła Bożego*, fol. [*****]ʳ.
4 Cyprian Bazylik, *Historyja o srogim prześladowaniu Kościoła Bożego*, fol. [******]ʳ. See also Baliński, *Pisma historyczne*, III, pp. 13–15.
5 Cyprian Bazylik, *Historyja o żywocie i zacnych sprawach Jerzego Kastryjota*, fol. Diijʳ⁻ᵛ.
6 The inventory mentions *Historia martyrum, pars prima, in folio* and *Historia martyrum, pars secunda, in folio*; this refers more than likely to John Foxe's *Rerum in Ecclesia gestarum* and Heinrich Pantaleon's *Historia martyrum*. However, neither Jean Crespin's martyrology nor Jan van Utenhove's account are included. See Kowalski, 'Krakowski drukarz Stanisław Murmelius i jego księgozbiór (1571)'. I would like to thank prof. Kowalski for letting me read his paper before publishing.

order of years — whatever happened, in which year and in which place — and translated them into the Polish language.[7]

Bazylik's martyrology also includes his translation of Jan van Utenhove's *Simplex et fidelis narratio de instituta ac demum dissipata Belgarum aliorumque peregrinorum in Anglia Ecclesia* [...], an account of the dispersion, expulsion, and miserable wandering of the London Foreign Church led by Jan Łaski (better known in Europe as John a Lasco). Bazylik associates those events with the Marian persecutions described by Foxe, interprets the story as the 'continuatio of the history of the English Church',[8] and in another dedicatory letter to Olbrycht Łaski emphasizes the role of his patron's paternal uncle.

Almost all these works translated and compiled by Bazylik (with the exception of Jean Crespin's martyrology) had been published in a relatively short span of time in Basel by Johannes Oporinus and his printing partner Nicolaus Brylinger. These were: John Foxe's *Rerum in Ecclesia gestarum* [...] *commentarii* (1559) and — designed as its second part — *Martyrum historia, hoc est maximarum per Europam persecutionum ac sanctorum Dei martyrum* [...] *commentarii* (1563) by Heinrich Pantaleon, as well as the previously mentioned Jan van Utenhove's *Simplex et fidelis narratio* (1560).

In the years 1555–1559, John Foxe was being employed by Oporinus, a humanist well known for his irenic and tolerationist views, a very close friend of Celio Secundo Curione and Sebastian Castellio. The latter two were both particularly admired by Polish students in Basel, whose numbers had started to increase significantly from the middle of the sixteenth century. Many of the students lodged in Curione's household and were friends with Castellio, while both scholars were dedicating their writings to these high-born sons of Polish and Lithuanian magnates. The Polish guests also inspired Oporinus's interest in authors from Poland–Lithuania. In the 1550s he published works by Stanisław Orzechowski, Andrzej Frycz Modrzewski, Jan Łaski, and Marcin Kromer. Other Basel typographers were showing similar interests. Brylinger issued Wolfgang Weissenburg's rendition of Frycz Modrzewski's *De republica emendanda* (1557) and Heinrich Petri printed a translation of Kromer's *De origine et rebus gestis Polonorum* (1562), done by Pantaleon.[9]

These links are worth mentioning in the context of Bazylik's martyrology, because exactly in 1563 Curione was hosting important guests from

---

7 Cyprian Bazylik, *Historyja o srogim prześladowaniu Kościoła Bożego*, fol. [*****]ʳ. Unless mentioned otherwise, all English translations of Polish and Latin original texts are mine.
8 Cyprian Bazylik, *Historyja o srogim prześladowaniu Kościoła Bożego*, fol. 350ᵛ.
9 Kot, 'Polacy w Bazylei za czasów Zygmunta Augusta'; Włodarski, 'Relacje polsko-szwajcarskie w dobie przedrozbiorowej'; Włodarski, 'Polen an der Universität Basel im 16. Jahrhundert'.

Lithuania. The most distinguished of his visitors was Jan Kiszka, the very young future patron of Anti-Trinitarianism, at the time only eleven years old, Prince Radziwiłł's nephew and a son of the *Voivode* of Witebsk.[10] It is very likely that one of Jan's courtiers and companions (some of whom were members of Radziwiłł's household) brought to Lithuania copies of Oporinus's bestsellers. No later than 1564 Bazylik received the commission from 'certain persons of high estate' to compile the martyrology.

The full title of Bazylik's work — *History of Harsh Persecution of God's Church, Containing Accounts of Those Martyrs Who, Starting from Wycliff and Hus, until This Our Age, in Germany, France, England, Italy, Spain and Other Lands Sealed with Their Own Blood the Truth of the Holy Gospel* — echoes the title of Jean Crespin's Latin martyrology, published in Geneva in 1560 (*Actiones et monimenta martyrum, eorum qui a Wicleffo et Husso ad nostram hanc aetatem in Germania, Gallia, Anglia, Flandria, Italia et ipsa demum Hispania, veritatem evangelicam sanguine suo constanter obsignaverunt*). However, contrary to dominant opinions in scholarship, Crespin's work did not figure in the *History* as the more important source: this was the two-part martyrology printed by Oporinus.[11] The latter's first component was John Foxe's *Rerum in Ecclesia gestarum*, which developed the author's project as already outlined in his *Commentarii rerum in Ecclesia gestarum* (1554). The Basel martyrology, which was much more extensive and comprehensive, though still focused on English and Scottish martyrs, introduced a universal ecclesiological perspective that built on a chronologically organized narrative about the true, invisible Church of persecuted Christians, contending for ages with the forces of the Antichrist. The image of that struggle was presented in an eschatological context, as the full title — *Rerum in Ecclesia gestarum, quae postremis et periculosis his temporibus evenerunt maximarumque per Europam persecutionum ac sanctorum Dei martyrum caeterarumque rerum si quae insignioris exempli sint, digesti per regna et nationes commentarii* (Commentaries on the History of the Church in These Perilous Last Days and on the Great Persecutions in Europe, as well as on God's Holy Martyrs and on Other Matters Provided as Examples, Arranged According to Kingdoms and Nations) — strongly emphasized by employing a reference from the Second Epistle of Paul to Timothy 3. 1: 'hoc autem scito quod in novissimus diebus instabunt tempora periculosa' (This know also, that in those last days perilous times shall come).[12]

In *Rerum in Ecclesia gestarum* the universalistic concept was still a work in progress. It would be fully implemented in Foxe's vernacular *Acts and Monuments*, with editions, starting from 1563, being published

---

10 In the following year, Curione dedicated to Kiszka his edition of Cicero's *De claribus oratoribus liber*. See Kot, 'Polacy w Bazylei za czasów Zygmunta Augusta', pp. 121–22.
11 Pollak, ed., *Bibliografia literatury polskiej Nowy Korbut*, I, p. 17; Ziomek, *Renesans*, p. 399.
12 Evenden and Freeman, *Religion and the Book in Early Modern England*, p. 79.

at John Day's London press. However, the second part of the Basel martyrology, Heinrich Pantaleon's *Martyrum historia*, already possessed a truly European scope. Pantaleon was an accomplished academic of Basel university, whose interest in historiography was attested to by his *Chronographia Christianae Ecclesiae* (1550), as well as by translations, with those of Johann Sleiden's *Commentarii* (1556) and the previously mentioned Kromer's *De origine et rebus gestis Polonorum* (1562) among them. In the dedicatory epistle to Philip of Hesse, which serves as a preface to *Martyrum historia*, Pantaleon calls Foxe *amicus meus* and defines his own endeavour as a continuation.[13]

The geographical scope of *Martyrum historia* is already truly impressive, as Pantaleon's linguistic skills allowed him to compile material from German, Dutch, and French sources.[14] Without having wide access to the network of agents and informers, he made the best use of the already published vernacular martyrologies and reorganized their material, supporting and developing the main idea of ecclesiastical history as proposed by his predecessor in *Rerum in Ecclesia gestarum*. Four years had passed since the first part of the martyrology had been published, so Pantaleon covered the most recent events and added the accounts of certain Italian martyrs.[15] Foxe, who at the same time was preparing the first edition of *Acts and Monuments*, cooperated with him by using his accounts compiled from vernacular sources and by employing alterations of his own previous stories retold by Pantaleon.[16] It should be interpreted as a sign of his fundamental approval of his Swiss friend's endeavour.

Of all the sources used by Bazylik in *History of Harsh Persecution* the only one that did not have a direct link with Basel and Oporinus's house was Jean Crespin's martyrology. This work, published for the first time in Geneva in 1554, was one of the canonical texts of the French Reformation, republished fourteen times within eighteen years. The Polish author used its Latin version, printed (like the all others) by Crespin himself in 1560.[17] It needs to be observed that Crespin's *Actiones et monimenta martyrum* incorporated large chapters of Foxe's works — both from the *Commentarii rerum in Ecclesia gestarum* and *Rerum in Ecclesia gestarum*, where Crespin found the reports about the Henrician and the Marian English martyrs. This dependence became even more obvious in the French edition of 1561, which — in modern scholarly opinion — 85% was related to Foxe's Latin martyrology.[18]

---

13 Heinrich Pantaleon, *Martyrum historia*, fol. 3ᵛ.
14 Freeman and Gehring, 'Martyrologists without Boundaries', pp. 11–12.
15 Freeman and Gehring, 'Martyrologists without Boundaries', p. 12.
16 Freeman and Gehring, 'Martyrologists without Boundaries', pp. 11–24.
17 See Gilmont, *Jean Crespin*, pp. 165–90; Watson, 'The Martyrology of Jean Crespin'.
18 Freeman and Gehring, 'Martyrologists without Boundaries', p. 7.

Though early versions of Crespin's work emphasized mostly the persecution of the Huguenots, the later successive editions broadened the scope. Nevertheless, *Actiones et monimenta martyrum* was still far less extensive than *Rerum in Ecclesia gestarum*. Crespin's narrative featured a certain dynamism and intent to mobilize his readership, but the historiographical idea did not manifest itself as distinctly as it did in Foxe's martyrology.

Connected Histories of Protestant Martyrs

In his attempt to adopt and develop Foxe's ecclesiological concept, Bazylik envisioned an annalistic arrangement of the history of the true Church in Europe: the Church of those oppressed because of their faith, the invisible Church, striving heroically against the Antichrist whose presence and cruelty against Christ's disciples attested to the approaching end time. Pantaleon's and Crespin's works allowed Bazylik to achieve what the English historiographer could not yet attain in his Latin martyrologies. They provided a chance to significantly widen the geographical scope of the *History*. For this reason, the author from Brest in a way anticipated the project that Foxe himself fully implemented no sooner than in his *Acts and Monuments*. This comes as no surprise, as both writers employed the same compiling methods based on incorporating stories, motifs, and whole passages from their predecessors' works, which they had recognized as being of historical, doctrinal, or rhetorical value. In the theological perspective offered by Foxe and adopted by Bazylik, the proto-Reformation and Reformation martyrs were regarded as a criterion of the true (though invisible) Church, an argument in the great ecclesiological controversy, and a foundation of Christian identity. Consequently, a martyrology by itself became a tool of regaining the ecclesiastical past for the needs of the Reformed denominations, and for erasing a troublesome stigma of 'novelty'.[19]

Bazylik introduced the readers to his key assumptions in an extensive dedicatory letter addressed to Olbrycht Łaski. The text depicts the antithesis of Christ's Church, for ever — like the Saviour himself — persecuted and considered 'the foolish things of the world' (1 Corinthians 1. 27), and the Church of the Antichrist, 'And that we call the Roman pope the Antichrist is no news, since it did not start in our lifetime, and the great men of old used to call him that'. Bazylik wrote and presented a long list of those 'great men', in whose number he even included Pope Gregory I ('though not yet as haughty as [his successor] today'), Arnulf of Reims,

---

[19] Kess, *Johann Sleidan and the Protestant Vision of History*, pp. 1–2.

Joachim of Fiore, Michael of Cesena, and Francesco Petrarca.[20] And in the end times, according to St Paul, the persecution was meant to come. The host of martyrs, depicted by Bazylik, is to be clear evidence that the day of the Lord is imminent.[21]

Following Foxe's and Pantaleon's example, Bazylik decided to rewrite the history of the Church, to bring out from the mists of time all 'true Christians' who fell victim to the Antichrist, to envision and present chronologically a number of the Protestant martyrs as constituting, along with the medieval dissenters, the mystical body of Christ; they suffered even more in the end times. Like the English historiographer, Bazylik designed an annalistic arrangement for his narrative. Yet the incorporation of large passages of two other martyrologies in order to present martyrs from various European countries caused small but inevitably numerous chronological inconsistencies.

Wycliff and Lollards open the procession of Christ's witnesses in the *History of Harsh Persecution*. Like in other martyrologies of the time, the story is derived from Foxe's work. To be more precise, it originates in the *Commentarii rerum in Ecclesia gestarum*, published in 1554 in Strasbourg.[22] In this small booklet Foxe used for the first time the *Fasciculi Zizaniorum*, a collection of documents related to Wycliff and his followers which he had received from John Bale.[23] By the end of the same year 1554, the two brothers Jean and Adam Rivery included this material into their illegal edition of Crespin's martyrology, and afterwards Crespin himself republished this truly pirated loot in his own editions. Of course, the material also became a part of *Rerum in Ecclesia gestarum*.[24]

Bazylik, when confronted with the account derived from *Fasciculi Zizaniorum*, had an option: he could choose between Foxe's original coverage or the offshoot from Crespin's martyrology. He decided to follow Foxe (Pantaleon skipped Wycliff's story). His report begins with the developed characteristics of the medieval Church and Christianity, with references to Edward III's clashes with the papacy, to the Crusades, Richard I, and

---

20 Cyprian Bazylik, *Historyja o srogim prześladowaniu Kościoła Bożego*, fol. [****]ʳ.
21 Foxe included a similar list, based on John Bale's *Scriptorum illustrium maioris Brytanniae* [...] *catalogus*, into his work (see Evenden and Freeman, *Religion and the Book in Early Modern England*, pp. 57–58). Yet Bazylik seems to use in this part of his preface Heinrich Bullinger's *In Apocalypsim Iesu Christi*, fol. Bᵛ–B2ʳ, though he does not mention this source of inspiration. The quotations from Bullinger's work have been identified by my former student Elżbieta Albingier in her unpublished doctoral thesis 'Postaci męczenników w "Historyi o srogim prześladowaniu Kościoła Bożego" Cypriana Bazylika i w "Żywotach świętych" Piotra Skargi'.
22 John Foxe, *Commentarii rerum in Ecclesia gestarum*.
23 Evenden and Freeman, *Religion and the Book in Early Modern England*, pp. 40–44. In 1564 Wendelin's son, Josias Rihel, republished this first version of Foxe's martyrology as *Chronicon Ecclesiae*. See King, *Foxe's 'Book of Martyrs'*, pp. 78–80.
24 Evenden and Freeman, *Religion and the Book in Early Modern England*, pp. 59–60.

Frederick Barbarossa, etc. He adds some colour to the descriptions of medieval devotion, but he very often skips or radically shortens passages belonging to political history. Theological matters seem to interest him more, but he tends to summarize or omit even doctrinal materials, so often interpolated by Foxe. For example, in his report about Wycliff, Bazylik loosely renders the relatively short *Protestatio I[oannis] Vuicleui*, which should have been followed by the extensive and theologically subtle *Conclusiones*. But instead of translating them too, he declares:

> Artykułów *Konkluzyj* Wiklefowych wiele barzo jest, które my dla przedłużenia opuszczamy, a zwłaszcza te, które zwierzchność papieską borżą, abowiem już o tym wątpienia niemasz miedzy wiernymi, że papież nie ma żadnej zwierzchności dusznej ani cielesnej w Kościele Bożym, i owszem, papież podległ pod karność słowa Bożego, tak jako i wszyscy inszy ludzie.[25]

>> (There are a number of Wycliff's *Conclusiones*, but we are going to skip them in order not to make things too long, and in particular we skip those that challenge the authority of the Pope, because nowadays there is no doubt amongst the congregation that the Pope does not have any authority either in spiritual or in worldly matters in God's Church, and indeed, he is a subject of God's Word like everyone else.)

It is one of many examples of the author's strategy to adapt the material derived from his sources to the literary taste and religious life of his Polish Protestant readers. In fact, in the course of his narrative he eventually translates a few of the previously deprecated *Conclusiones*, yet he skips the most complex. In his translation he does not render the original entirely, but summarizes Wycliff's epistles, interpolated by Foxe; sometimes, instead of quoting a document, he includes only a short mention. This happened to the extensive *Testimonium Universitatis Oxoniensis de doctrina et vita Ioannis Vuiclevi*, which was replaced with the short note:

> Oksonieńskie też Kolle[g]ium pisało świadectwo za Wiklefem i jego nauką, dawając świadectwo, że on był prawdziwym krześcijaninem i doktorem w Piśmie uczonym, a iże też on nie był heretykiem, ani ich prełaci abo kollegiaci zezwolili na to, aby był wykopan z ziemie i spalon.[26]

>> (Oxford College wrote a testimony in order to support Wycliff and his doctrine, confirming that he was a true Christian and a biblical

---

25 Cyprian Bazylik, *Historyja o srogim prześladowaniu Kościoła Bożego*, fol. 1ʳ.
26 Cyprian Bazylik, *Historyja o srogim prześladowaniu Kościoła Bożego*, fol. 5ʳ.

scholar, not a heretic, and not permitting his body to be unearthed and burned.)

Bazylik also significantly shortens the *Testimonium et verba D. Ioannis Hussi de Viclevo Anglo* that followed in the Latin original text. He omits completely the multipoint, extensive *Articuli Ioannis Viclevi sparsim ex operibus eius ab adversariis et malevolis excerpti* along with the *Defensio* of Wycliff's articles, consisting of almost twenty-five pages; and he completes his narrative with the discourse about medieval prophecies relating to the Antichrist. This last passage is derived from Foxe's tirade on true Christianity: as a whole, it probably seemed too much extra baggage for the annals of martyrs. Bazylik also owes to Foxe the following reports about the martyrs of the thirteenth century and of the Lollards. Unlike the English historiographer, the Polish author seems not to assume a 'double readership' for his work — both educated and uncultured — so he is far less concerned with the documentary aspect of the martyrology and cares more for the dynamics of his story, emphasizing the contrast between the Church of the Antichrist and the Church of the holy martyrs whose blood proves the latter genuine.

When Bazylik has three alternative accounts of the same events at his disposal, he usually decides to compile all of them by picking passages which he finds rhetorically attractive or important for the course of action. However, it is noteworthy that in such cases, in spite of this general strategy, he favours positioning one or two sentences taken from *Ecclesia rerum gestarum* in the most visible parts of his narrative (e.g. in its initial parts), as if he wanted to emphasize its dependence on Foxe's work. This is the case with the accounts of the martyrdom of John Hus and of Jerome of Prague, which Bazylik read in both Foxe's and Pantaleon's, as well as in Crespin's works. Nonetheless, he decided to follow Foxe in the opening sentences of his own narration:

> Jako ci dwa złączeni byli za żywota, Jan Hus i Jeronim z Pragi, którzy też i spólnie się uczyli, i spólnie Pana wyznawali, tak też i w śmierci sobie byli równi, abowiem dowiedziawszy się, iż Jana Husa pozwano do Konstancyjej, przyjechał tam i upominał Husa, już wsadzonego do więzienia, aby pamiętał na stateczność, którą był winien Mistrzowi swemu, Krystusowi.[27]

> (As these two were united in life, John Hus and Jerome of Prague, when they were studying together and professing the Lord together, so they were equal in their deaths. For when [Jerome] found out that John Hus was called to Constance, he went there to

---

[27] Cyprian Bazylik, *Historyja o srogim prześladowaniu Kościoła Bożego*, fol. 11ʳ.

exhort the imprisoned Hus not to forget his steadiness, which he owed to Christ his Master.)

And though Foxe's *exordium* is much more extensive one may easily recognize elements used by Bazylik:

> Proximo ab huius martyrio anno post Christum videlicet 1416 praeceptorem Hussum insequutus est Hieronymus Pragensis, florida tum aetate, tum eloquentia iuvenis. Qui ut eandem causam quam Hussus habuerat, ita eosdem fere hostes et accusatores sortitus est. *Tum ut in omni vita illi coniunctissimus erat, ita nec morte a veteri sodali ac pietatis socio admodum distrahebatur.* Ut ergo praetermissis iis, quae ad vitam ipsius, ad mores, ad indolem ac studia spectant, causam ipsam ilico adgrediamur: *Hieronymus hic simulatque Ioannum Hussum ad concilium accitum, ac iamiam iturum intelligeret, sedulo officio adest amico suo, consolatur, rogat, ac adanimat, ut memor virtutis ac constantiae suae, rem gnaviter gerat pro Christo ac veritatis incolumitate.*[28]

> (In the next year after his [Hus's] martyrdom, that is in the year AD 1416, Jerome of Prague, a youth in the prime of his life and eloquence, followed in the footsteps of his teacher Hus. As he and Hus were connected by the same cause, he faced the same foes and accusers. As he was united with him in his whole life, thus he was not separated in death from his old companion and fellow believer. However, passing over what refers to his life [...], let us move straight to the point: as soon as Jerome learned, that John Hus had been summoned to the Council and was already about to go, he faithfully joins his friend, heartens him and exhorts him to remember his virtue and steadiness, and to persevere for the sake of Christ and the inviolability of truth.)

Bazylik's text could hardly pass for a translation; nevertheless, it includes the most important motifs, such as the unity of the two martyrs in life and death, exhorting the imprisoned Hus, and emphasizing his prior steadiness in professing Christ. On the whole, it is an intelligent abridgement, with elements of a paraphrase. No doubt the Polish author is sensitive to the rhetorical values of Foxe's prose, yet he cares more for action and the turn of events. That is why in the subsequent parts of his account of Jerome he decides to follow a more colourful and vibrant version of events: the same as in both Crespin's and Pantaleon's martyrologies. Bazylik shortens and condenses this report, but retaining anything having emotional or edifying value, such as Jerome's words during his execution, and Hus's prophecy

---

28 John Foxe, *Rerum in Ecclesia gestarum*, p. 67.

about Luther. Chromatic, dynamics, and emotional values remain the criteria of Bazylik's literary choices.

In the *History of Harsh Persecutions* some reductions with regard to its Latin sources are conditioned by specific social and religious problems in Poland–Lithuania. When, for example, in the English Church the growing influence of Nonconformists led to a dispute over the use of episcopal vestments in the 1560s and 1570s, in the Polish and Lithuanian Reformed congregations this issue did not stir emotions. Bazylik, retelling Foxe's account of John Hooper, was confronted with an episode foreshadowing the later vestment controversy, but found no reason to go into details. He chooses to ignore theological subtleties and to interpret the event from a moralistic perspective, as a struggle of vainglory versus modesty.[29] In the Polish version of the account, the devout and humble English bishop resists 'the rags' and vain ceremonies with disgust, for the time being surrendering to compulsion, but Hooper's ideas will eventually triumph.

In *Rerum in Ecclesia gestarum*, the story of Hooper, his mission, trial, and martyrdom, was told at length in over a hundred and twenty pages, filling most of Book III. Along with the account Foxe afforded supplemental poems, trial documents, and reports from prison, as well as letters and theological writings. Bazylik summarized it all in no more than twenty pages. He more or less carefully translated the narrative part concerning Hooper's life and execution, including some documents (the *Apellatio ad Parlamentum* among them), but he deliberately omitted theological writings. The reason he provided for his decision indicates the difference between England and Poland–Lithuania with regard to the dynamics of doctrinal controversies:

> Pisał ten Hoperus w więzieniu wielkie księgi o sakramencie Wieczerzy Pańskiej, dosyć uczone i dowodne przeciw tym, którzy Chrystusa cieleśnie chcą mieć w sakramencie chleba i wina, i w których czyni porównanie wieczerzej Krystusowej ze mszą Antykrystową. Ale iż są księgi ty wielkie, przeto osobno mogą być potym wydane. Bo też już za łaską Bożą Kościoły nasze polskie i litewskie tak grubego błędu nie dzierżą.[30]

> (That Hooper wrote in prison extensive books about the sacrament of the Lord's Supper, quite learned and compelling against those who want Christ to be physically present in the sacrament of bread and wine, and he made comparison between the Christ's Supper and the Antichrist's mass. But since these books are weighty, they could be published separately some other time. Because with the

---

29 John Foxe, *Rerum in Ecclesia gestarum*, pp. 280–81; Cyprian Bazylik, *Historyja o srogim prześladowaniu Kościoła Bożego*, fol. 215ᵛ–16ʳ.
30 Cyprian Bazylik, *Historyja o srogim prześladowaniu Kościoła Bożego*, fol. 222ʳ.

grace of God, our Polish and Lithuanian Churches do not uphold so big an error).

Bazylik never published Hooper's 'books'. By omitting them from the *History of Harsh Persecution*, he not only took into consideration the circumstances of the local Reformed congregations and their doctrinal identity, but also, being aware of his readers' expectations, gave priority to the historical facts.

Bazylik's omissions and reductions in the process of rendering his Latin sources are sometimes truly drastic and could be hardly explained otherwise than by the author's haste or by his overriding intention of keeping to the annalistic arrangement of his work. However, what strikes the reader, and what should be emphasized, is that this very cohesive narrative and the autonomous figure of its storyteller tie the text together. Though Bazylik's account echoes voices of other authors, he still manages the inherited narrative resources with admirable self-confidence, well envisioning his Polish readers, their learning and cognitive skills, and providing the necessary explanations. In the *History of Harsh Persecution*, the audience's theological aspirations are well taken into account: Bazylik does in fact translate extensive doctrinal tracts, minutes of interrogations and debates, but just enough to arm his readers as possible participants in these religious disputes. He opens up to them the perspective of almost the whole of Europe and leads them to towns and villages with foreign-sounding names, earnestly translating historical passages, and sketching for example the history of English Reformation and the French religious wars. The didactic and educational dimension of Bazylik's work is beyond question, yet it is also true that he seemed not to appreciate the learned and the humanist aspects of his Latin sources. When compared to Foxe's or even Crespin's martyrologies, the *History of Harsh Persecution* has almost none of their epideictic feature. Bazylik, though a poet himself, omitted all poems and epitaphs, reduced introductions and speeches, and focused on the account itself, quite often reducing it to the basic facts. He affected his readers' emotions in quite a different manner than through figures of speech and apostrophes. He did not include images either: only the title page is decorated with eight small woodcuts showing the executions of the holy martyrs. His work emphasizes the very course of events, presenting examples of heroic faithfulness and manifestations of the only true Church.

Bazylik's decision to combine in one work the essential martyrological compilation with a translation of Jan van Utenhove's *Simplex et fidelis narration* should also be regarded as a specific measure of adaptation and Polonisation. As I previously mentioned, the author offered *The History of Harsh Persecution* to the *Voivode* of Sieradz, Olbrycht Łaski, who was John a Lasco's own nephew, and who became his new patron after the death of Prince Mikołaj Radziwiłł. In a separate preface to this part of *The History*,

Bazylik emphasizes the connection between Oporinus's martyrologies and the great Polish reformer:

> Gdym ja tedy, miłościwy Panie, ty historyje Kościoła Bożego i męczenników jego z troich ksiąg łacińskich na polski język przekładał, nalazłem w księgach Jana Foxa i Henryka Pantaleona, iże na kilku miejscach stryja W[aszej] M[iłości] księdza Jana Łaskiego wspominali. A tak dostawszy tej historyjej spraw jego, w Niemcech przed kilkiem laty łacińskiem językiem wydanej, ujrzałem, iż ta historyja jest prawie *continuatio* historyjej Kościoła angielskiego, i zajrzałem tego Niemcom, iże oni nie tylko to, ale wiele inszego pisania jego mają drukowanego w ziemie swej, które tu nas ledwy dochodzą.[31]

> (When I was, Your Grace, translating these stories of God's Church and her martyrs from three Latin books into Polish, I found in the books of John Foxe and Henry Pantaleon that they had mentioned Your Grace's paternal uncle, Father Jan Łaski, on several occasions. Therefore, when I received the story of his doings, which had been published in Germany several years ago, I realized that this is truly a *continuatio* of the history of the English Church, and I envied the Germans that they have not only this but also many other of his writings published in their lands and seldom reaching our country).

This '*continuatio* of the history of the English Church' should be understood both as a continuation of the history of the London Foreign Church, and in Bazylik's understanding, as another chapter of persecutions following Queen Mary's accession to the throne. Of course, there is a dose of over interpretation in what Bazylik suggests. Though the very fact of the Foreign Church's expulsion does fall under the notion of religious persecution, yet the odyssey of this small congregation, lasting several months, to which the Scandinavian Lutherans denied any hospitality, could hardly fit into the axiological scheme of the whole martyrology. Including Van Utenhove's account that presented the brave and holy figure of John a Lasco was a form of *captatio benevolentiae*, addressed to a new patron, his nephew, and a kind of Polonization of the narrative. In 1567 Poland–Lithuania, 'the heretics' safe heaven', was one of the most tolerant of the European states, and therefore Bazylik was unable to include in his work a single Polish or Lithuanian Protestant martyr.[32] The invisible Church of the persecuted Christians did not form part of the existential experience of his readers, but by binding this ecclesiastical idea with the narrative of John a Lasco and his companions, Bazylik could at least establish a reference to

---

31 Cyprian Bazylik, *Historyja o srogim prześladowaniu Kościoła Bożego*, fol. 350ʳ.
32 See, for example Kosman, *Protestanci i kontrreformacja*; Wisner, *Rozróżnieni w wierze*; Tazbir, *Państwo bez stosów*; Kras, 'Religious Tolerance in the *Jagiellonian* Policy'.

the realities of Poland–Lithuania and in this manner increase the impact the whole martyrology could have in a process of shaping a Reformed identity amongst a Polish audience.

Conclusion

The *History of Harsh Persecution* attests to the existence of the transnational community of Protestant martyrologists and is an example of their specific 'cooperation', whether they knew each other or not. It represents the same techniques of composing a martyrology, based on compilation and on re-using both the results of research and the texts of predecessors. Crespin's, Foxe's, Pantaleon's, and other authors' martyrological collections featured undeniable rhetorical and compositional unity, yet their components were interrelated, as they mutually served each other as sources of information, of ecclesiological and historiographical ideas, and models for interpreting documents and events. Cyprian Bazylik, unlike the authors of the martyrologies he could use, was unable to add new facts to the repository they created, but he structured his historical account in a parallel manner in order to shape the religious attitudes of his congregation, and to mobilize it against the outside world ruled by the Antichrist.

What seems original and should be emphasized as such, is the fact that the *History*, though in the Polish vernacular, has a truly European scope, and foreshadows to a certain extant Foxe's *Acts and Monuments*. The lack of Polish Protestant martyrs made any attempt to focus on local issues (which typically narrowed the perspective of other vernacular martyrologies) impossible: it redirected the author's attention towards the universal Church. As a member of the 'Protestant Pleiade' (as Donald R. Kelley once called the first generation of the Protestant martyrologists), Bazylik shared 'a common ideological commitment, a common historical perspective, and a common reliance upon what Foxe called the "miracle" of printing'.[33] In this context, it also seems important that Bazylik was a typographer himself, perfectly aware of the significance of the 'miracle' of print in religious propaganda.

Acting as a member of the Reformed 'textual community', Bazylik assumes the role as an interpreter of ecclesiastical history for the needs of his local congregation.[34] His work has an obvious commemorative dimension: holy men of faith are presented as admirable figures or simply saved from oblivion, and with the conscientiousness of a chronicler Bazylik records even the anonymous victims. However, the author's tendency to abridge and summarize the literary material seems to confirm that in his

---

33 Kelley, 'Martyrs, Myths, and the Massacre', p. 1325.
34 Stock, *The Implications of Literacy*, p. 90.

narrative martyrs do not have the predominant role of paraenetic examples, whose heroic deeds would require elaborate account. They become 'texts' themselves, both semiotic structures and rhetorical arguments, and as such components of the ecclesiological and eschatological discourse that Bazylik addresses to his readership. Martyrs bear witness to the true Church and sometimes even preach its doctrine, while the martyrologist interprets their glorious death. His narrative deciphers and reconstructs the community of the invisible Church, drawing it forth from the world. The diverse means of adaptation, both the very fact that it is in a vernacular narration, addressing a less educated readership, and that it provides a symptomatic reduction of the epideictic as well as humanist features of the re-used literary texts, all serve the purpose of making the local congregation feel a part of the wider Reformed community, and of arming its members with new theological concepts and historical knowledge.

Works Cited

Primary Sources

Cicero, *De claribus oratoribus liber, qui dicitur Brutus*, ed. by Celio Secundo Curione (Basel: apud Michaelem Insegrinium, 1564)

Cyprian Bazylik, *Historyja o srogim prześladowaniu Kościoła Bożego, w której są wypisane sprawy onych męczenników, którzy, począwszy od Wiklefa i Husa, aż do tego naszego wieku w niemieckiej ziemi, we Francyjej, Anglijej, Flandryjej, we włoskiej ziemi, w Hiszpanijej i w inszych ziemiach prawdę ewanjelijej świętej krwią swą zapieczętowali* (Brześć: drukarnia Radziwiłłowska, 1567)

——, *Historyja o żywocie i zacnych sprawach Jerzego Kastryjota, którego pospolicie Szkanderbegiem zową* (Brześć: drukarnia Radziwiłłowska, 1569)

Heinrich Bullinger, *In Apocalypsim Iesu Christi, revelatam quidem per angelum Domini, visam vero vel exceptam atque conscriptam a Ioanne apostolo et evangelista [...]* (Basel: Johannes Oporinus, 1557)

John Foxe, *Commentarii rerum in Ecclesia gestarum, maximarumque per totam Europam, persecutionum, a Vuiclevi temporibus ad hanc usque aetatem descriptio. Liber primus. Autore Ioanne Foxo Anglo* (Strasbourg: V. Rihelius, 1554)

——, *Rerum in Ecclesia gestarum, quae postremis et periculosis his temporibus evenerunt, maximarumque per Europam persecutionum, ac sanctorum Dei Martyrum, caeterarumque rerum si quae insignioris exempli sint, digesti per regna et nationes Commentarii. Pars Prima, in qua primum de rebus per Angliam et Scotiam gestis, atque in primis de horrenda, sub Maria nuper Regina, persecutione, narratio continetur* (Basel: Nicolaus Brylinger, Johannes Oporinus, 1559)

Heinrich Pantaleon, *Martyrum historia, hoc est maximarum per Europam persecutionum ac sanctorum Dei martyrum caeterarumque rerum insignium, in Ecclesia Christi postremis et periculosis his temporibus gestarum, atque certo consilio per regna et nationes distributarum commentarii* (Basel: Nicolaus Brylinger, 1563)

Secondary Studies

Albingier, Elżbieta, 'Postaci męczenników w "Historyi o srogim prześladowaniu Kościoła Bożego" Cypriana Bazylika i w "Żywotach świętych" Piotra Skargi' (unpublished doctoral thesis, The John Paul II Catholic University of Lublin, 2017)

Baliński, Michał, *Pisma historyczne* (Warsaw: Sennewald 1843)

Czamańska, Ilona, 'Jakub Bazylikos Heraklides — droga wyzwolenia Grecji?', *Balcanica Posnaniensia*, 9–10 (1999), 133–51

Evenden, Elizabeth, and Thomas S. Freeman, *Religion and the Book in Early Modern England: The Making of John Foxe's Book of Martyrs* (Cambridge: Cambridge University Press, 2011)

Freeman, David, and Scott Gehring, 'Martyrologists without Boundaries: The Collaboration of John Foxe and Heinrich Pantaleon', *The Journal of Ecclesiastical History*, 69.4 (2018), 746–67

Gilmont, Jean-François, *Jean Crespin. Un éditeur réformé du XVIe siècle* (Geneva: Droz, 1981)

Kelley, Donald R., 'Martyrs, Myths, and the Massacre: The Background of St Bartholomew', *The American Historical Review*, 77.5 (1972), 1323–42

Kess, Alexandra, *Johann Sleidan and the Protestant Vision of History* (Aldershot: Ashgate, 2008)

King, John N., *Foxe's 'Book of Martyrs' and Early Modern Print Culture* (Cambridge: Cambridge University Press, 2007)

Kosman, Marceli, *Protestanci i kontrreformacja. Z dziejów tolerancji wyznaniowej w Rzeczypospolitej XVI–XVIII wieku* (Wrocław: Zakład Narodowy im. Ossolińskich, 1978)

Kot, Stanisław, 'Polacy w Bazylei za czasów Zygmunta Augusta. U źródeł polskiej myśli krytycznej XVI wieku', *Reformacja w Polsce*, 1.2 (1921), 108–28

Kowalski, Waldemar, 'Krakowski drukarz Stanisław Murmelius i jego księgozbiór (1571)', *Odrodzenie i Reformacja w Polsce*, 62 (2018), 5–45

Kras, Paweł, 'Religious Tolerance in the Jagiellonian Policy in the Age of the Reformation (Polish–Lithuanian Commonwealth)', in *Die Jagiellonen — Kunst und Kultur einer europäischen Dynastie an der Wende zur Neuzeit*, ed. by Dietmar Popp and Robert Suckale (Nürnberg: Germanisches Nationalmuseum, 2002), pp. 131–38

Pollak, Roman, ed., *Bibliografia literatury polskiej Nowy Korbut. Piśmiennictwo staropolskie* (Warsaw: Państwowy Instytut Wydawniczy, 1964)

Stock, Brian, *The Implications of Literacy: Written Language and Models of Interpretation in the Eleventh and Twelfth Centuries* (Princeton: Princeton University Press, 1983)

Stoy, Manfred, 'Jacob Basilikos Heraclides (Despot Vodă), Fürst der Moldau 1561–1563, und die Habsburger', *Mitteilungen des Instituts für Österreichische Geschichtsforschung*, 100 (1992), 305–27

Tazbir, Janusz, *Państwo bez stosów* (Warszawa: Iskry, 2009)

Watson, David, 'The Martyrology of Jean Crespin and the Early French Evangelical Movement, 1523–1555' (unpublished doctoral thesis, University of St Andrews, 1997) <https://research-repository.st-andrews.ac.uk/handle/10023/314> [accessed 4 August 2021]

Wisner, Henryk, *Rozróżnieni w wierze. Szkice z dziejów Rzeczypospolitej schyłku XVI i połowy XVII wieku* (Warsaw: Książka i Wiedza, 1982)

Włodarski, Maciej, 'Polen an der Universität Basel im 16. Jahrhundert', *Historisches Seminar Basel*, January 2010 <https://unigeschichte.unibas.ch/fileadmin/user_upload/pdf/W322odarski_Polen_an_der_Universitt_Basel_im_16._Jahrhundert.pdf> [accessed 4 august 2021]

———, 'Relacje polsko-szwajcarskie w dobie przedrozbiorowej', in *Wśród krajów Północy. Kultura Pierwszej Rzeczypospolitej wobec narodów germańskich, słowiańskich i naddunajskich: mapa spotkań, przestrzenie dialogu*, ed. by Mirosława Hanusiewicz-Lavallee (Warsaw: Wydawnictwo Uniwersytetu Warszawskiego, 2015), pp. 297–98

Ziomek, Jerzy, *Renesans* (Warsaw: Wydawnictwo Naukowe PWN, 1995)

MARCIN POLKOWSKI

(Re-)Constructing a Community of Readers

The Image of the Laity in Books Printed in Delft (1477–1500)[*]

Introduction

The term 'laity' in the Middle Ages is a complex notion, whose meaning varies in relation to the socio-historical context. During the 'Long Sixteenth Century' (*c.* 1450–*c.* 1550), which is the time-span set for the present chapter, the *laicus* (layman or -woman) was generally understood as an object of pastoral ministry (*cura animarum*), and the meaning attached to this term was no longer pejorative. It meant, essentially, every member of the Christian community who had been baptized but who was not part of the clergy or of a monastic order.[1] This primary

---

[*] This chapter incorporates revised and enlarged parts of the following lectures delivered by the author: '"Centers of learning", "communities of interpretation", and "creative minorities": the users of exempla collections in late medieval Holland', conference 'Centres of Learning and Knowledge Exchange in Late Medieval and Early Modern Europe' (Jagiellonian University and Dominican Centre, Cracow (Poland), 25–26 September 2014), and 'Unity and variety in the portfolio of printers in Delft (1477–1530)', Working Group 3 Leuven Meeting (Catholic University of Leuven (Belgium), 6–7 April 2017); both conferences were held as part of COST Action 'New Communities of Interpretation: Contexts, Strategies and Processes of Religious Transformation in Late Medieval and Early Modern Europe'.

1 Ginther, *The Westminster Handbook*, 'Laity', p. 115. For an intellectual history of the term 'Laity', see Imbach, *Laien in der Philosophie des Mittelalters*. See also Hamilton, 'Religion and the Laity'.

Marcin Polkowski, associate professor in Dutch literature at the John Paul II Catholic University of Lublin, has a PhD degree in Dutch and comparative literature (2007) and a habilitation on the literary and religious culture in the Netherlands during the transition from the Middle Ages to the early modern period (2013). His current fields of research are medieval and early modern Dutch literature, comparative literature, and the history and culture of the Low Countries.

Networking Europe and New Communities of Interpretation (1400–1600), ed. by Margriet Hoogvliet, Manuel F. Fernández Chaves, *and* Rafael M. Pérez García, New Communities of Interpretation, 4 (Turnhout: Brepols, 2023), pp. 71–98
BREPOLS PUBLISHERS   10.1484/M.NCI-EB.5.134311

sense overlapped with a secondary one, in which the term *laici* (used in opposition to *clerici*) began to refer increasingly to the level of education which an individual had received. In this sense, a *laicus* could be firstly, someone who had had hardly any schooling or none altogether. In the latter case, this term denoted someone who did not have the ability to read or write (*illiteratus*). In an extended, metaphorical meaning, the term *laicus* could also refer to an intellectually less able person, a simpleton (sometimes, when the additional function was that of a *topos modestiae*, this sense was not pejorative). Thirdly, as education began to be gradually accessible to the burgher class in north-western Europe, a *laicus*, often in this case contextualized in opposition to *clericus*, referred to someone who was literate but who did not know Latin (or not at an adequate level of fluency). Fourthly, it could refer to an individual, who despite being educated to some degree (and possibly able to understand, read or even write Latin) did not have a university education.[2] In the latter two cases such a *laicus* could display aspirations of an intellectual or theological nature. As Christoph Burger observed, the various usages of *laicus* make it a term which is highly imprecise and yet at the same time indispensable.[3]

Setting up a context, therefore, under the two final meanings mentioned above, a member of a monastic institution, for instance, although certainly not a layman or -woman in the modern sense, could practically consider him- or herself a *laicus* when he or she wished to emphasize a lack of formal schooling, inferior knowledge of Latin, etc.[4] Another example could be that of a well-educated town clerk, a layman in today's terms, who would refer to himself as *laicus*, yet instead of doing so to indicate that he was not ordained or a member of a religious order, since this would be obvious to him and his audience and therefore did not need to be stressed, he used this term to identify his level of education as inferior to someone who had university training.[5] The variegated meanings of the term *laicus* were strongly contingent on the context. For this reason, it is obviously advisable to study the formal and ideological environment, in which such

---

2 The categories listed here are based on the definitions of *leek* (Middle Dutch for *laicus*) in *Middelnederlandsch woordenboek* (lemmata 'Leek I' and 'Leek II').
3 Burger, 'Direkte Zuwendung zu den "Laien"', p. 87.
4 On this premise, for instance, St Lutgardis of Aywières (1182–1246), a Benedictine and Cistercian nun, otherwise an educated person by the standards of her time, is referred to as *laica* (Middle Dutch *leec*) in one of her vernacular *vitae*, an adaptation of Thomas of Cantimpre's *Vita Lutgardis*: 'Dies en verstont si nyet een waert, want si was *leec*, de guede Lutgaert' (emphasis – M. P.). Broeder Geraert, *Leven van Sinte Lutgart*, fol. 43ʳ.
5 In the medieval Low Countries, a relatively rapid change occurred between the thirteenth and fourteenth centuries, when a positive understanding of *laici* appeared in the context of the acquisition of knowledge from vernacular texts. One of the earliest authors who referred to the 'laity' in a positive way was the Antwerp town clerk Jan van Boendale (1279–1350/1351), author of the moral treatise *Lekenspiegel* (*Mirror for the laity*). See Wuttke, *Im Diesseits das Jenseits bereiten*, pp. 9–10.

a term occurs, its rhetorical and communicative function, at the same time exercising due caution so as not anachronistically to project a modern, all too clear-cut definition of laity on its historical usage.

Laici understood in the primary, but even more in the secondary sense of this term, are the actors of a discourse which appears in various vernacular texts in the Middle Dutch language, ranging from theological treatises and devotional literature, through moral handbooks and paraenetic texts, to works of natural science, historical chronicles, etc. This discourse works up to and through the beginning of the age of print, as will be shown below through reference to a group of incunabula in the vernacular which appeared in Delft from 1477 (the beginning of printing in that city) until approximately the second decade of the sixteenth century.

The study into *laici* as the addressees of late medieval devotional literature received a strong foundation in research by Georg Steer and Volker Honemann.[6] Honemann discerned two categories of laity, who were explicitly addressed by this term in the prefaces of late medieval vernacular religious treatises. The first comprised laymen who were genuinely interested in religious life, were literate, and able critically to study texts and assimilate their contents. This group had access to a majority, if not all, of the texts available to Latinate *clerici*. The other group of addressees comprised 'simple people' (described as such in these treatises) considered to be in need of religious instruction and hence less qualified than the former in the area of literacy skills. The distinction proposed by Honemann will be used in the research performed below.[7]

In the context of Middle Dutch literature, the notion of a literature addressed to a lay readership comprising burghers in an urban environment was explored by Herman Pleij.[8] Pleij's overarching vision of the laity as a homogenous community of readers and authors of an ideologically consistent corpus of texts was nuanced by other scholars, including Joris Reynaert.[9] Since then, the search for lay readers in the context of the medieval Low Countries has been pursued by various scholars working from philological and historical angles.[10]

---

6 On this problem, see esp. Steer, 'Der Laie als Anreger und Addressat' and Honemann, 'Laien als Literaturförderer'.
7 Honemann, 'Der Laie als Leser', p. 251. For a practical application, see Roolfs, *Der 'Spieghel der leyen'*, p. 495.
8 For the notion of the burgher as an addressee of a corpus of literary texts sharing specifically urban preoccupations and engaging the reader by appealing to urban mores, see Pleij, 'Op belofte van profijt' and Pleij, 'The Rise of Urban Literature in the Low Countries'.
9 Reynaert, 'Leken, ethiek en moralistisch-didactische literatuur'.
10 A bibliography of the recent studies that are the most relevant here, should include Corbellini, 'Lezers, kopiisten en boekverkopers', Van Beek, *Leken trekken tot Gods Woord*, Caspers, 'Bidden in twee talen', Desplenter, 'Publiek van bijbelvertalingen', Dlabačová, *Literatuur en observantie*, Folkerts, 'The Cloister or the City?', Folkerts, 'Te "duncker" voor

In this chapter, when I refer to the laity, I mean first and foremost that they are a group whose existence is confirmed and supported by these texts, and who, through the medium of these texts, a certain kind of collective, albeit variable, identity. The concept of an actor, which we may employ in this chapter, as well as that of a network, will draw in general upon Bruno Latour's Actor–Network Theory (without embarking, however, on a theoretical critique of the conglomerate of concepts known under this name).[11] The term 'actor', in the Latourian sense, enables us to conceive of the *laicus* as not only a sociological entity, but most of all as a rhetorical construct and a literary *topos*. Similarly, Latour's notion of a network, which implies a complex set of relations between various actors unfolding (and dynamically changing) in time and space, can be useful for considering the social environment of the texts in which this discourse was formulated.

Where Latour somewhat controversially speaks of non-human actors, I will consider the *laicus* as an actor in the discourse of late medieval vernacular authors (including the authors of paratexts, such as book printers and publishers) from the Low Countries. However, apart from the normal referential meaning of this term, i.e. a sociological group meeting the multi-tiered definition formulated above, I will also use this term to refer to an intellectual construct, or more precisely the belief in the *raison d'être* of such a group among the authors of vernacular texts. In this latter case, instead of using the term 'laity' I will resort to its Latin equivalent. The hypothesis will be, therefore, that apart from functioning as a neutral descriptor of an existing social reality we should consider the notion of *laici* as employed by authors, book printers, and publishers of the late medieval period as a framing device for rhetorical purposes. The secondary thesis of this chapter will be that the book printers and publishers of the late medieval era contributed to the self-discovery of the laity, notwithstanding the earlier use of this term in vernacular writing: in other words, facilitating the creation of a 'lay identity' and articulating some of its major concerns in the area of its intersection with religious knowledge.

If the early printed publications which appeared at Delft during this period can be credited with not simply describing an already existing social situation (that is to say, the emergence of the laity as readers and users of vernacular printed books as a consequence of the economic and political emancipation of the burgher class in cities of the Netherlands), but actually invented or constructed a specific concept of a *laicus* as the

---

leken?', Folkerts, 'Approaching Lay Readership of Middle Dutch Bibles', Folkerts, 'Vrome leken en foute priesters', Goudriaan, 'De franciscanen, de leken en de drukpers', Kors, 'Die Bibel für Laien', Korteweg, 'Geestelijken en leken'.
11 Latour, *Reassembling the Social*.

intended addressee of those books, then the practical problem will be to reconstruct the identity of this peculiar actor, understood as an intellectual notion. Who was the *laicus* on the level of discourse, and therefore in a subtle way ontologically different from the actual readers of the texts in question (among whom, of course, were some actual laypersons) will be one of the chief concerns addressed in this chapter. In other words, we will seek to understand how the authors and producers (book printers and writers of paratexts) conceived of the 'model' or 'ideal' reader of their texts as potentially distinct from the 'actual' or 'empirical' readers thereof.[12]

Communities of Readers

Discussing the *laicus* as a 'virtual' actor in a network of textual communication does not mean that we must disregard the actual communities of users of literature, in which early printed books were read and interpreted. One of several 'turns' which have taken place with regard to the emphasis of research on late medieval literature is the turn toward a more 'reader-oriented' approach, and away from a philological-historical attention to the text. For an important part this 'reader-oriented turn' has its origins in the theoretical reflection of Stanley Fish, who argued that the process of interpretation (in other words, of construing the valid meanings of a text), can never be detached from the existence of a community of recipients-interpreters. To describe the social agency inherent in textual interpretation, Fish coined the term 'interpretive community', which he defined as:

> not so much a group of individuals who shared a point of view, but a point of view or way of organising experience that shared individuals in the sense that its assumed distinctions, categories of understanding, and stipulations of relevance and irrelevance were the content of the consciousness of community members who were therefore no longer individuals, but, insofar as they were embedded in the community's enterprise, community property.[13]

Characteristically, in Fish's radically collectivist vision of reading and interpreting literature, the individual does not make personal choices to interpret literature. Individual decisions on how to read a text are replaced by impersonal 'interpretive strategies' acting on the text, which are not

---

12 After Umberto Eco, a 'model reader' may be defined as a rhetorical device, a textual 'portrait' of a reader supposedly ideally adapted to the reception of the work of literature, and at the same time distinct from the real, or 'empirical' readers, who may or may not correspond to its characteristics.
13 Fish, *Doing What Comes Naturally*, p. 141.

a creation of any single person but of a society in general. In another definition Fish posited that 'interpretive communities are made up of those who share interpretive strategies, not for reading (in the conventional sense) but for writing texts, for constituting their properties and assigning their intentions'.[14] This definition points to the commonality of strategies deployed by the writers and readers of a text. Writing, according to Fish, is therefore the product of applying a highly specific set of interpretive strategies; were a different set applied, it would result in a different text. The approach advocated by Fish has now become commonplace, and its underlying assumption that meaning is socially conditioned is shared tacitly across a spectrum of academic ventures, despite its limitations, the most important of which is a reduction of the role of the individual to a mere 'carrier' of collectively held notions. In consequence, the theory exhibits a tendency to disregard individual choice, which should be accounted for as a factor responsible for selecting a specific interpretive strategy from among the competing and sometimes contradictory sets of rules and norms available in a given community.

The 'empirical' readers of early printed books may be envisaged in totality as an interpretive community, which shared specific norms for the production and interpretation of texts. This community eludes definition in sociological terms as 'laity' (in the several senses of the word), or otherwise we would have to speak of various sub-communities, needlessly complicating the matter. To avoid this problem, borrowing a term from Benedict Anderson, we will describe the notion of *laici* formulated in vernacular texts in the Low Countries at the close of the medieval period as an 'imagined community' of readers. By this we will imply, somewhat similar to what Anderson did (without going into the merits or demerits of his proposition in other respects) a virtual community — in this specific case, of readers who are unaware of each other, but who are united by certain traits ascribed to them in discourse.[15]

The process of imagining a community of laity was a long-term one, beginning in the Low Countries with the early fourteenth century, but thankfully its evolution may be traced in vernacular literature, where Jan van Boendale's work, especially his *Lekenspiegel* (*Mirror of the Laity*), appears as an important waystage, marking the gradual intellectual emancipation of the burgher class. But it was only with the coming of the printing press (in the Low Countries in the final quarter of the fifteenth century) and with the accompanying rapid orientation of the nascent printing trade toward the literate urban elites, that the *laicus* as an actor in the collective mentality of various interpretive communities comprising actual lay readers acquired a visible presence.

---

14 Fish, 'Interpreting the Variorum', p. 483.
15 Anderson, *Imagined Communities*, pp. 5–6.

Communities of Interpretation in Delft during the Later Middle Ages

During the 'Long Sixteenth Century' Delft counted among the most important centres of printing in the northern Netherlands, one where not only the first book in the Dutch language bearing a date mark, a vernacular translation of much of the Old Testament (*Bible in Duytsche* 1477), was produced, but where soon afterwards, thanks to the activities of several printers, who successively set up their business in the town, a quantitatively and qualitatively substantial range of books was published. Instead of having a clearly defined profile (e.g. exclusively theological works), the portfolio of the pioneering Delft printers (Jacob Jacobszoon van der Meer in partnership with Mauritius Yemantszoon, and subsequently alone; Christiaen Snellaert; and Hendrick Eckert van Homberch) is characterized by considerable thematic diversity. The preserved output of Delft printers between 1477 and 1530 may be described as a 'melting pot' in which oppositions, for instance between literature designed for *clerici* and that addressed to *laici*, between the official Latin and an ever stronger vernacular, between the *sacrum* of liturgical texts and the *profanum* of worldly epics, between works embedded in the traditions of a fading scholasticism and those with roots in a nascent humanism, between texts striving ostensibly at factual verity (*historia*) and those offering undisguised fiction (*fabula*), were reconciled, and texts of a varied nature, aimed at different groups of readers, coexisted alongside one another in apparent harmony. The printers' workshops of Delft may be therefore described as a middle ground, where different languages, themes, styles, and registers were harmoniously combined, and where diversity, although obviously circumscribed by the boundaries of Western Christian orthodoxy, was not only possible but even encouraged. In effect, the portfolio of the Delft printers may be described as a vehicle for the transfer of religious and scholarly knowledge to lay communities (in all senses of the term marked out above), thanks to the interaction of urban clergy and members of religious orders on the one hand, and an increasingly literate commercial elite on the other.

The business of the Delft printers did not exist in a void, but appeared in a city where already a number of stable social networks, supportive of literary culture, were in existence. The coordinates of urban literary culture in the late medieval northern Netherlands were demarcated by a network of sites of religious worship such as parish churches or monastic institutions. Churches and chapels were not simply signs of the sacred in the space of the city, but housed in themselves spaces where the individual was able to enter into a relation with the sacred, experiencing it through the mediation of various objects and phenomena. These spaces were created by the spoken word, although, for instance in the liturgy, it was only one of the factors mediating the religious experience.[16] The parish clergy were the organizers of an interpretive community which also comprised the lay inhabitants of the city as co-participants in and listeners to literary activities in the vernacular. A mystery play entitled *Van die Verrijsenis* (About the Resurrection), for instance, was staged next to the church of St Hippolytus, the oldest church in Delft, in 1496 and the following years, on a podium (*stellync*) specially constructed for this purpose.[17] The focus of religious worship in this church was the venerated figure of *Maria [van] Jesse* (Mary of Jesse); the events connected with the origins of the cult of this figure were commemorated in an annual procession, the *Delftse ommegang*. Beginning in the latter half of the fourteenth century this church became the destination of individual and collective pilgrimages from the neighbouring towns and villages, and even from abroad. The sick who had experienced healing submitted depositions about their miraculous recovery. These narratives were recorded in *miracula* collections.[18]

The social culture of the later Middle Ages created religious confraternities as specific interpretive communities relying on the concept of Christian brotherhood (*fraternitas*) understood as the realization of the evangelical injunction to brotherly love and extended to one's immediate social and professional environment. For the laity, participation in such a confraternity offered a range of religious and social benefits.[19] Religious brotherhoods and craft guilds, apart from their primary functions, were also the principal actors in the networks of literary communication in an urban milieu. An influential religious confraternity, whose members communicated through literary texts and which existed as a supra-regional community of devotees, was the confraternity of the Seven Sorrows of the Virgin Mary.[20]

The medium through which the guilds and confraternities interacted with the predominantly lay urban society was the theatre. In particular, the so-called *Spul van Jesse* or *Yesse* (Jesse Play), was staged to coincide with the annual *Delftse ommegang*, as a series of *tableaux vivants* in which each guild had its own performance according to its tasks and character. For instance, the guild of skippers enacted a scene centred on a 'Ship of St Ursula'. The church accounts mention an amount of money going to the 'clergen van sproken te scriven' (*clerici*, who wrote the *sproken* [tales

---

16 Mostert, 'Wytwarzanie, przechowywanie i użytkowanie', pp. 32–33.
17 Van Boheemen and Van der Heijden, *De Delftse rederijkers*, pp. 16–19.
18 Verhoeven, *Devotie en negotie*, pp. 197–224.
19 Krause and others, 'Bruderschaften, Schwesternschaften, Kommunitäten', p. 197. For brotherhoods as 'media in the process of civilisation', see Dąbrówka, *Teatr i sacrum*, pp. 216–48.
20 Polkowski, *A Struggle for Survival*, pp. 61–125 (with a bibliography on pp. 62–63).

that were meant to be performed orally]).[21] The authors of the narrative connecting the scenes were denoted as *clerici*, which in this context implied some kind of ecclesiastic background coupled to literacy skills and an affinity with literary culture, and possibly fluency in Latin (although the texts themselves were in the vernacular).

The Delft church of St Hippolytus was equipped with a library. This facility was accessible to readers upon the payment of a certain sum. The ledger indicates that the community of readers who borrowed books was not restricted to the clergy but consisted of lay burghers, artisans of various professions. The books, which were in the possession of this library, were above all in the vernacular. The collection was not large, because it could be stowed in a single chest.[22] An etching on the title leaf of an edition of the *Passionael* (the Middle Dutch adaptation of the *Aurea legenda*), printed in Delft, shows laypeople, a man and a woman, consulting a similar library of a non-monastic character.[23]

The second of the churches in Delft, that of St Ursula (the 'New Church'), was also a key site for interpretive communities including the clergy and laity. In the winter of 1498, a miracle play about the Adoration of the Magi (*Spul van den drie Coningen*) was staged there.[24] The principal actors were representatives of the clergy, who arrived on horseback at the door of the church, in which the manger was arranged next to the main altar. The organization of this innovative spectacle, which attracted large crowds, was most likely also the work of male religious from the local Franciscan convent situated in the same part of the city.[25] In 1487 the Guild of the Sweet Name of Jesus (*Gilde des zueten naems Jhesus*) was founded in the church of St Ursula, obtaining from the Guild of the City Guard the right to hold Masses in the chapel of St George. The Guild of the Sweet Name of Jesus was no longer a purely religious confraternity of laypersons, but already displayed the traits of a chamber of rhetoric in that its members were denoted as *gesellen van de rhetorica* (brethren of rhetoric), similarly to the members of a craft guild.[26]

The 'Long Fifteenth Century' proved to be especially productive for religious institutions in Delft, for during that period not only around a dozen monastic houses were founded, but these institutions also became important sites in the network of literary communication situated both within the city walls and reaching beyond them. One of the collective

---

21 Van Boheemen and Van der Heijden, *De Delftse rederijkers*, p. 11. The generic term *sproke* refers generally to a short, rhymed text with a serious, moralizing-didactic content.
22 Oosterbaan, *De Oude Kerk te Delft*, p. 87.
23 Jacobus de Voragine, *Passionael. Winterstuc*, fol. 1ʳ. See Polkowski, *A Struggle for Survival*, pp. 349, 447.
24 Van Boheemen and Van der Heijden, *De Delftse rederijkers*, pp. 19–20.
25 Van Boheemen and Van der Heijden, *De Delftse rederijkers*, pp. 19–20.
26 Van Boheemen and Van der Heijden, *De Delftse rederijkers*, pp. 21–26.

actors in such a network was the community of the Brethren of the Common Life, to which several houses in Delft belonged, and which effectively promoted the diffusion of innovation in the area of religious and literary culture.[27] One of the expressions of the new concept of inward, spiritual life, cultivated by the Brethren, was the emphasis on the transmission of the written word and on education. From 1460 the Brethren in Delft ran a school which educated pupils in the Latin language and offered a basic knowledge of classical literature, continuing the tradition of the parish 'Latin school' which had been in existence since 1342.[28] During the Corpus Christi processions, the events from the life of Christ were enacted by 'clerks' (here meaning the students of the school), equipped for instance with the attributes of Christ's Passion (*arma Christi*).[29]

The culture of the written word at the centre of the activities of the Brethren of the Common Life was firmly embedded in the notion that an individual should have an affinity with religious books and their intellectual universe.[30] The Delft monastic institutions reflected this intellectual climate by organizing facilities for the production of handwritten texts. The convents of St Anne, St Ursula, and St Barbara are well known to art historians for their illuminated manuscripts, which belong to the 'Delft school'.[31] The monastic institutions in Delft also had well-equipped libraries, one of which was housed in the convent of St Barbara. Its inventory provides an insight into the tastes of its community of readers, who were literate in the vernacular and had access to a varied selection of devotional literature which, moreover, closely matched the output of Delft book printers in the latter decades of the fifteenth century.[32]

After the invention of print, book printers set up their workshops in the heart of the city. The nodes in the networks of social interaction, where these workshops arose, were not selected at random, but were located at crucial sites near the religious, commercial, and administrative centres of the city. From the colophons of early printed books one can learn that Frans Sonderdanck's workshop was situated 'besiden die oude kercke'[33]

---

27 Mertens, 'The Modern Devotion and Innovation'.
28 Verhoeven, *Devotie en negotie*, p. 18; Beckers and Leeuw, 'Onderwijs: scholen', pp. 113–14.
29 Van Boheemen and Van der Heijden, 'Literatuur en toneel in Delft', p. 162.
30 Obbema, *De middeleeuwen in handen*, p. 16.
31 On this subject see Chavannes-Mazel and Venner, 'Delftse handschriften en boekverluchting', pp. 134–37, Rudy, 'De productie van manuscripten in het Sint-Ursulaklooster', and Płonka-Bałus, *The Catalogue of Medieval Illuminated Manuscripts and Miniatures*, pp. 125–29.
32 The Hague, KB, MS 130 E 24. An edition of this catalogue was published by Moll, *De boekerij*. For a comparison with the output of Delft book printers, cf. Polkowski, *A Struggle for Survival*, pp. 35–38. A different document of the same type is the subject of analysis by Corbellini and Verhoeven, 'A Sixteenth-Century Book Catalogue from Delft'.
33 *Een suuerlijc exmpel* [sic], fol. 8^v.

(next to the Old Church). Henric Pieterszoon Lettersnijder's successful workshop at the turn of the first and second decade of the sixteenth century was located 'Bij dat martuelt aen die suitsijde van die niewe kerke' (on the market square, at the southern side of the New Church),[34] and son, Cornelis Hendricsz Lettersnijder worked 'next to the fish market', at a location nearby in a street called Cameretten,[35] a busy commercial location between the Old and New Church.

The Portfolio of Delft Book Printers

The Incunabula Short Title Catalogue of the British Library lists 155 imprints published in Delft after 1477 and before 1501. A period of slightly more than two decades witnessed the rapid increase in the volume of books printed in the city.[36] Below, on a range of selected examples from this portfolio, an imagined community of *laici* as readers will be reconstructed in the form of a composite image basing on how the identity of the model reader is represented in the paratexts of early printed books from Delft. Additional information on how the identity of the model reader as an actor in the process of literary communication was constructed by the book printers and editors of these books will be derived from visual clues conveyed by the graphic material: the etchings on the title leaves, which often produced an impression of the intended readership, emphasizie the message contained in the text.

Books for Clerici *and* Laici?

The contents of the portfolio of Delft printers offers an impression of its diversity. Because vernacular texts are of interest to us here, the Latin texts, which may be classified globally as not intended for *laici*, will be discussed only very briefly. These texts may be divided into two sub-categories, 'ecclesiastic' and 'scholastic', after the institutions which provided the platform and environment for their use. To the 'ecclesiastic' category belonged liturgical books (missals), books of hours, theological commentaries, and Church documents such as bulls or indulgences. The second subcategory comprises 'scholastic' literature. These were the Latin schoolbooks which made up a large part of the printers' publishing output: Alexander de Villa

---

34 *Die sijn die seven getijden der passien ons Heren.*
35 *Een boecxken van devocien geheten die negen couden.*
36 For a survey of the evolution of book printing in Delft between 1477 and 1572, see Polkowski, *A Struggle for Survival*, pp. 41–59, 138–47 and 359–90 (statistical analysis). A survey for the period 1477–1501 is provided by Van Duijn, 'Printing, Public, and Power'.

Dei's *Doctrinale*[37] and the works of Donatus, for instance, or the *Libellus de accentibus syllabarum*,[38] which allowed the reader to familiarize himself with the metrical system of the Latin language. The *Expositio hymnorum cum notabili commento* signalled the growing intellectual engagement of the Latinate clergy and its pupils with some of the sacred texts of the Church.[39] In 1503 an edition of Horace's *De arte poetica* heralded a shift in interest toward classical Latin.[40] These schoolbooks, manuals, and editions of Latin works were an answer to demand from grammar schools; in turn, their availability allowed for the training of a new generation of pupils. The demographic cohort, which acquired knowledge from such books, born at the turn of the fifteenth and sixteenth centuries, crucially went on to establish the social networks which enabled the dissemination of humanist ideas in the Low Countries. Among the Latin texts and their translations a sub-trend may be discerned in the form of works by theologians representing traditional scholasticism, such as St Anthony of Florence (Antonino Pierozzi, 1389–1459), whose manual *Confessionale: defecerunt scrutantes scrutinio* was published in 1482.[41] A different group of Latin texts involves humanist authors, who, in turn, may be grouped either in a more conservative or in a more radical category, respectively represented by Jacob Wimpfeling and Alexander Hegius.[42] Erasmus is represented only in translation: his *Paraphrases* were eagerly translated into Dutch almost as soon as they appeared, but no Latin edition was printed in Delft. This suggests that works by this author (three editions before 1530) were marketed to readers fluent only in the vernacular.

(Re-)Constructing an Imagined Community of Laici

The Delft Bible: *Imagining a Community of* Laici *as Readers*

It is characteristic of the portfolio of book printers in Delft that theological works by non-Dutch authors in translation were often explicitly or implicitly marketed to *laici*. This trend was already started by the publishers of the *Delft Bible* (*Bible in Duytsche*).[43] The notions expressed in its prologue,

---

37 Alexander de Villa Dei, *Doctrinale*.
38 *De accentibus syllabarum*.
39 *Expositio hymnorum*.
40 Horatius, *De arte poetica*.
41 Anthony of Florence, *Confessionale*.
42 Jacob Wimpfeling has been designated a conservative humanist on the value of his polemical writings defending scholasticism by Nauert, 'The Humanist Challenge', p. 275. For a commentary on Hegius's role as an educator and pioneering humanist, see Worstbrock, 'Zur biographie des Alexander Hegius'.
43 *Bible in Duytsche*.

which might be interpreted as a programmatic statement of the book's publishers, were not original, however, as its text was modelled on the preface to Petrus Naghel's Bible translation (the Herne Bible) and from the *North Netherlandish History Bible* (*Noordnederlandse historiebijbel*).[44]

In the prologue to the *Delft Bible* two different communities of readers were juxtaposed, and to these communities different reactions and models of interpretation were subsequently ascribed. On the one hand, a negative image was created of a group of *clerici* (denoted by the terms *clercken* or *clergye*). This term can mean academically-trained 'clerks', who with their theological knowledge and fluency in Latin would jealously guard their monopoly over the reading and interpretation of the Bible:

> Nochtan weet ic wel dattet sal worden zeer benijt onder die clergye: hoe wel dat si nochtan weten ende mercken sullen die oorbaerlicheit daer of [...] want sommighe clercken torent dat: datmen die heymelicheit der scriftueren den ghemeenen volcke soude ontbinden. Ende dat by sondere die de minste clercken sijn, ende en willen niet weten dat Cristus apostolen in allen tonghen spraken.[45]

> (Nevertheless, I know that it [i.e., the translation of the Bible] will be envied among the 'clerks', although they too will become aware of and will notice its usefulness [...] because some 'clerks' are angry that the secrets of the Scripture should be exposed to the ordinary population. The greatest of these [critics] are the least learned [who] disdain to know that Christ's disciples spoke in many languages.)

For obvious reasons, the community of *clercken* should not be understood as synonymous with ordained persons or members of religious institutions, that is to say 'clergy' in the modern-day sense.[46] The sense that scholarly training or learning is referred to as the common denominator of the identity of this group follows from the reference to 'die de minste clercken sijn', literally, 'those who are clerks (of) the lowest (degree)', which paraphrased means 'those who have the least learning'. Here, one may add that *clerken*, appearing as the protagonists of *exempla*, certainly do not represent all of the priesthood but merely a small, highly-educated circle within the medieval Church. In the prologue to the *Delft Bible*, *clerici* on the whole received the negative identity of a group carefully guarding its custody and interpretive monopoly of the Bible, whose members despite

---

44 Van Duijn, *De Delftse Bijbel*, offers a comparative analysis of these Bible translations on pp. 43–44, 77–79, and 58–59.
45 *Bible in Duytsche*, fol. 1ᵛ.
46 For a discussion of the term 'clergye' in the context of the *Delft Bible*, see Van Duijn, *De Delftse Bijbel*, p. 78, and Kors, *De bijbel voor leken*, p. 157.

their claims possessed only superficial learning, and as a matter of fact failed properly to understand Scripture.

The other community was identified again by a lack of a formalized academic training ('ongheleert is van clergyen') but exhibiting personal devoutness ('menich salich mensche'). The reading of the Bible, it was explained, was profitable ('zijn profijt in doen'), and a positive way of spending time ('den tijt daer in corten'), especially on feast- and holidays, days free of labour ('op die heilighe daghen die gheordineert ende gheset sijn vander heyligher kercken'), which would otherwise be filled with idle pursuits ('ydelheden').[47] An obstacle addressed in the prologue was that the *laicus*, who was the model reader, was all too easily distracted by reading books classified as 'worldly':

> Veel luyden sijn die lesen waerlike boeken van konsten: ende van krachten: historien: ende van ouden heren die der werelt dyenden. Mer dat is al tijtverlyes: want sij daer inne niet en vinden der zielen salicheit: want alle die tijt die wij onnuttelikken toe brenghen daer moeten wij voer gode rekeninghe of gheuen. Ende wantet Gode mishaghet dat die mensche die Gode dyenen soude gaerne waerlijke boeken leeset.[48]

> (Many read worldly books about the arts, and about the powers, histories, and those about ancient lords who served the world. But all this is a waste of time, because there they will not find the salvation of the soul; because we will have to account to God for all the time that we spend uselessly. And because God is displeased when people who serve God read worldly books.)

It is not entirely clear who was referred to by 'the people who serve God'. This might have included both ordained persons and the members of religious institutions, but pious laity were also a plausible option. From this it follows that the model readership was not explicitly restricted to the laity in the modern sense, although it was certainly open to this group. Texts belonging to the 'genres' loosely indicated in the prologue (including scholarly handbooks relating to the *konsten*, or in other words, *artes*) were to be found in the libraries of monastic institutions, so this reference does not have to refer unambiguously to the laity either. In general, literate, pious laymen and -women (though not only literate ones, because the prologue makes provision for the aural reception of the text — 'leesen ende hooren leesen') as well as ordained persons and members of religious

---

47 *Bible in Duytsche*, fol. 1ʳ.
48 *Bible in Duytsche*, fol. 1ᵛ.

institutions, in each case characterized by a lower level of theological knowledge and Latin literacy, were imagined as the text's community of users.[49]

The Laicus *as a Model Reader: 'All Christians'*

Not infrequently, the community of readers of vernacular texts was defined in very general terms, a trend started also by the editors of the *Delft Bible*, who in the colophon determined, in a more inclusive way than in the prologue which had been based on Naghel's text, that the translation was intended for 'stichticheit ende lerijnge der kersten gelovigen menschen' (the edification and education of the Christian faithful). According to Mart van Duijn, this formulation was inclusive of both clergy and religious as well as the laity, because the editors did not wish to restrict their readership to a single group.[50] Another method of imagining the community of readers in discourse was by referring to 'den ghemeenen volcke' (the common people), a collective entity which in the prologue of the *Delft Bible* had been described as distinct from the *clerici*, and was certainly inclusive of the laity in the modern sense of the word.

The community of readers received a collective identity with very general features inclusive of the laity in a considerable number of vernacular devotional handbooks. Socio-religious and -moral categories of this type included, for instance, 'der goeder menschen' (all good people)[51] or 'allen sondigen menschen' (all sinful people).[52] A collection of exempla referred to the readership as 'den ghenen die Marien minnen' (those who love the Virgin Mary), likewise a capacious category.[53] Sometimes, the model reader was characterized by his or her inability to read and consequently by an aural mode of reception, which, as we have seen, was an important feature of the identity of a *laicus*. An *ars moriendi*, for instance, was advertised as useful for all those who, being still in good health, should 'dicwille dit boecxken binnen sijnen gesonden leuen lese oft horen lesen' (read this little book or listen to it being read by others), a formula which repeats the one used in the prologue of the *Delft Bible*.[54]

---

49 Van Duijn, *De Delftse Bijbel*, pp. 73–81.
50 Van Duijn, *De Delftse Bijbel*, p. 79.
51 *Dat Leven ons Heren Jhesu Christi*, above the colophon.
52 *Een cransken van minnen*, fol. 2ʳ.
53 *Miraculen onser liever Vrouwen* [alt. title *Dat boeck van onser liever Vrouwen miraculen*], fol. 1ᵛ.
54 *Een seer profitelijck boecxken om alle menschen wel te leeren sterven*, fol. 1ᵛ.

The Laicus *as a Model Reader: 'Those Who Cannot Read'*

Elsewhere, the identity of the *laicus* as a model addressee is based on an explicit reference (using the term *leek* or a similar phrase) to not just a lower level of education in comparison to *clerici*, but most especially to a lack of literacy skills. In a handbook about the devotion to the Seven Sorrows of the Virgin Mary, provision was made for an absence of literacy skills by the inclusion of religious images in the form of woodcuts: 'En*de* oec op dat die leecke lieden die niet lesen en connen: die personaegien aensiende he*m* daer in sullen mogen oeffenen Wa*n*t die beelden sijn der leeker luden boeken' (So that the *laici* who cannot read, looking at the figures in the images, should exercise themselves in it [i.e. piety], because images are the books of the *laici*).[55] The concept which was applied was similar to that of the *Biblia pauperum*. A graphic depiction, the argument went, was no less conducive to religious meditation than the written word. Through the term *laici* the author of the paratext addressed a community of devotees which was defined as comprising (apart from literate recipients) also illiterate members. It is not clear, in this instance, whether the subordinate clause is to be understood as supplying clarification ('*laici*, in other words those who cannot read'), or making a distinction ('[certain] *laici* who cannot read') among various groups of addressees, but perhaps this kind of hair-splitting was irrelevant for the author of this text, who simply wished to formulate his 'imaginary community' in the broadest possible way.

The Laicus *as a Model Reader: Instructing Others*

A collection of Jean Gerson's (1363–1429) theological writings, touching on the Ten Commandments, confession, and spiritual assistance to the dying, appeared as *Salicheit der menschen*.[56] The image of the model reader constructed in the prologue to this book comprised four categories of recipients:

> Ten eyrsten voer priesters en*de* cureiten die simpel sijn en*de* biecht horen moeten. Ten andere*n* voer allen ongheleerde*n* persone*n* weerlick oft geestelick. Ten derde*n* voer kindere*n* en*de* jonghen diemen va*n* huere*n* kinsche iaren yerst sal leren dat ghemeen inhout van onse*n* ghelove [...]. Ten vierden voer den die wil visitere*n* godshuysen of gasthuysen en*de* die biden sieken sijn.[57]

---

55 *Van de seven droefheden ofte weeden O.L.V.*, fol. 2ʳ.
56 Jean Gerson, *Salicheit der menschen*.
57 Jean Gerson, *Salicheit der menschen*, fols Aiiʳ–Aiiᵛ.

(First of all for priests and curates who are simple-minded and who hear confessions. Secondly, for all unlearned worldly or religious persons. Thirdly, for children and the young, who are to be instructed from childhood in the faith [...]. Fourthly, for those involved in caring for the poor in hospitals and almshouses.)

Without using the word *leek*, this prologue resorted to similar formulations: *weerlick* ('worldly', i.e. lay), and its complement, *geestelick* ('religious', i.e. ordained to the priesthood or belonging to a religious order). Among the non-lay readers, parish priests are mentioned. The members of this group are *simpel* ('simple', i.e. uneducated), and therefore they may be understood to constitute a category which meets the definition of *laicus* in its secondary meaning (cf. above). Next, the author nuances the model of the lay and non-lay model reader by including other categories: churchmen (*prelaten*) dealing with uneducated laity, parents and schoolmasters, masters of hospitals, and charitable institutions. Finally, in a broad category which includes both the laity and clergy, the text mentions as the addressees all persons charged with repairing their sinful behaviour, mentioning in particular those 'die ander mensche*n* tot sonde*n* ghebrocht hebben met woerden of wercke*n*' (who had led others to sin through words or deeds), and all those who 'and*er*en mensche*n* schuldich ware*n* te leeren en*de* dat v*er*sumet hebbe*n*' (had been responsible for instructing others but who had neglected to perform this task properly). For such persons, instructing others, in particular other *laici*, through the mediation of literature, was to be a way of achieving 'goede penitentie' (good penitence).[58]

The image of the model reader formulated in this prologue entails a view of the *laicus* as a dynamic actor in various social networks: those of the family, Church, and charitable institutions. The lack of learning, an important feature of the identity of the *laicus* in this kind of discourse, is transformed into a positive trait. Objections to the use of the book by untrained *laici* are rejected by the argument that ignorance in religious matters is a sin (and therefore, that religious information should be actively acquired), and furthermore by the observation that the dissemination of knowledge relating to the sacraments of confession and anointing of the sick is 'een werc van barmherticheit Gode bequamer dan lichamelike aelmisse' (a work of charity that is rightfully superior to ordinary forms of almsgiving), since the latter only concerned bodily needs, while the former catered to spiritual ones.[59] The notion that this book is addressed to a community comprising both ecclesiastics and *laici* (in all senses of this

---

58 Jean Gerson, *Salicheit der menschen*, fol. Aii^v.
59 Jean Gerson, *Salicheit der menschen*, fol. Aii^v.

term) is reinforced by a woodcut image on the title leaf showing a male religious surrounded by two laypeople, a man and a woman, and their two children, in the act of receiving religious instruction.

The Laicus *as a Model Reader: Knowledgeable* Laici

The portfolio of the book printers in Delft contains a large sub-segment of vernacular paraenetic texts, that is to say, works offering moral instruction, often coupled to basic theological knowledge (catechization). Among these texts, some were explicitly marketed to a reading public comprising *laici*. This was especially the case with a Middle Dutch translation of Jean Boutillier's (*c.* 1325/1345–1395) *Somme rural*, which was printed in Delft. The *Somme rural*, written between 1385 and 1393, was the work not of a *clericus* but of a layman who had nevertheless gained a systematic knowledge of the practice of canon and civil law, and had won considerable renown by codifying oral customary laws. The term 'rural' referred not to the physical space of the countryside, but to its inhabitants, the common people, for whom this compendium was intended.[60] The Middle Dutch translation reflects this image of the model readership: 'ende is gheintituleert somme rurale om dattet allen leeken dienende is' ([this work] is entitled *Somme rural* because it serves all *laici*).[61] Out of this arises an image of *laici* as a distinct community with its own, specific interests and preoccupations, an 'imagined community' by virtue of its universality and openness. Reinforcing this statement was a woodcut illustration showing a medieval throne chamber with a king seated among his court. On the monarch's right-hand side, a group of ecclesiastics, including a tonsured monk and several men who might be *clerici*, are standing, and to his left are a group of laymen in aristocratic costume — a clear, symbolic depiction of two of the three estates of medieval society.

A community of *laici* interested in the improvement of their spiritual life is the collective addressee of a translation of the theological handbook *Somme le roi*.[62] The original, compiled around 1279 by Laurent d'Orléans, was translated in 1408 by the aristocrat-turned-*conversus* Jan van Brederode in the Carthusian house of Zeelhem (near Diest).[63] This book, dedicated by the translator to his nephew, is advertised in the following way: 'Onder alle boeken die ic gehoert hebbe, so dunct mi dit enen leken mensche also nutten boec wesen in te lesen die gaern naden geboden Gods leuen soude' (among all the books I had ever listened to, this is, I believe, the most useful book to read for *laici* who wish to live according

---

60 Martyn, 'Jean Boutillier'.
61 Jean Boutillier, *Somme rurale*, fol. Ai^r [1^r].
62 Laurent de Orléans, *Summe le roy of des conincs summe*.
63 Van Oostrom, 'De erfenis van "Des coninx summe"'.

to God's commandments).[64] Repeatedly, Brederode envisaged the model of reception as a mixture of reading and listening, describing *Somme le roi* as the best book which he had ever 'als ic ye las of hoerde' (read or listened to).[65] Such a formula corresponds to the identity of the *laici* as those who did not possess well-developed literacy skills, but who wished to deepen their knowledge of the Christian faith, in this case on the fundamental level of the catechism.

The Laicus *as a Model Reader: 'Simple People with No Time to Read'*

The strategy of creating an imaginary community of *laici* was not always explicit. Sometimes the addressees' 'simplicity' was alluded to, as in the afterword of a Dutch translation of the German theologian Johannes Eck's polemic against Martin Luther, the *Enchiridion locorum communium adversus lutheranos*.[66] Here, the book was marketed as intended 'voer den simpelen' (for the simple).[67] This, as we have seen above, connoted not an intellectual deficit on the part of readers, but rather a lack of formal education associated with *clerici*. The model readership was further characterized as comprising individuals occupied by many matters, and therefore not having the time to read 'grote boecken' (large books). This discourse created for the *laicus* the identity of an actor in a challenging and dynamic socio-professional environment which was most likely associated with the commercial or artisanal class.[68]

An Implicit Image of Laici *as Model Readers: The Family — Adults and Children*

An interesting case is the anonymous treatise by a Franciscan author, *Der kersten eeuwe*, which offered, as Anna Dlabačová pointed out, practical moral and religious advice for lay readers.[69] The text is conceived as a dialogue between the narrator, addressed as a brother, and persons asking various questions in matters involving moral and religious values. Although the text was intended for an interpretive community of *laici*, both actual laymen and -women as well as their spiritual advisers, male religious who would have likewise counted as *laici* on account of their lower level of learning and non-Latin literacy, this model readership was not explicitly designated as such. It is only through the contents of these

---

64 Laurent de Orléans, *Summe le roy of des conincs summe*, fols 1^r–1^v.
65 Laurent de Orléans, *Summe le roy of des conincs summe*, fol. 1^v.
66 Johannes Eck, *Hier beghint een corte declaracie*.
67 Johannes Eck, *Hier beghint een corte declaracie*, fol. 108^v.
68 Johannes Eck, *Hier beghint een corte declaracie*, fol. 108^v.
69 Dlabačová, *Literatuur en observantie*, pp. 88–89.

questions and answers that one may deduce, as Dlabačová does, a lay, urban environment: the addressee is, for instance, addressed as going 'thuys gaen tot uwer onlede*n* om u nootdrufte te winnen' (home, to [their] daily chores, to earn a living).[70]

A similar situation occurs in the case of another handbook for an explicitly lay audience, the treatise *Hoe men dat huysghesinne regeren sal* (a translation of *Epistola de gubernatione rei familiaris*) by a twelfth-century scholar, poet and cosmographer Bernard Silvestris (also known as Bernard of Tours), but misattributed to St Bernard of Clairvaux. The addressee of the treatise is 'elcker mensche' (every man) who is urged to learn the proper way of managing 'hem selven, sijns huijs, en*de* huijsghesinne' (himself, his home, and family).[71] The treatise offers succinct advice emphasizing the virtues of simplicity, thrift, and modesty in taking care of the everyday needs of family members and servants, but its model reader is not explicitly addressed as *laicus*. This term, in fact, is not present in the text, which leads to the conclusion that such a verbal 'framing device' was not always deemed essential by editors and book printers; the model readership was adequately defined by the title and contents of the book, and needed no further clarification. The only extra-textual element explicitly pointing toward a lay readership was the woodcut on the first leaf of the Delft edition, which showed a monk with a halo (St Bernard?), sitting in a scriptorium, addressing a group of standing laymen in fashionable, aristocratic attire.

A woodcut showing a group of laymen, a laywoman, and a boy standing and listening (in this case, to an older layman, possibly a philosopher) was likewise used as a visual aid to evoke the identity of *laici* as model readers in a printed edition of a vernacular moral handbook, a translation of the Italian layman Albert of Brescia's *De arte loquendi et tacendi*. This treatise is described in the prologue as having been written by Albert 'tot leringe en*de* informacie sijns soons en*de* alle goede kerste*n* mensche*n*' (for the instruction of his sons and of all good Christian people); the addressees, apart from this group, were furthermore determined to be schoolchildren, for whom this book is believed to be especially beneficial — arguably, an early example of 'youth literature'.[72]

Conclusion

The case study performed on selected examples above reveals that the categories into which we may divide the identities of the *laicus* as an actor

---

70 *Spiegel des kersten geloofs*, fol. Biij[r].
71 Bernard of Clairvaux [Bernard Silvestris], *Hoe men dat huysghesinne regeren sal*, fol. 2[r].
72 Albert of Brescia, *Van die konste van spreken ende van swighen*, fol. 2[r].

and imagined community in the discourse of paratexts in early printed books are highly diverse, and do not automatically correspond to the sociological categories into which historians divide late medieval laity. Of course, there is considerable overlap: we may discern a sizeable group of texts, beginning with the *Delft Bible*, whose model readership falls into Volker Honemann's category of 'devout laity', knowledgeable laymen and -women interested in spiritual matters and eager to increase their knowledge, which approaches that of *clerici*.[73] Other books, with a *paraenetic* character, were marketed to laity whose description matches the secondary sense of this term as individuals with a lower level of knowledge, and fits Honemann's second category of lay readers as those in need of basic moral or religious instruction.[74]

This process of communication was possibly mediated by a member of the clergy or male religious in the capacity of a leader providing hermeneutic guidance to the members of such an interpretive community. The very universal, non-exclusive descriptors of the imagined community of interpretees ('all Christians', etc.) served to open or facilitate the process of the transmission of knowledge to various groups of empirical readers, which could consist of laity or non-laity (in today's sense of the word). Here, the common denominator was a lack or lower level of formal schooling and a need for delivering or receiving catechesis.

Of the examples analysed here, a considerable number of texts are translations of non-Netherlandish authors, predominantly French, but also some Italian, which leads to the conclusion that the notion of the *laici* as a community of readers, while certainly developed by authors from the Netherlands, was also partly the product of an international transfer of ideas. This gives additional reason to regard the references to *laici* in these texts as the evidence of the existence of an imagined community which was projected onto the collective mentality of readers. Consequently, we should treat these *laici* as actors in a particular discourse of literary communication, and hence as different from, and to a certain degree independent of, the actual existence of such a group in sociological terms. Finally, it is significant that graphic material in the form of woodcuts often served as a framing device additionally strengthening the notion of a community of *laici* as readers, which was constructed in the text.

Empirical readers, on the other hand, were a very diverse group, whose members could but did not always have to match the image created in the paratexts. Within the category of pious *meditationes* printed in Delft we find, for instance, a Book of Hours, which was decorated by an illuminator who added marginal flourishes and ornamental initials, giving it the appearance of a manuscript. The name of this artist, who can be considered

---

73 Honemann, 'Der Laie als Leser', p. 251.
74 Honemann, 'Der Laie als Leser', p. 251.

one of the first readers, is preserved on one of the leaves, carrying the inscription: 'bidt voor broeder Meynaert' (pray for Brother Meynaert).[75] Unfortunately we do not know which religious institution this brother (perhaps a *conversus*) was connected to. Was he a *laicus*? Certainly, though his situation was probably somewhere on the vague continuum of 'lay' stations in life that Christoph Burger specifies for the later Middle Ages.[76] Afterwards, this prayer book had a long history of use into the sixteenth and seventeenth century, as attested by the inscriptions on the title leaf. There are three handwritten notes and one specimen of poetry, all signed with the initials 'P. v[an] M.'. Additionally, copperplate etchings dating from the sixteenth century were pasted on the empty leaves. All this confirms a continuous use by a community of readers, who used this book for devotional purposes.

---

75 *Ghetyden van onser liever vrouwen*, fol. 203ʳ.
76 Burger, 'Direkte Zuwendung zu den "Laien"', pp. 89–90.

Works Cited

Manuscripts and Archival Sources

The Hague, Koninklijke Bibliotheek, MS 130 E 24

Primary Sources

Albert of Brescia, *Van die konste van spreken ende van swighen* (Delft: Jacob Jacobszoon van der Meer or Christiaen Snellaert, 1487); ISTC ia00209250

Alexander de Villa Dei, *Doctrinale*, Part II (Delft: [Christiaen Snellaert or Hendrik Eckert van Homberch, 1497]); ISTC ia00445570. Parts III and IV (Delft: [C. Snellaert], 1496); ISTC ia00454570

Anthony of Florence, *Confessionale: Defecerunt scrutantes scrutinio*. Add. Johannes Chrysostomus, *Sermo de poenitentia* (Delft: Jacob Jacobszoon van der Meer, 1482); ISTC ia00801100

Bernard of Clairvaux [Bernard Silvestris], *Hoe men dat huysghesinne regeren sal* (Delft: Christiaen Snellaert or Henrick Eckert van Homberch, 1493); ISTC ib00381990

Bible in Duytsche (Delft: Jacob Jacobszoon van der Meer and Mauricius Yemantszoon, 10 January 1477); ISTC ib00648000

Broeder Geraert, *Leven van Sinte Lutgart*, ed. by Instituut voor Nederlandse Lexicologie (samenstelling en redactie), *Cd-rom Middelnederlands* (Den Haag/Antwerpen: SduUitgevers/Standaard Uitgeverij, 1998)

Dat Leven ons Heren Jhesu Christi (Delft: Hendrik Eckert van Homberch, 1498); ISTC il00187500

De accentibus syllabarum. Add: *De generibus pedum et metrorum* (Delft: Christiaen Snellaert or Hendrick Eckert van Homberch, 1497); ISTC ia00016300

Die sijn die seven getijden der passien ons Heren met die seven weden onser Vrouwen (Delft: Henric Pietersz Lettersnijder, 1510); USTC 420333

Een boecxken van devocien geheten die negen couden (Delft: Henric Pietersz Lettersnijder, 1511); USTC 420354

Een cransken van minnen (Delft: Cornelis Henricz Lettersnijder, 1518); USTC 420625

Een seer profitelijck boecxken om alle menschen wel te leeren sterven (Delft: Cornelis Cornelissen, 1501–1505)

Een suuerlijc exmpel [sic] *hoe dat Jesus een heydensche maghet een soudaens dochter wech leyde wt haren lande* (Delft: F. Sonderdanck, 1501); USTC 424812

Expositio hymnorum (Delft: C. Snellaert, 11 August 1496); ISTC ie00155000

Ghetyden van onser liever vrouwen (Delft: Jacob Jacobszoon van der Meer, 1484); ISTC ih00430000

Horatius (Quintus Horatius Flaccus), *De arte poetica* (Delft: Cornelis Cornelissen, 20 December 1503); USTC 420088

Jacobus de Voragine, *Passionael. Winterstuc* (Delft: Christiaen Snellaert, 1489); ISTC ij00141000

Jean Boutillier, *Somme rurale* (Delft: Jacob Jacobszoon van der Meer, 1483); ISTC ib01050900

Jean Gerson, *Salicheit der menschen* (Delft: Jacob Jacobszoon van der Meer, 1482); ISTC ig00244000

Johannes Eck, *Hier beghint een corte declaracie ende antwoert teghen zomighe articulen der lutheranen* (Delft: Cornelis Henricz Lettersnijder / Amsterdam: Meester Luyt, 1527); USTC 420954

Laurent de Orléans, *Summe le roy of des conincs summe*, trans. by J. van Brederode (Delft: Jacob Jacobszoon van der Meer and Mauricius Yemantszoon, 1478); ISTC il00089000

Miraculen onser liever Vrouwen [*Dat boeck van onser liever Vrouwen miraculen*] (Delft: Jacob Jacobszoon van der Meer and Mauricius Yemantszoon, 1477); ISTC im00619800

Spiegel des kersten geloofs of der kersten eeuwe (Delft: Christiaen Snellaert, 1488); ISTC is00672300

Van de seven droefheden ofte weeden O.L.V. (Delft: Christiaen Snellaert, 1494); ISTC id00366420

Secondary Studies

Anderson, Benedict, *Imagined Communities: Reflections on the Origin and Spread of Nationalism* (London: Verso, 1991)

Beckers, J. A., and Rein-Arend Leeuw, 'Onderwijs: scholen', in *De stad Delft, cultuur en maatschappij tot 1572*, I: *Tekst*, ed. by Rein-Arend Leeuw and Ineke V. T. Spaander (Delft: Stedelijk Museum Het Prinsenhof, 1981), pp. 113–15

Beek, Lydeke van, *Leken trekken tot Gods Woord: Dirc van Herxen (1381–1457) en zijn Eerste Collatieboek*, Middeleeuwse studies en bronnen, 120 (Hilversum: Verloren, 2009)

Boheemen, Fabianus Cornelis van, and Theodorus Cornelis Jacobus van der Heijden, 'Literatuur en toneel in Delft', in *De stad Delft, cultuur en maatschappij tot 1572*, I: *Tekst*, ed. by Rein-Arend Leeuw and Ineke V. T. Spaander (Delft: Stedelijk Museum Het Prinsenhof, 1981), pp. 162–65

——, *De Delftse rederijkers 'Wy rapen gheneucht'* (Amsterdam: Huis aan de Drie Grachten, 1982)

Burger, Christoph, 'Direkte Zuwendung zu den "Laien" und Rückgriff auf Vermittler in spätmittelalterlicher katechetischer Literatur', in *Spätmittelalterliche Frömmigkeit zwischen Ideal und Praxis*, ed. by Bernd Hamm and Thomas Lentes (Tübingen: Mohr Siebeck, 2001), pp. 85–110

Caspers, Charles M. A., 'Bidden in twee talen: een beschouwing van het bidgedrag van clerici, religieuzen en leken in de laatmiddeleeuwse Nederlanden', *Queeste*, 15 (2008), 3–16

Chavannes-Mazel, Claudine A., and Joseph Godefridus Cornelis Venner, 'Delftse handschriften en boekverluchting', in *De Stad Delft. Cultuur en maatschappij tot 1572*, I: *Tekst*, ed. by Rein-Arend Leeuw and Ineke V. T. Spaander (Delft: Stedelijk Museum Het Prinsenhof, 1981), pp. 134–37

Corbellini, Sabrina, 'Lezers, kopiisten en boekverkopers in de middeleeuwse stad', in *Verlichte geesten: de IJsselstreek als internationaal religieus-cultureel centrum in de late middeleeuwen*, ed. by Catrien Santing and Jan Cornelis Bedaux (Deventer: Stadsarchief en Athenaeumbibliotheek, 2012), pp. 41–53

——, and Gerrit Verhoeven, 'A Sixteenth-Century Book Catalogue from Delft', in *Education and Learning in the Netherlands 1400–1600*, ed. by Koen Goudriaan, Jaap van Molenbeek, and Ad Tervoet (Leiden: Brill, 2004), pp. 253–76

Dąbrówka, Andrzej, *Teatr i sacrum w średniowieczu. Religia — cywilizacja — estetyka* (Wrocław: Fundacja Nauki Polskiej, 2001)

Desplenter, Youri, 'Publiek van bijbelvertalingen in de middeleeuwse Lage Landen: leken, semireligieuzen, religieuzen en clerici', in *De Bijbel in de Lage Landen: elf eeuwen van vertalen*, ed. by Paul Gillaerts, Henri Bloemen, Youri Desplenter, Wim François, and August den Hollander (Heerenveen: Royal Jongbloed, 2015), pp. 64–65

Dlabačová, Anna, *Literatuur en observantie: de 'Spieghel der volcomenheit' van Hendrik Herp en de dynamiek van laatmiddeleeuwse tekstverspreiding* (Hilversum: Verloren, 2014)

Duijn, Mart van, 'Printing, Public, and Power: Shaping the First Printed Bible in Dutch (1477)', *Church History and Religious Culture*, 93 (2013), 275–99

——, *De Delftse Bijbel. Een sociale geschiedenis 1477 – circa 1550* (Zutphen: Walburg Pers, 2017)

Fish, Stanley E., 'Interpreting the Variorum', *Critical Enquiry*, 2.3 (1976), 465–85

——, *Doing What Comes Naturally: Change, Rhetoric, and the Practice of Theory in Literary and Legal Studies* (Durham: Duke University Press, 1989)

Folkerts, Suzan, 'Vrome leken en foute priesters', *Madoc*, 19 (2005), 225–33

——, 'Te "duncker" voor leken? Middelnederlandse Bijbelvertalingen vanuit het perspectief van de gebruikers', *Jaarboek voor Nederlandse boekgeschiedenis*, 18 (2011), 155–70

——, 'The Cloister or the City? The Appropriation of the New Testament by Lay Readers in an Urban Setting', in *Cultures of Religious Reading in the Late Middle Ages: Instructing the Soul, Feeding the Spirit, and Awakening the Passion*, ed. by Sabrina Corbellini (Turnhout: Brepols, 2013), pp. 175–99

——, 'Approaching Lay Readership of Middle Dutch Bibles: On the Uses of Archival Sources and Bible Manuscripts', in *Discovering the Riches of the Word: Religious Reading in Late Medieval and Early Modern Europe*, ed. by Sabrina Corbellini, Margriet Hoogvliet, and Bart Ramakers (Leiden: Brill, 2015), pp. 18–43

Ginther, James R., *The Westminster Handbook to Medieval Theology* (Louisville: Westminster John Knox Press, 2009)

Goudriaan, Koen, 'De franciscanen, de leken en de drukpers', *Ons geestelijk erf*, 85 (2014), 230–66

Hamilton, Bernard, 'Religion and the Laity', in *The New Cambridge Medieval History*, ed. by David Luscombe and Jonathan Riley-Smith (Cambridge: Cambridge University Press, 2004), pp. 499–533

Honemann, Volker, 'Der Laie als Leser', in *Laienfrömmigkeit im späten Mittelalter. Formen, Funktionen, politisch-soziale Zusammenhänge*, ed. by Klaus Schreiner and Elisabeth Müller-Luckner (Munich: Oldenbourg, 1992), pp. 241–51

―――, 'Laien als Literaturförderer im 15. und 16. Jahrhundert', in *Laienlektüre und Buchmarkt im späten Mittelalter*, ed. by Thomas Kock and Rita Schlusemann (Frankfurt am Main: Peter Lang, 1997), pp. 147–60

Imbach, Ruedi, *Laien in der Philosophie des Mittelalters. Hinweise und Anregungen zu einem vernachlässigten Thema*, Bochumer Studien zur Philosophie, 14 (Amsterdam: Grüner, 1989)

Kors, Mikel M., 'Die Bibel für Laien: Neuansatz oder Sackgasse? Der Bibelübersetzer von 1360 und Gerhard Zerbolt von Zutphen', in *Kirchenreform von unten. Gerhard Zerbolt von Zutphen und die Brüder vom gemeinsamen Leben*, ed. by Nikolaus Staubach (Frankfurt am Main: Peter Lang, 2004), pp. 243–63

―――, *De bijbel voor leken: studies over Petrus Naghel en de Historiebijbel van 1361*, Publicaties van de Stichting Encyclopédie Bénédictine, 4 (Leuven: Encyclopédie Bénédictine, 2007)

Korteweg, Anne S., 'Geestelijken en leken als bestellers van liturgische handschriften', in *Zuid-Nederlandse miniatuurkunst: de mooiste verluchte handschriften in Nederlands bezit*, ed. by Anne-Margreet W. As-Vijvers and Anne S. Korteweg (Utrecht: Museum Catharijneconvent, 2018), pp. 264–71

Krause, Gerhard, and Robert Stuppernich, 'Bruderschaften, Schwesternschaften, Kommunitäten', in *Theologische Realenzyklopädie*, ed. by Horst Robert Balz, Gerhard Krause, and Gerhard Müller (Berlin: De Gruyter, 1976–2004), pp. 195–212

Latour, Bruno, *Reassembling the Social: An Introduction to Actor–Network–Theory* (Oxford: Oxford University Press, 2005)

Martyn, Georges, 'Jean Boutillier, La somme rural', in *Colard Mansion: Incunabula, Prints and Manuscripts in Medieval Bruges*, ed. by Evelien Hauwaerts, Evelien De Wilde, and Ludo Vandamme (Brugge: Snoeck, 2018), p. 147

Mertens, Thom, 'The Modern Devotion and Innovation in Middle Dutch Literature', in *Medieval Dutch Literature in its European Context*, ed. by Erik Kooper (Cambridge: Cambridge University Press, 1994), pp. 226–41

Middelnederlandsch woordenboek <http://gtb.inl.nl/search/?owner=mnw> [accessed on 16 March 2018]

Moll, Willem, *De boekerij van het St Barbara-klooster te Delft* (Amsterdam: Van der Post, 1857)

Mostert, Marco, 'Wytwarzanie, przechowywanie i użytkowanie. O roli tekstu pisanego w średniowieczu', in *Kultura pisma w średniowieczu. Znane problemy, nowe metody*, ed. by Anna Adamska and Paweł Kras (Lublin: Wydawnictwo KUL, 2013), pp. 17–36

Nauert, Charles G., Jr., 'The Humanist Challenge to Medieval German Culture', in *Renaissance Thought: A Reader*, ed. by Robert Black (London: Routledge, 2001), pp. 275–95

Obbema, Pieter, *De middeleeuwen in handen. Over de boekcultuur in de late middeleeuwen* (Hilversum: Verloren, 1996)

Oosterbaan, Dinant Petrus, *De Oude Kerk te Delft gedurende de middeleeuwen* (The Hague: Voorhoeve, 1973)

Oostrom, Frits van, 'De erfenis van "Des coninx summe"', *Optima*, 14 (1996), 119–26

Pleij, Herman, 'Op belofte van profijt: inleiding', in *Op belofte van profijt: stadsliteratuur en burgermoraal in de Nederlandse letterkunde van de middeleeuwen*, ed. by Herman Pleij (Amsterdam: Prometheus, 1991), pp. 8–51

──, 'The Rise of Urban Literature in the Low Countries', in *Medieval Dutch Literature in its European Context*, ed. by Erik Kooper (Cambridge: Cambridge University Press, 1994), pp. 62–77

Płonka-Bałus, Katarzyna, *The Catalogue of Medieval Illuminated Manuscripts and Miniatures in the Princes Czartoryski Library and Museum*, part I: *The Netherlands (15th–16th Centuries)* (Cracow: Universitas, 2013)

Polkowski, Marcin, *A Struggle for Survival: The Continuity of Catholic Religious Literature in Holland: The Example of Delft (1450–1650)* (Lublin: Wydawnictwo KUL, 2012)

Reynaert, Joris, 'Leken, ethiek en moralistisch-didactische literatuur: ter inleiding', in *Wat is wijsheid? Lekenethiek in de Middelnederlandse letterkunde*, ed. by Joris Reinaert and Dini Hogenelst (Amsterdam: Prometheus, 1994), pp. 9–36

Roolfs, Friedel Helga, *Der 'Spieghel der leyen': eine spätmittelalterliche Einführung in die Theologie der Sünde und des Leidens. Diplomatische Edition und philologische Untersuchung* (Cologne: Böhlau, 2004)

Rudy, Kathryn, 'De productie van manuscripten in het Sint-Ursulaklooster te Delft', *Delf*, 12.2 (2010), 24–27

Steer, Georg, 'Der Laie als Anreger und Addressat deutscher Prosaliteratur im 14. Jahrhundert', in *Zur deutschen Literatur und Sprache des 14. Jahrhunderts. Dubliner Colloquium*, ed. by Walter Haug, Timothy R. Jackson, and Johannes Janota (Heidelberg: Winter, 1983), pp. 354–67

Verhoeven, Gerrit, *Devotie en negotie. Delft als bedevaartplaats in de late middeleeuwen* (Amsterdam: VU Uitgeverij, 1992)

Worstbrock, Franz Josef, 'Zur biographie des Alexander Hegius', *Humanistica Lovaniensia*, 29 (1980), 161–65

Wuttke, Ulrike, *Im Diesseits das Jenseits bereiten. Eschatologie, Laienbildung und Zeitkritik bei den mittelniederländischen Autoren Jan van Boendale, Lodewijk van Velthem und Jan van Leeuwen* (Göttingen: Universitätsverlag, 2016)

Exiles, Diasporas, and Migrants

IGNACIO GARCÍA PINILLA

Spanish Merchants and Dissidents outside Spain in the Sixteenth Century*

Spanish religious dissidents of the sixteenth century were represented in the nineteenth century as spiritual misfits outside the national mainstream. Even after concepts of social discipline and confessionalization became widespread, the tendency to regard them as uprooted people remained. However, several decades ago researchers started to consider this issue from a very different point of view. My intention in this chapter is to present some examples of the close links of some of these dissidents with the environment in which they found themselves and with compatriots within their reach there. Specifically, studying their relationships with commercial communities is essential for understanding their circumstances, their ideas, and their behaviour in general.

I will focus on the commercial area of the Low Countries. In that part of the world, some colonies of Spanish merchants went back to the thirteenth century, but it was in the second half of the fourteenth century that they obtained a significant presence. Bruges reached a prominent position, at the time when the Castilian consulate (an organ of management, legal documentation, and control) was established there, and Spaniards who were settled at other locations in the Low Countries, such as Antwerp, Middelburg, Bergen, etc., maintained contact with their kin in

---

* This paper is part of the project 'La República política entre Clío y Calíope. Representaciones y prácticas políticas en la Monarquía Hispánica en la Alta Edad Moderna' (PGC2018-093833-B-I00), financed by the Spanish Ministry of Science, Innovation and Universities with FEDER funds.

Ignacio J. García Pinilla is Professor of Classics at the University of Castilla–La Mancha (Toledo). He has edited several works written by sixteenth-century Spanish dissidents and exiles (most recently, *Inquisitionis Hispanicae artes aliquot*, Brill, 2018). He has published many studies on the link between humanist culture, religious nonconformism, and political conflict in early modern Spain.

Networking Europe and New Communities of Interpretation (1400–1600), ed. by Margriet Hoogvliet, Manuel F. Fernández Chaves, *and* Rafael M. Pérez García, New Communities of Interpretation, 4 (Turnhout: Brepols, 2023), pp. 101–118

BREPOLS PUBLISHERS   10.1484/M.NCI-EB.5.134312

Bruges. With the transfer by Emperor Maximilian I of foreign merchants to Antwerp between 1488 and 1494, as well as due to the silting-up of the Zwin channel, which had connected the city of Bruges to the sea, around 1500, the greater part of the economic activity moved to other localities (the already mentioned Antwerp, Middelburg, and Bergen op Zoom). Still, a large part of the Spanish community continued to consider Bruges central to their presence in the Low Countries for decades afterward.

Vives and the Spanish Merchant Colonies

Juan Luis Vives, a Spanish humanist from Valencia, settled in Bruges in 1526.[1] He had previously lectured at the Universities of Paris, Louvain, and Oxford. He was related to the world of merchants by birth and marriage, and was of Jewish descent. He was a friend of Erasmus and Thomas More and promoted a renewed spirituality focused on everyday life. He was the preceptor of outstanding figures like the young bishop of Cambrai, Guillaume de Croy, as well as of members of the bourgeoisie, especially merchants. Names frequently mentioned in this connection include Diego Gracián de Alderete (from a family with ties to the court), Honorato Juan (from Valencia), and Pedro Maluenda and Diego de Astudillo (from Burgos families). Fagel adds — with reservations — Juan del Castillo, Gaspar de Castro, and Pedro Alonso de Burgos.[2] The list might perhaps be further enlarged with the names of Hernán Ruiz de Villegas and Pedro Juan Olivar,[3] though Olivar did not belong to the bourgeoisie.

Vives is notable for the wide reception that his writings enjoyed. They were printed many times, especially during the first part of the sixteenth century. Spanish merchants translated and published some of these editions, and, as one would expect, these merchants were linked to Bruges: Diego de Astudillo and Diego Ortega de Burgos, and both of these surnames were notable amongst the community of merchants from Burgos.

Diego de Astudillo translated into Spanish the *Introductio ad sapientiam* along with two treatises of Plutarch's *Moralia*.[4] In the preliminaries he

---

1 For a general perspective on Vives, see Moreno Gallego, *La recepción hispana de Juan Luis Vives*; González González, 'Juan Luis Vives: Works and Days'; González González, *Joan Lluís Vives*. On the specific relationship of Vives with the commercial environment, cf. Fagel, 'Un humanista entre mercaderes'.
2 Fagel, *De Hispano–Vlaamse wereld*, pp. 356–57.
3 Concerning Ruiz de Villegas, cf. Moreno Gallego 'Tristia rerum'; Pino González, 'Grudia me tenuit cultrix studiosa Mineruae'. For Olivar, see Almenara i Sebastiá, 'El humanista Pere-Joan Olivar', pp. 104–08.
4 *Introduction a la sabiduria compuesta en latin por el Doctor Iuan Luys Viues. Dialogo de Plutarcho, en el qual se tracta, como se ha de refrenar la ira. Vna carta de Plutarcho, que enseña*

expressly presents himself as a merchant, and his brother stated that Diego wrote the translation 'siendo casado y lleno de negocios de la mercadería y dessassossiegos que aquella manera de vivir trae consigo' (being married and full of the merchant deals and anxieties that this way of life brings).[5] As the Astudillos were one of the most prominent families from Burgos then in the Low Countries, it is not strange that Diego was *consul* of the Spanish consulate in Bruges for four years, and a member of the consulate for ten more years.[6]

The second translator is Diego Ortega de Burgos, who is present as a merchant in the commercial registers of Antwerp in the middle decades of the sixteenth century. He published his translation of *Ad animi in Deum excitationem commentatiunculae* in Antwerp, with a second edition published two years later in Burgos.[7] In the introduction to the reader he explains that '[e]l ruego de algunos amigos fue en alguna manera causa para que procurase de tradizir la presente obra' (the request of some friends was in some way the cause that impelled me to translate this book).[8] Who were these friends? Obviously, they have to be sought among the Spaniards who were nearby, those who lived in the Low Countries. They might be mostly merchants. These two translations coincide in proposing a higher spiritual lifestyle to this group, open to innovative proposals. In the Low Countries there was a Spanish mercantile bourgeoisie eager to incorporate the new trends that were around, and its attitudes towards new religious ideas would be extremely varied.

Other merchants placed their children as pupils of Vives. One of them, Pedro de Maluenda, was later imperial theologian at the Council of Trent, and he strongly opposed the heterodox Spaniards, especially in the case of Juan Díaz. The three people mentioned in relation to Vives were all members of merchant families from Burgos. And two more could probably been added: Pedro Alonso de Burgos, born in Zeeland, and Gaspar de Castro.[9]

---

alos casados como se han de auer en su biuir. Todo nueuamente traduzido en castellano, por Diego de Astudillo, En Anuers, en casa de Iuan Steelsio, 1551.

5 Juan Luis Vives, *Introduction a la sabiduria*, fol. A2^r.
6 Fagel, 'Spanish Merchants in the Low Countries', p. 93. On Diego de Astudillo, cf. Morales Ortiz, *Plutarco en España*, pp. 101–04.
7 *Comentarios para despertamiento del animo en dios. Y preparacion del animo para orar … compuestas primero en latin, por el excelente y famoso varon el doctor Iuan Luys viuas, traduzidas de alli en castellano por Diego ortega de Burgos, vezino de Burgos*, Emprimido en la villa de Emberes por Miguel Hillenio, 1537; cf. González y González, Albiñana, and Gutiérrez, eds, *Vives. Edicions princeps*, p. 265.
8 Juan Luis Vives, *Comentarios para despertamiento del animo en dios*, fol. A2^r.
9 Fagel, *De Hispano–Vlaamse wereld*, pp. 356–57.

Burgos Merchants and Lutheranism

Two merchant families from Burgos that were settled in the Low Countries became implicated in trials for Lutheranism: the San Román and Enzinas families. Given the close links within the Spanish expatriate merchant community (they used marriages to create and seal business alliances), the impact of these condemnations must have been high.

Francisco de San Román (d. 1542) is a special case. Born in Burgos, he received the usual training for merchants, and he did not go to university: 'Literarum aut religionis nihil unquam didicit praeter communem illam nostrorum hominum institutionem' (He never learnt anything of arts or religion apart from the usual basic training among our people).[10] In 1540, the year of Juan Luis Vives' death, he experienced a sudden conversion to Protestantism when, while on a business trip, he heard a sermon in German. San Román understood the sermon thoroughly and discovered a whole different way of being a Christian. From that moment on, he devoted himself to the study of the new doctrine, despite not having had any previous theological training; and as a new convert he undertook intense proselytizing activity. Imprisoned on his return to Antwerp and released some weeks later, he had three meetings with Emperor Charles V in Regensburg. After a second arrest there, he was sent to Spain, was tried by the Inquisition, and burnt at the stake as a Lutheran in Valladolid. His friend Francisco de Enzinas said about him: 'Scripsit etiam aliquot volumina, primo copiosas literas ad Antuerpienses [...]. Deinde scripsit binas aut ternas literas ad imperatorem [...]. Postremo scripsit copiosum catechismum atque alios libellos Hispanica lingua, in quibus multum de singulorum articulorum doctrina tradebatur' (He also wrote several works: first, many letters to his colleagues in Antwerp [...]. Secondly, he wrote two or three letters to the Emperor [...]. Lastly, he wrote an ample catechism and other short books in Spanish, in which he expounded the doctrine of every single article in detail).[11]

Enzinas explains that all these works were produced within a short period of thirty or forty days, perhaps at the beginning of 1541. Keeping in mind the aforementioned publications by merchants, San Román's activity is more easily understandable, because they followed the same path, and we may assume that the target group for these works was, basically, the Spanish merchant community in the Low Countries with its connections, just as in the previous cases mentioned before.

It has already been said that Francisco de Enzinas was San Román's friend. In fact, our knowledge of the vicissitudes of Francisco de San

---

10 Francisco de Enzinas, *De statu Belgico*, § 80, l. 4. On San Román, see Tellechea Idígoras, 'Francisco de San Román'.
11 Francisco de Enzinas, *De statu Belgico*, § 81, ll. 4–5.

Román is due largely to the narrative of Francisco de Enzinas, whom he had known since childhood. However, the causes of the religious change in Francisco de Enzinas (1518–1552) and his brother Diego (d. 1547) were completely different. It seems that they became Protestants while studying in Louvain. The Enzinas were another merchant family from Burgos, strongly linked to many other families established in the Low Countries, with surnames such as Pardo, Lerma, Torre, Valladolid, Espinosa, Ayala, Arceo, Santa Cruz, Salamanca, Salinas, Ortega, and Castro de Londres.[12] Consequently, the network of families extended to Seville, Medina del Campo, Bruges, London, Antwerp, Middelburg, Florence, and Rome, to mention only the most relevant places. Moreover, it is very likely that the aforementioned Diego Ortega de Burgos, Vives' translator, was closely linked to Francisco de Enzinas.[13] Pedro de Lerma (a fervent Erasmist, Abbot of Alcala de Henares, and professor at the Sorbonne) was also his relative.

Lerma had been condemned by the Inquisition in 1537 and afterwards, though he was by this time quite old, he decided to leave Spain and return to Paris. On his deathbed he was attended by Francisco and Diego de Enzinas. We know in any case that the Spanish merchant community from Burgos (including those from Burgos families born in the Low Countries) had a significant presence in Paris as well. To cite just one example: a book of short poems published by Jerónimo de la Peña in Paris in 1537 explicitly mentions no fewer than five members of these merchant families: Francisco Orense, Francisco Astudillo, Jacques de la Torre, the aforementioned Pedro de Maluenda, and Jerónimo de Salinas.[14]

Along with the network formed by Burgos families, Francisco de Enzinas had an important relationship with Hieronymus Sailer, although we do not know how it started. Sailer, a merchant from St Gallen, had spent many years in Spain in the service of the Welser, including as head of their Madrid office, and on his return to Germany he had settled in Augsburg and married a Welser — a fact which shows his high rank.[15] Evidence of

---

12 These are the families mentioned as relatives (*parientes*) in a memorandum dictated by Inés de Enzinas; Valladolid, ARCV, Caja 1206, exp. 6, fols 33^v–34^r of the second part.
13 Diego Ortega is mentioned three times in Enzinas's correspondence as present in Antwerp and related to Enzinas's economic support, cf. Francisco de Enzinas, *Epistolario*, pp. 72 (1540), 94 (1543), and 101 (1551). He was probably Enzinas's uncle on his mother's side.
14 Jerónimo de la Peña, *Philadelphiarum*, poems 1,50 (Orense), 2,3 (Astudillo), 2,93 (Torre), 2,46 (Maluenda), 2,39, 2,46 and 2,83 (Salinas). The numbers (book, poem) refer to the list included at the end of this article: Amherdt and García Pinilla, 'Les *Philadelphiarum libri duo* de Hieronymus Rupeus', pp. 425–56.
15 There is a summary of Hieronymus Sailer's economic activity in Häberlein, *Brüder, Freunde und Betrüger*, pp. 128–32. This includes his movements and relationships, with a particular focus on details relevant to his cooperation in providing finances to the French Crown in the 1540s. His Spanish period is studied by Kellenbenz and Walter, *Oberdeutsche Kaufleute*, pp. 30–38.

the strong relationship between Enzinas and Sailer is that the former was godfather to a daughter of the latter.

At the same time, Sailer was closely connected to the traffic in goods and slaves with Santa Marta (in what is now Venezuela), whose governor was García de Lerma, an individual from Burgos who may well have been related to Francisco de Enzinas's family. It is tempting to think that Sailer acted as protector and financial guarantor of Francisco as a result of a relationship established while in Castile. In appreciation of the magnate's protection, while Enzinas was in Basel he wrote a prologue dedicated to Sailer's young sons, published anonymously, in which he extolled the importance of intellectual and humanist education.[16]

There is no satisfactory explanation for the origin of Enzinas's relationship with a Fugger factor called Jörg Stecher, who worked first in Spain and subsequently at the trading-house in Antwerp. Stecher even expressed an interest in checking the prologues written by Enzinas before the publication of some of his books. Another friend of Enzinas's was Jörg Herwart, from an important and aristocratic banking family, who later held the position of consul of Augsburg. The family had established a trading-house in Antwerp in the early sixteenth century and was related to Sailer.[17]

In addition to these relationships with merchants or German bankers, Enzinas mentions other Burgos families in passing. In his *Memorias* he alludes several times to his relatives in Antwerp and at court. We can only conjecture about the latter, but some details about the former are clear. Besides the aforementioned Diego Ortega de Burgos (who was several times consul of the Spanish nation at Antwerp), he had a clear relationship with the Salamancas, an important merchant family, especially with the branch related to the Santa Cruz family. For example, Jerónimo de Salamanca Santa Cruz started a legal struggle to repatriate Enzinas's orphaned daughters to Castile, using their grandmother, Beatriz de Santa Cruz, who lived in Burgos. Through this same connection, Enzinas was almost certainly related to Diego de Santa Cruz Salamanca (husband of Barbara Lixhals, and thus linked to another merchant family of German origin), who lived in Antwerp until 1558 and was buried in that city's church of St Jacob.[18]

This firmly established position in the Low Countries helps us to understand why, for example, Francisco de Enzinas could escape from

---

16 *Dramata sacra* [VD16 O 794]. This anonymous prologue has been sometimes attributed to the printer Oporinus, but its content, style, and external evidence are perfectly consistent with the hypothesis that Enzinas wrote it. In Enzinas's correspondence there is ample evidence of his attention to the education of these young men, which did not always go forward easily.
17 Cf. Francisco de Enzinas, *Epistolario*, for Stecher, pp. 354–56, 390, 432–35, 444–45, 475, 620–22; for Herwart, pp. 268 (father) and 192–95 (son).
18 There is material about him in Brussels, KBR, MSS 10243 and 10244.

prison in Brussels — finding all the gates unlocked and without a guard — and how he could use the commercial routes of the Santa Cruz family to attempt to send hundreds of copies of his *Breve y compendiosa institición de la religión cristiana* (printed at Antwerp in 1542) to Spain.[19]

Following the example of their predecessors, the two Enzinas brothers opted for translation as a way to spread ideas, but in their case, they translated works of Luther (*On Christian freedom*) and Calvin (the 1537 *Catechism*). They relied on the family network to try secretly to send copies to Spain, but the Inquisition prevented this.[20] Francisco has left us many translations, and he often included additions in them. It is not by chance that the longest one in his translation of Calvin occurs while commenting on the eighth commandment:

> El que usa fraudes y cautelas o contratos engañosos y malos para ganar dineros, y el que anda en cambios y recambios, usuras y finanças y otras innumerables maldades y engaños que hoy se usan y de cada día nuebamente se inventan, de que el mundo está lleno. Y lo que peor es, entre próximos cristianos y entre parientes y hermanos, y aun entre padres e hijos se querrían robar y sacarse unos a otros las entrañas.[21]

> (One who uses fraud and subtleties, or contracts that are dishonest and bad to make a profit, and who goes about doing exchanges and re-exchanges, usury, financing, and innumerable other evils and deceits in use today, more of which are invented every day, and of which the world is full. And the worst of it is, family members and brothers, and even parents and children, would like to rob and eviscerate each other.)

He must have been thinking of the merchants and traders he had seen acting in Antwerp and Burgos, many of them his relatives. It is impossible to understand Francisco de Enzinas's activities without taking into account his connection to the world of wealthy merchants who, through marriages,

---

19 For a general description of the communication networks of the Spanish merchant families at this period, cf. Casado Alonso, 'Los flujos de información en las redes comerciales'.
20 The Inquisition was informed that 'it was printed by order of a Spanish student who was at Louvain whose name is Francisco de Enzinas, a native of Burgos, and the nephew of the treasurer of the Cathedral of said city of Burgos. And for the purpose of better concealment, he changed the name and the year and the place of printing. And they say that this Francisco de Enzinas has a brother named Diego de Enzinas who is on his way to these lands with three or four hundred of the aforementioned books, according to the information received by the person who gave notice of it here, and he says he knows that, suspecting this, some family members of said Diego de Enzinas who are in Flanders wrote to said treasurer in Burgos so that he would secretly take the books and have them burned'. Reproduced in the introduction to Francisco de Enzinas, *Breve y compendiosa institución de la religión cristiana*, pp. 19–20. The treasurer was Álvaro de Santa Cruz.
21 Francisco de Enzinas, *Breve y compendiosa institución de la religión cristiana*, pp. 129–30.

had established wide-ranging commercial networks stretching from Seville to Lübeck and from London to Venice. Even his strange plan to go and live in Constantinople in 1548 must have had some basis of support from a family member established there.

Religious Unrest in Merchant Families Residing in the Low Countries

Pedro Jiménez (1524–1595) was another representative of a wealthy merchant clan, in this case from Andalusia, the Jiménez de León family.[22] They first established themselves in Middelburg, and they were well connected with other Andalusian families established in that city and in Bergen op Zoom, Antwerp, Frankfurt, etc. (such as the Palmas, Pérezes, Hinojosas, Paredes, etc.), and they soon married into local families, for example the Roekocx, Van Stemburch, and Van Brecht families. However, Pedro Jiménez (or Ximenius) did not take up a trading career but rather followed university studies in Salamanca, Bologna, and Paris, and became an expert in Greek and Hebrew. He has remained in the historical shadows because all his written work has disappeared, although it was appreciated by great intellectual figures of his time. Indeed, Pedro Jiménez played an important part in Justus Lipsius's conversion to Catholicism. Jiménez is an unusual representative of Irenicism, linked to Georg Cassander. Although he remained within the Catholic Church, he was always suspect in the eyes of agents of the Spanish Crown, the University of Louvain, and the clergy of Cologne (the last place where he resided), because his daring doctrinal positions, his openness, and his pacifism were in sharp contrast to the confessional intransigence that marked the second half of the sixteenth century.

While is it true that we do know only the title of Jiménez's principal written work (*Demonstratio Christianae et Catholicae veritatis*, to which he dedicated several years of his life), recently Peter A. Heuser has demonstrated that he was also the author of a *Dialogus de Pace* printed anonymously, probably in Cologne, in 1579.[23] In that year there was a peace conference in Cologne between the northern provinces of the Low Countries and the Spanish Crown, during the Eighty Years' War. In this fictitious dialogue the King of Spain and the Duke of Parma, Alessandro Farnese, dealt with arguments in favour of peace through concessions by both sides, with an explicit recognition of the freedom of conscience. The

---

22 The most detailed description of Pedro Jiménez can be found in Heuser, *Jean Matal*, pp. 177–208.
23 Heuser, 'Kaspar Schetz von Grobbendonk oder Pedro Ximénez?'.

book contains very audacious arguments, and includes criticisms of past actions by the Catholics themselves.

It appears that Jiménez was able to live and work during all this time thanks to his family's wealth. It appears that his father was the Middelburg merchant Pedro Jiménez de León. A sister of Pedro senior, Isabel Jiménez, married Pedro de Hinojosa (or Hiniosa), whose family will be discussed below. One of the brothers of the humanist Pedro was Francisco Jiménez de León (1520–1560), who was a soldier and who received the title of *hidalgo* (*eques*, knight) from Charles V in 1549 — yet another example of men with *converso* backgrounds who were elevated to the nobility. Francisco established a connection with another important merchant family through his marriage to María Ortiz, and further connections came via the couple's children.[24] Of their daughters, Mayor Jiménez married a member of the Van Laurenten family, Baltazar, while Isabel (who cared for her uncle Pedro in Cologne) married into the Daza family. After the repression of the Calvinists in Antwerp in 1567, which entailed the flight of a great many Spanish merchants, one of the cousins of the humanist Pedro Jiménez: the wealthy merchant Juan de Hinojosa (son of the aforementioned Pedro de Hinojosa) set up residency in Cologne.[25] This Juan de Hinojosa had traded in Spain before 1570 and claimed to have been a victim of the Spanish Inquisition (though this claim is not corroborated by any other source, for his name does not appear in any of the lists of condemned persons). Given the time-frame when his supposed arrest took place, it is reasonable to think that it may have coincided with the great repression of Protestants in Seville, Valladolid, and other Castilian cities. In any case, Juan de Hinojosa left Antwerp just before the Duke of Alba's repression, and he was in fact was condemned by the Conseil des Troubles. Once in Cologne, his adherence to Calvinism was public knowledge, though Calvinists residing in a Catholic city required a certain amount of discretion. He never lost his links to the Low Countries: his son Pedro (Pieter) was, years later, president of the Supreme Court of Holland. It is interesting to note that, of the Andalusian families of Middelburg — all closely related by marriage and blood — the Jiménez de León family remained Catholic while most of the Hinojosas and Palmas converted to Calvinism.

---

24 His wife may have belonged to the Ortiz family from Seville that had been established in Middelburg since at least 1478; if so, this would be another fact supporting Raymond Fagel's belief that the Andalusian families who resided there and in Bergen op Zoom were in the habit of making close connections among themselves; cf. Fagel, 'La Nación de Andalucía en Flandes', p. 40.

25 There is information about Juan de Hinojosa and his wife, Clara Arends Borsslap (van Halmale), in Van Vloten, *Beeldenstorm in Middelburg*, pp. 235, 248, and in Heuser, *Jean Matal*, pp. 184–86.

The Calvinist Merchants from Seville and the Antwerp Revolt

In the 1560s the Calvinist Church of Antwerp experienced rapid growth, to the point where it became the model for the rest of the Calvinists of the Low Countries. In its favour was the fact that there were a significant number of nobles, regents, and merchants among its members, along with citizens of all ranks. There is an extant report sent to Philip II by his agent Jerónimo Curiel at the end of 1566, containing the names of fifteen Calvinist merchants who traded with Spain from Antwerp. Three of them were from commercial families of clear Spanish origin: Marcos Pérez [de Segura], his brother-in-law Martín López [de Villanova], and Hernando de Sevilla:

> Este [Marcos Pérez] se a señalado en estos negozios más que nadie y no agora, sino en años atrás, el qual a tenido pláticas y corrispondenzias con los erejes españoles que an sido en Francia, Alemana e Ynglaterra. [...es] el que a sustentado y sustenta los pedricadores y allegados dellos, y aun se presume que agora anda procurando de ynbiar libros a Spaña desta setta en spañol. [... Martín López] ha muchos años que está tocado e que tiene grande quenta con los erejes españoles que por acá andan y ha estado en Franzia y en Alemaña a tratar con ellos.[26]

>> (This [Marcos Pérez] has had meetings and correspondence with the Spanish heretics who have been in France, Germany, and England. [... Marcos Pérez] has supported and supports their preachers and friends [of the Protestants] and even now he is presumably trying to send books of this sect in Spanish to Spain. [... Martín López] has been contaminated for many years and has a close relationship with the Spanish heretics who are active in these parts, and he has travelled to France and Germany to interact with them.)

For the most part Curiel's report contains no surprises: Marcos Pérez, from a rich family of merchants with origins in Andalusia named Pérez de Segura, was president of the Flemish Calvinist consistory. He was a key person in the life of the city and became one of the leading Calvinists of the Low Countries. He had in fact been one of the eight Calvinist delegates who had negotiated the September Accord with the Prince of Orange. Pérez made an offer to the Spanish Crown of the fabulous sum of three million gold florins in exchange for conceding religious liberty to the Low

---

26 Van der Essen, 'Épisodes de l'histoire religieuse et commerciale d'Anvers', pp. 349–50, 351, 354.

Countries.[27] Undoubtedly, he was one of the leading citizens of Antwerp; in a letter to Granvelle it was reported that 'en Anvers Marcos Peres peult tout, et est sa maison chancellerie' (in Antwerp Marcos Pérez can do everything he wants, and his house is a chancery).[28] His wife Úrsula, the sister of Martín López, established a school for girls open to all. Pérez maintained a close friendship with Pedro Jiménez for many years, so much so that the latter would stay at his house whenever he was in Antwerp. Nevertheless, it appears that their friendship cooled after the events at Antwerp in 1566: Jiménez, although very irenic and open to dialogue, remained a Catholic, while Pérez clearly marked himself out as a Calvinist who was willing to do anything to establish the Reformed religion in the Low Countries.

During that same extraordinary year 1566, there was a rumour that Marcos Pérez was behind a plan to send 30,000 Protestant books to Spain, along with ten preachers well instructed in Reformed ideas. It also appears that he was giving support from his position in the Low Countries to a Paris printing project involving a Spanish New Testament. This project was intercepted and aborted by the local Parisian authorities at the request of the Spanish Crown. The Inquisition, for its part, stepped up its control of Spanish ports in order to keep out any such books and preachers. Moreover, the Inquisition tried to fill in its picture of Pérez's relatives in Seville, as can be seen from the following exchange of letters, beginning with an epistle sent from the Low Countries:

> Se tiene noticia la diligençia con que procuran los luteranos enviar libros prohibidos a estos reinos, mayormente un Marcos Pérez, mercader español que reside en Emberes, a cuya costa dicen se envían y ha partido ya de Flandes gran copia d'ellos endereçados a esa ciudad.
>
> Y [...], converná que con gran recato y secreto os procuréis informar si tienen ahí algunos deudos que tentan trato de compañía con él, porque sería posible que a ellos, antes que a otros, viniesen endereçados los libros que el dicho Marcos Pérez envía.[29]

> (We have heard of the diligence with which the Lutherans strive to send banned books to these kingdoms, especially one Marcos Pérez, a Spanish merchant who lives in Antwerp, at whose expense many of them are presumably sent to that city [Seville], and that they have already left Flanders.

---

27 See the history of these negotiations in Gilly, '*Comme un cincquiesme evangile*', pp. 296–305.
28 Letter from Maximilien Morillon to Granvelle, 5 October 1566, in Poullet, ed., *Correspondance du cardinal de Granvelle*, pp. 6–7.
29 López Muñoz, *La Reforma en la Sevilla del siglo XVI*, II, p. 358.

> [...] It would be advisable to try to know, using great discretion and secrecy, if they have any relatives there who have business dealings with him, because it is possible that the books that the aforementioned Marcos Pérez sends would come to them rather than to others.)

This is the reply from the Seville tribunal of the Inquisition:

> En lo que toca a Marcos Pérez, mercader español que reside en Amberes, lo que hasta agora habemos podido saber es que aquí en Sevilla tiene un primo hermano suyo que se llama Francisco Núñez Pérez, e otro primo hermano que se dice Luis Pérez, el cual está casado con una hermana de Pero Rámirez, relajado en persona por luterano. [...] E que en Lisbona tiene un factor que se llama Diego Martínez, que tiene parte en el contrato de la espeçiería del reino de Portugal. Y dicen que hace los negoçios del dicho Marcos Pérez este Françisco Pérez que está aquí en Sevilla, y que un Antonio del Río, burgalés, y el dicho Marcos Pérez, son casados con dos hermanas.[30]

> (Here in Seville Marcos Pérez has a first cousin called Francisco Núñez Pérez, and another cousin, called Luis Pérez, who is married to a sister of Pedro Ramírez, burned at the stake as a Lutheran. [...] And in Lisbon he has a factor called Diego Martínez, who participates in the spice contract of the kingdom of Portugal. And it is said that this Francisco Pérez, who is here in Seville, does business for Marcos Pérez, and that a certain Antonio del Río, from Burgos, and the aforementioned Marcos Pérez, are married to two sisters.)[31]

Pérez was the principal protector of Casiodoro de Reina and Antonio del Corro; and his widow, Úrsula López de Villanova, would remain so. Both Reina and Corro were exiled Spaniards who had fled the monastery of San Isidro del Campo, near Seville, in 1557. Both men had joined the Church of the Reformation, but both had problems with the rigid confessionalization that was becoming the norm. When Reina was forced to leave London in the autumn of 1563, he took up residence in Marcos Pérez's house, although not for long. Pressure from the government caused him to move on. Nevertheless, the two men continued to collaborate for many years.[32] Corro also enjoyed the protection of Marcos Pérez during his first months in Antwerp, between the autumn of 1566 and the spring of 1567, before the arrival of Spanish troops sent them both into exile. The first well-founded work denouncing the Spanish Inquisition is most likely

---

30 López Muñoz, *La Reforma en la Sevilla del siglo XVI*, II, p. 360.
31 Indeed, the wives were Eleonora and Úrsula López de Villanova, respectively.
32 Moreno Martínez, *Casiodoro de Reina*, pp. 132–34.

the result of their collaboration and may have had the financial support of Marcos Pérez.[33]

These events have been studied in detail by Ben Vermaseren, Gordon Kinder, and Carlos Gilly, and there is no need to speak at length about them here.[34] It is enough to say that Reina and Corro are perhaps the two most prominent figures among the Spanish Protestants of the sixteenth century, and that for some time they were supported by the Pérez family. Reina was the publisher of the first complete Bible in Spanish and Corro wrote theological works in a language free from doctrinal orthodoxies and in defence of the freedom of conscience. His *Letter to the Lutheran pastors* or *Epistre et amiable remonstrance* (1567), for example, is a treatise pointing out to the Lutherans that their extreme language concerning the Sacramentarian controversy in Antwerp in 1566 was fanning the flames of strife.

Conclusion

Some cases of religiously restless Spaniards have been briefly presented: of Juan Luis Vives, Francisco de San Román, Francisco de Enzinas, Pedro Jiménez, Casiodoro de Reina, and Antonio del Corro. Many others could have been mentioned who, like them, had strong links with merchant families.

Previous studies have highlighted the importance in early modern Europe of these networks of Burgos and Seville families for the spread of religious change from the Low Countries. Yet researchers still have much work to do, and it is important for scholars in Economic History to work together with their colleagues in Religious Studies. There is an abundance of archival materials yet to be fully explored, which can provide information about the people and strategies involved in these processes of religious transformation. There is also a great deal of information in literary works and their preliminary materials that partially reveals the networks both of people who supported publishing activity and of those people to whom the works were directed. All of this research requires a strongly transnational approach.

---

33 Reginaldus Gonsalvius Montanus, *Inquisitionis Hispanicae Artes*, pp. 9–13.
34 Vermaseren, 'The Life of Antonio del Corro'; Kinder, *Casiodoro de Reina*; Gilly, *Spanien und der Basler Buchdruck*, pp. 353–436.

Works Cited

Manuscript and Archival Sources

Brussels, Koninklijke Bibliotheek, MS 10243
———, MS 10244
Valladolid, Archivo de la Real Chancillería de Valladolid, Pleitos civiles, Alonso Rodríguez (F), Caja 1206, exp. 6 (1568–1569)

Primary Sources

Dramata sacra. Comoediae atque tragoediae aliquot e Veteri Testamento desumptae... tomus secundus (Basel: Oporinus, 1547) [VD16 O 794]
Francisco de Enzinas, *Francisci Enzinatis Burgensis historia de statu Belgico deque religione Hispanica*, ed. by Francisco Socas, Bibliotheca scriptorum Graecorum et Romanorum Teubneriana (Stuttgart: Teubner, 1991)
———, *Epistolario*, ed. by Ignacio J. García Pinilla, Travaux d'Humanisme et Renaissance, 290 (Geneva: Droz, 1995)
———, *Breve y compendiosa institución de la religión cristiana (1542)*, ed. by Jonathan L. Nelson, Serie de Disidentes Españoles, 2 (Cuenca: Universidad de Castilla–La Mancha, 2007)
Jerónimo de la Peña, *Philadelphiarum, seu lusuum fraternorum libri duo, Scholiis Chalcographi dilucidati* (Paris: Pierre Vidoué, 1537)
Juan Luis Vives, *Introduction a la sabiduria compuesta en latin por el Doctor Iuan Luys Viues. Dialogo de Plutarcho, en el qual se tracta, como se ha de refrenar la ira. Vna carta de Plutarcho, que enseña alos casados como se han de auer en su biuir. Todo nueuamente traduzido en castellano, por Diego de Astudillo* (Antwerp: Steelsius, 1551)
———, *Comentarios para despertamiento del animo en dios. Y preparacion del animo para orar... compuestas primero en latin, por el excelente y famoso varon el doctor Iuan Luys viuas, traduzidas de alli en castellano por Diego ortega de Burgos, vezino de Burgos* (Antwerp: Hillenius, 1537)
[Pedro Jiménez], *Viri pietate, virtute, moderatione, doctrinaque clarissimi dialogus de pace. Rationes, quibus Belgici tumultus, inter Philippum serenissimum et potentissimum Hispaniae Regem et subditos, hoc rerum statu, componi possint, explicans* ([s. l.: s. i.], 1579)
Reginaldus Gonsalvius Montanus, *Inquisitionis Hispanicae Artes: The Arts of the Spanish Inquisition*, ed. by Marcos Herráiz Pareja, Ignacio García Pinilla, and Jonathan Nelson, Heterodoxia Iberica, 2 (Leiden: Brill, 2018)

Secondary Studies

Almenara i Sebastiá, Miquel, 'El humanista Pere-Joan Olivar. Vida, bibliografía y epistolario' (unpublished doctoral thesis, Universitat de València, 1992)

Amherdt, David, and García Pinilla, Ignacio J., 'Les *Philadelphiarum libri duo* de Hieronymus Rupeus. Un instantané du monde humaniste parisien en 1537', *Bibliothèque d'Humanisme et Renaissance*, 83.3 (2021), 425–56

Casado Alonso, Hilario, 'Los flujos de información en las redes comerciales castellanas de los siglos XV y XVI', *Investigaciones de historia económica*, 10 (2008), 35–68

Essen, Léon van der, 'Épisodes de l'histoire religieuse et commerciale d'Anvers dans la seconde moitié du XVIe siècle. Rapport secret de Gerónimo de Curiel, facteur du roi d'Espagne à Anvers, sur les marchands hérétiques ou suspects de cette ville (1566)', *Bulletin de la Commission Royale d'Histoire*, 80 (1911), 321–62

Fagel, Raymond P., *De Hispano–Vlaamse wereld: de contacten tussen Spanjaarden en Nederlanders 1496–1555* (Brussels: Archief- en Bibliotheekwezen in België, 1996)

——, 'Spanish Merchants in the Low Countries: stabilitas loci or peregrinatio?', in *International Trade in the Low Countries (14th–16th Centuries): Merchants, Organisation, Infrastructure*, ed. by Peter Stabel, Bruno Blondé, and Anke Greve (Leuven: Garant, 2000), pp. 87–104

——, 'La Nación de Andalucía en Flandes: separatismo comercial en el siglo XVI', in *Comercio y cultura en la Edad Moderna*, ed. by Juan J. Iglesias Rodríguez, Rafael M. Pérez García, and Manuel F. Fernández Chaves (Seville: Universidad de Sevilla, 2015), pp. 29–41

——, 'Un humanista entre mercaderes. Juan Luis Vives y el mundo comercial de Brujas', in *Juan Luis Vives. El humanista y su entorno*, ed. by M. A. Coronel Ramos (Valencia: Institució Alfons el Magnànim centre Valencià d'estudis i d'investigació, 2017), pp. 167–97

García Pinilla, Ignacio J., 'Paz religiosa, libertad religiosa: la apuesta por el pacifismo de Pedro Ximénez en el *Dialogus de pace* (1579)', *Hispania Sacra*, 70 (2018), 39–50

Gilly, Carlos, *Spanien und der Basler Buchdruck bis 1600. Ein Querschnitt durch die spanische Geistesgeschichte aus der Sicht einer europäischen Buchdruckerstadt* (Basel: Helbing & Leichtenhahn, 1985)

——, '*Comme un cincquiesme evangile*: Glaubensbekenntnisse und Toleranz in Antwerpens "wonderjaar"', in *La formazione storica della alterità. Studi di storia della tolleranza nell'età moderna offerti a Antonio Rotondò*, ed. by Henri Méchoulan, Richard H. Popkin, Giuseppe Ricuperati, and Luisa Simonutti, I (Florence: Olschki, 2001), pp. 295–329

González González, Enrique, *Joan Lluís Vives. De la Escolástica al Humanismo* (Valencia: Generalitat, 1987)

──, 'Juan Luis Vives: Works and Days', in *A Companion to Juan Luis Vives*, ed. by Charles Fantazzi (Leiden: Brill, 2008), pp. 15–64

González y González, Enrique, Salvador Albiñana, and Víctor Gutiérrez, eds, *Vives. Edicions princeps* (Valencia: Universitat de València, 1992)

Häberlein, Mark, *Brüder, Freunde und Betrüger. Soziale Beziehungen, Normen und Konflikte in der Augsburger Kaufmannschaft um die Mitte des 16. Jahrhunderts* (Berlin: De Gruyter, 1998)

Heuser, Peter A., *Jean Matal, Humanistischer Jurist und europäischer Friedensdenker (um 1517–1597)* (Cologne: Böhlau, 2003)

──, 'Kaspar Schetz von Grobbendonk oder Pedro Ximénez? Studien zum historischen Ort des "Dialogus de pace" (Köln und Antwerpen 1579)', in *Frieden und Friedenssicherung in der Frühen Neuzeit. Das Heilige Römische Reich und Europa. Festschrift für Maximilian Lanzinner*, ed. by Guido Braun and Arno Strohmeyer (Münster: Aschendorff, 2013), pp. 387–411

Kellenbenz, Hermann, and Rolf Walter, *Oberdeutsche Kaufleute in Sevilla und Cadiz (1525–1560): eine Edition von Notariatsakten aus den dortigen Archiven* (Stuttgart: Franz Steiner, 2001)

Kinder, A. Gordon, *Casiodoro de Reina: Spanish Reformer of the Sixteenth Century* (London: Tamesis, 1975)

López Muñoz, Tomás, *La reforma en la Sevilla del siglo xvi*, 2 vols (Seville: MAD, 2011)

Morales Ortiz, Alicia, *Plutarco en España: traducciones de Moralia en el siglo xvi* (Murcia: Universidad de Murcia, 2000)

Moreno Gallego, Valentín, 'Tristia rerum. El poeta neolatino Ruiz de Villegas y su testamento', *Silva. Estudios de Humanismo y tradición clásica*, 4 (2005), 209–33

──, *La recepción hispana de Juan Luis Vives* (Valencia: Generalitat Valenciana – Conselleria de Cultura, Educació i Esport, 2006)

Moreno Martínez, Doris, *Casiodoro de Reina, contra la Inquisición y la intolerancia* (Seville: Fundación Pública Andaluza Centro de Estudios Andaluces, 2017)

Muñoz Solla, Ricardo, 'Judeoconversos burgaleses a fines de la Edad Media', *Espacio, Tiempo y Forma, Serie III, Hª Medieval*, 22 (2009), 207–28

Pino González, Eduardo del, '*Grudia me tenuit cultrix studiosa Mineruae*. Textos relacionados con la estancia en Lovaina del humanista español Juan de Verzosa', *Cuadernos de Filología Clásica. Estudios latinos*, 23.1 (2003), 171–209

Poullet, Edmond, ed., *Correspondance du cardinal de Granvelle, 1565–1586*, II (Brussels: F. Hayez, 1880)

Tellechea Idígoras, José Ignacio, 'Francisco de San Román, un mártir protestante burgalés (1542)', *Cuadernos de investigación histórica*, 8 (1984), 223–60

Vloten, Jan van, *Beeldenstorm in Middelburg. Onderzoek van's Konings wege ingesteld omtrent de Middelburgsche beroerten van 1566 en 1567, naar het oorspronkelijk handschrift uitgegeven* (Utrecht: Kemink en Zoon, 1873); online edn (Stichting De Gihonbron Middelburg, 2005. Versie 2, 2016) <http://www.theologienet.nl/documenten/Vloten%20Beeldenstorm%20Middelburg1566.pdf> [accessed 30/08/2017]

Vermaseren, Bernard A., 'The Life of Antonio del Corro (1527–1591) before his Stay in England', *Archives et Bibliothèques de Belgique*, 57 (1986), 531–68; 61 (1990), 175–275

MANUEL F. FERNÁNDEZ CHAVES

The Library of the Pious House and Chapel of Saint Andrew of the Flemish Nation in Seville under Philip V

This chapter makes known the contents of the library of pious house and chapel of the Flemish Nation in Seville according to an inventory drafted in 1732. However, the authors and titles represented in the library correspond mainly to the seventeenth century and before. Authors and books are identified, and the composition and role of the library within the pious foundation that owned it are analysed, with the focus on its creation and subsequent existence. This is the unique case in the entire Iberian Peninsula of a library belonging to a Flemish Nation.

The Flemish Nation in Seville

Over the last decades, the study of the different corporate nations constituted during the modern period in most of the major cities of the Spanish monarchy has seen important developments.[1] However, many

1 Through classical works like those by Girard, *El comercio francés en Sevilla y Cádiz*; Domínguez Ortiz, *Los extranjeros en la vida española y otros artículos*. Many have followed in the last thirty years, of which we can mention, without any claim to exhaustivity: García Bernal and Gamero Rojas, 'Las corporaciones de nación en la Sevilla moderna'. Also, Crespo Solana, ed., *Comunidades transnacionales*, and Recio Morales, ed., *Redes de nación*, including

Manuel F. Fernández Chaves is Associate Professor in the Early Modern History Department at the Universidad de Sevilla. His main interests are the study of merchants and mercantile culture in the sixteenth and seventeenth centuries, their participation in the global exchange of commodities, and their role in the slave trade. The Portuguese, English, and Flemish communities settled in Seville and Andalusia constitute his main interest. He has published several articles and book chapters, and has edited several books about these communities and their role in business and the slave trade.

Networking Europe and New Communities of Interpretation (1400–1600), ed. by Margriet Hoogvliet, Manuel F. Fernández Chaves, *and* Rafael M. Pérez García, New Communities of Interpretation, 4 (Turnhout: Brepols, 2023), pp. 119–168
BREPOLS PUBLISHERS 10.1484/M.NCI-EB.5.134313

questions are still unanswered and the field is still to be fully explored to achieve a better understanding of the creation, functioning, identity, and role of these institutions and their members. This chapter specifically addresses some of those aspects in relation to the Flemish Nation of Seville.[2] Founded between 1570 and 1590, after 1586 the nation had, in addition to two consuls, a pious foundation under the patronage of Saint Andrew. This foundation started with a hospital created in 1602, to which a chapel was added in 1604. The chapel's construction was finished in 1607. The institution was governed by four *mayordomos* (stewards), an administrator, and a treasurer, and was financed by the contributions of the nation's members.[3] Its objectives were to provide support to the poorer Flemish transients and residents in the city, to give alms, and to combat heresy. The premises for the hospital, the chapel, and the pious house of the chapel were built in a plot adjoining the Colegio Dominico de Santo Tomás (Saint Thomas Dominican College), close to Genova Street, in front of the Casa Lonja (Market House) and very near the Alcazar. Here the Flemish Nation built the Capilla de San Andrés (Saint Andrew's Chapel) between 1604 and 1609, after reaching an agreement with the Dominican Order, which set an annual rent of 500 ducats for the plot. The Confraternity of the Holy Rosary was also established there, to encourage and cultivate this particular devotion of the Order of the Preachers.[4] This series of foundations, supported by the increasing presence of Flemings on the coasts of Lower Andalusia and in various Spanish cities from the

---

Iglesias Rodríguez, García Bernal, and Díaz Blanco, eds, *Andalucía y el mundo atlántico moderno*. See further: Fernández Chaves, Pérez García, and Perez, eds, *Mercaderes y redes mercantiles*. A historiographical assessment is found in Villar García, 'Los extranjeros en la España Moderna', and Recio Morales, 'Los extranjeros y la historiografía modernista'. Specifically on the various Flemish nations, we can mention Crespo Solana, *Entre Cádiz y los Países Bajos*; Crespo Solana, 'El patronato de la nación flamenca'; Crespo Solana, 'Nación extranjera y cofradía de mercaderes'. Other works are cited below.

2 On the Flemings in Seville, see, among others: Otte, *Sevilla, siglo XVI*, pp. 284–89; Stols, 'La colonia flamenca de Sevilla'; Stols, 'Les marchands flamands dans la Péninsule Ibérique'; Stols, *De Spaanse Brabanders*; Everaert, 'Infraction au monopole?'; Crailsheim, *The Spanish Connection*; Díaz Blanco, 'La familia del bibliógrafo sevillano Nicolás Antonio'; Díaz Blanco and Fernández Chaves, 'Una élite en la sombra'; Gamero Rojas and Fernández Chaves, 'Flamencos en la Sevilla del siglo XVIII'; Gamero Rojas, 'La mujer flamenca del mundo de los negocios en la Sevilla'; Gamero Rojas, 'Flamencos en el siglo XVII'; Gamero Rojas, 'Los hombres de negocios flamencos'. Gutiérrez Nuñez, 'Nicolás de Omazur Ullens, de Amberes a Sevilla (1641–1698)'. For the sixteenth century, see the recent works of Abadía Flores, 'La comunidad flamenca en Sevilla en el siglo XVI'; Jiménez Montes, 'La comunidad flamenca en Sevilla'; Jiménez Montes, 'Sevilla, puerto y puerta de Europa'; Jiménez Montes, 'Los inicios de una nación'. See also his important work, *A Dissimulated Trade*.

3 Díaz Blanco, 'La construcción de una institución comercial', pp. 128–29.

4 See in particular, Gamero Rojas, 'Flamencos en la Sevilla del siglo XVII'. A more general analysis of the creation and operation of the Consulate of the Flemish and German Nation is found in Díaz Blanco, 'La construcción de una institución comercial'.

1560s onwards,[5] aimed at protecting the Flemings' economic and material interests, and at the same time to prove their loyalty to Catholicism against the suspicion of heresy among the nation's members and transient people of the same origin.[6]

The institution was officially acknowledged by Philip IV in 1615, the date of its statute.[7] Its creation may be considered tardy if compared to that of other nations, like those of the Genoese and Catalans, but the foundation of the Hospital y Casa Pía de San Andrés (Saint Andrew's Hospital and Pious House) was supported by an important group of merchants whose economic strength paralleled their positive cultural and political assimilation, which helped them become full and active participants in the life of the city.[8]

In addition to these institutions in Seville, other establishments like the Flemish hospital in Cadiz (1565) or the better-known[9] Hospital de San Andrés de los Flamencos (Hospital of Saint Andrew of the Flemings) in Madrid (1594)[10] had been created slightly earlier. These institutions, which depended on their corresponding nation,

> servían como centros de reconocimiento y representación común, y brindaban la posibilidad de convertir sus capillas, iglesias y hospitales en espacios en torno a los cuales se configuraba una comunidad legalmente instituida y formalmente reconocida por la autoridad real. Dichas comunidades promocionaban un sentido de identidad colectiva y sentido 'nacional' de carácter exclusivo que fomentaba lazos de sociabilidad basados en la exaltación de su naturaleza y que generaba mecanismos de gestión independientes de otras instancias jurisdiccionales en las que su diferenciación por naturaleza apenas se tenía en cuenta.[11]

---

5 Otte, *Sevilla, siglo XVI*, pp. 284–89. Jiménez Montes, *A Dissimulated Trade*.
6 Gamero Rojas, 'Flamencos en la Sevilla del siglo XVII'.
7 Díaz Blanco, 'La construcción de una institución comercial', pp. 126–27. On its institutional functions and operation, see pp. 128–31.
8 Domínguez Ortiz, 'Documentos sobre los mercaderes flamencos'; Ybarra Hidalgo, *Notas genealógicas y biográficas*; Álvarez de Toledo y Pineda, 'Un linaje de origen flamenco'. In her recent work on Saint Andrew's chapel and hospital, Professor Mercedes Gamero Rojas has analysed the lawsuit filed by a group of Flemings who did not wish to contribute to the sustenance of the nation any longer, because they considered their children to be natives of Castile. On the cultural life of the Flemish and other communities in Seville during the eighteenth century, see Gamero Rojas, 'Flamencos en el siglo XVII'.
9 Thanks to the work by Vidal Galache and Vidal Galache, *Fundación Carlos de Amberes*, and to the thorough work by García García, 'La Nación Flamenca en la corte española'.
10 Crespo Solana, 'El patronato de la nación flamenca', Vidal Galache and Vidal Galache, *Fundación Carlos de Amberes*.
11 García García, 'La Nación Flamenca en la corte española', p. 390.

(served as spaces of common recognition and representation, and offered the possibility of transforming chapels, churches, and hospitals into places around which a community that was legally constituted and formally acknowledged by royal authority could gather. These communities promoted a sense of collective identity and an exclusive 'national' feeling that fostered sociability and strengthened social ties based on the exaltation of their common nature, and generated management mechanisms that were independent from other jurisdictional instances, which barely took into account their differentiation in nature.)

The Flemish Nation of Seville and the Bourbon Monarchy

After the change of dynasty and the break in the political bond between the Low Countries and Castile, what was the legal status of those Flemings who did not acknowledge the Habsburgs of Vienna as their natural lords?[12] This created many difficulties for the pious foundations, which lost their meaning if the nation in Seville continued to express its loyalty to the Habsburgs who were the lords of Flanders and Brabant, but not to the new Bourbon king. The War of Succession laid this problem on the table.

In 1702 the Consejo de Flandes (Council of Flanders) was abolished and the Hospital of Saint Andrew of the Flemish in Madrid was assigned to the Consejo de Castilla (Council of Castile). From that moment onwards, and despite the issuing in the same year of a charter that ratified the privileges of the Flemish Nation in Spain,[13] the Flemings in charge of the Hospital and Confraternity of Saint Andrew in Madrid had to prove that this foundation could not be dissolved without disregarding the will of its founder, and that this would entail abandoning the Flemish residents and transients in Spain. In 1717 the foundation was on the brink of disappearing and its facilities were about to become the seat of another pious establishment, after a decree of 1715 had impelled the ministers of the Cámara de Castilla (Chamber of Castile) to look for the best place to accommodate the Colegio de Nuestra Señora del Amparo (College of Our Lady of the Refuge) for orphan girls, created at the request of the late Queen Mary Louise of Savoy. The Flemish hospital was chosen for this purpose, and the Flemings appealed to the Chamber of Castile to

---

12 Their double status as subjects of Emperor Charles V had been acknowledged in 1533 and was renewed by the Austrian archdukes in 1616; see Crespo Solana, 'El patronato de la nación flamenca', p. 307.
13 Madrid, Archivo Histórico Nacional, file 610/21, Madrid, 29 June 1702.

solve the problem,[14] which nevertheless persisted until the Marquis of Monterrey (1640–1716), linked with Flanders through his military and governmental career, supported their cause and prevented this decision from taking effect, thus liberating the deputies of the hospital from the threat of being absorbed by another institution in 1721.[15]

In Cadiz, the 'Ilustre y Antigua y Noble Nación Flamenca y Alemana' (Illustrious and Ancient and Noble Flemish and German Nation) owned Saint Andrew's pious house and hospital since the sixteenth century, but there is no detailed information available about these institutions before the establishment of a board of trustees, thanks to the donation made by Captain Pedro de la O in 1636. The nation's members also strove for the recognition of the special privileges that acknowledged their double nature as Flemings and Spaniards after the War of Succession. In addition, they had to overcome their internal divisions and the meddling of the ecclesiastical courts in the accounts and administration of the board of trustees in order to verify whether their income was in fact destined for welfare and charitable purposes.[16] Moreover, they had to negotiate their status with the consul appointed by the Emperor and acknowledged by the nation's members, Jacques Vermolen.[17]

The Flemish Nation of Seville also endured difficulties due to the loss of members and by being in the line of fire of the political authorities and other institutions. First the Council of Flanders was abolished in 1702; then, in 1714, the southern Low Countries were returned to the Austrian Habsburg Monarchy. Consequently, after the War of Succession the nation in Seville found itself in an institutional limbo, even if the influence of some of its members helped to build a favourable image of its existence and activities. Thus, in 1722 the regent of the *Audiencia* (royal court) and *Asistente* (governor) of Seville, Manuel de Torres, defended before the Junta de Dependencia de Extranjeros (Board for Foreign Affairs)[18] the

---

14 The Chamber of Castile was the administrative channel in this case. Being under the royal patronage of Phillip III, the foundation found itself under the supervision of the Capilla Real (Royal Chapel) and the civil jurisdiction of the Consejo Real (Royal Council) and the Chamber of Castile; see García García, 'La Nación Flamenca en la corte española', p. 388. In 1730, the Chamber also studied the petition of the Flemish Nation of Seville, see Seville, Biblioteca de la Universidad de Sevilla, A 111/124 (3).
15 Vidal Galache and Vidal Galache, *Fundación Carlos de Amberes*, pp. 66–74.
16 Crespo Solana, 'El patronato de la nación flamenca', pp. 311–28. About the nation in Cadiz, see also Bustos Rodríguez, 'Le consulat des Flamands à Cadix'. Jurisdictional problems were also commonplace in the case of the Flemish hospital and pious house in Madrid, in which the Royal Chapel, the Council of Flanders, and the Franciscan Order, among other institutions, intervened, García García, 'La Nación Flamenca en la corte española', pp. 414–25.
17 Bustos Rodríguez, 'Le consulat des Flamands à Cadix', pp. 109–32.
18 This board, created in 1714, supervised the appointment of foreign consuls and 'jueces conservadores' (magistrates) of all nations, and, in addition to controlling the presence of

reports that the nation sent to Madrid. He insisted on the advisability of restoring the privileges that it used to enjoy, because

> le constaba ser cierto todo lo que referían en cuanto a las obras pías, como también que con la separación de algunos iban decayendo los efectos en que podía consistir su subsistencia [...] pero que en su concepto no tenía duda que si se les concediese el Juez conservador en la forma que se proponía, volverían los pocos que se habían separado, el gremio de la misma hermandad y cesaría el recelo de que decreciese o se perdiese con el tiempo el culto de la capilla y los santos fines de su instituto. A que se seguía atraer (con el halago de la excepción) de los dominios de Flandes otros hombres de negocios a residir en aquella ciudad en la confianza de ser tratados con las mismas prerrogativas que antes tenían [...] con el mayor número de hombres de negocios también lo era que con esta especie de fincas se aseguraban los réditos para el culto de la capilla, hospitalidad y demás obras pías.[19]

> (he was aware that everything referring to its pious activities was true, as was the fact that with the separation of some of its members the resources that sustained their existence had been reduced [...] but, all in all, he had no doubt that should the *juez conservador* [magistrate] grant those privileges in the form requested, those that had separated would return [to], the guild of their brotherhood, and the fear of the decline or disappearance of worship in the chapel and of the sacred purposes of the institution would cease. And other merchants from the land of Flanders would be attracted [by praising the exceptional conditions] to reside in the city, hoping to enjoy the same prerogatives that their nationals used to have [...] and a larger number of merchants would secure the properties that would supply the income required to maintain worship at the chapel as well as the hospitality and other pious activities.)

The endeavours of the Flemings of Cadiz and Seville for the recognition of their privileges lasted as long as the reign of Philip V.[20] In their search

---

foreign population, very soon acted as 'una plataforma para la reivindicación de antiguos privilegios que las diferentes naciones tenían en suelo hispano desde los orígenes de su establecimiento (secreto de sus libros contables, testamentarías)' (a platform for the claiming of ancient privileges that the different nations enjoyed while on Spanish soil from the beginning of their establishment in the country [secret character of their account books, execution of wills]). Cf. Crespo Solana and Montojo Montojo, 'La Junta de Dependencias de Extranjeros', p. 377.

19 Crespo Solana, 'El patronato de la nación flamenca', p. 311.
20 Crespo Solana and Montojo Montojo, 'La Junta de Dependencias de Extranjeros', pp. 363–94.

for acknowledgement, the Flemish Nation of Seville knew how to profit from the presence of the king in the city during the so-called 'Lustro Real' (Royal Five-Year Period).[21] Philip V finally granted its rights and ordered the printing of two royal charters that re-established 'los Privilegios antiguos, de que gozaba la Nacion, hasta el año de mil setecientos y catorce' (the ancient privileges enjoyed by the Nation until 1714), at the behest of the nation's steward, the Fleming Luis Doye.[22] This sentence confirms that the Board of Foreign Affairs had in fact abolished those privileges at the end of the War of Succession, although it seems that the nation had continued to be acknowledged as such until 1728, for one of the royal charters signed by Philip V stated that the nation had existed for 124 years after its foundation in 1604.[23] Does this mean that the institution had actually disappeared? We believe that it was probably the case in the eyes of the royal court, but most likely the religious activities performed in the chapel, pious house, and hospital, as well as the will of the nation's members, kept the memory of the nation alive during that period.

The first of the two charters, dated in Seville on 29 August 1731, was addressed to Manuel de Torres. It restored the privileges of the Flemings and appointed the regents of the *Audiencia* as *jueces conservadores* of their nation, a position that had been held until 1714 by Antonio Valcárcel y Formento.[24] Subsequently, Luis Doye asked for permission to print a certain number of copies of the above-mentioned charter and of another one dated the same day and addressed to the nation's members. This second charter, in addition to confirming the granting of privileges, took into consideration the work performed at the chapel, pious house, and hospital: 'Hospitalidad, de curacion de enfermos, socorro de Viudas, y enseñanza de Huerfanos, y Pobres de vuestra nacion' (hospitality, healing of the sick, support to widows, and education of orphans and poor people of your nation). The foundation did not only pursue the healing of 'los Enfermos, que transitaban de la misma Nacion' (ailing transients belonging to the nation), but also

---

21 From 1729 to 1733. On this issue, see also Márquez Redondo, *Sevilla 'ciudad y Corte'*.
22 Seville, Biblioteca de la Universidad de Sevilla, A 111/124 (3).
23 '[O]s conservasteis, con tan gloriosa memoria, mas de ciento y veinte y quatro años' (you stayed alive, with such glorious memory, for more than one hundred and twenty-four years), Seville, Biblioteca de la Universidad de Sevilla, A 111/214 (3).
24 Torres dealt, in the first instance, with civil and criminal cases 'que se hubieren movido, y movieren con los de la dicha Nacion, como reos' (that were or might be related to those of the aforementioned nation, [such as prisoners], without the intervention of any judicial authority), 'aunque sea con pretexto de reconocer casa mortuoria de alguno, o algunos de los comerciantes de dicha Nacion Flamenca' (not even on the pretext of searching the home of a dead person among the merchants of this Flemish Nation), Seville, Biblioteca de la Universidad de Sevilla, A 111/124 (3). On the figure of the *juez conservador*, see Crespo Solana, 'El juez conservador'.

> se catequizassen los que, perturbados en nuestra Sagrada Religion, quisiessen reconciliarse con nuestra Santa Iglesia Catholica Apostolica Romana, cuyo efecto produxo repetidos frutos en muchos, venidos de los Payses de Olanda y otras partes, logrando al mismo tiempo con la conversion, mantenerse a expensas de los Nacionales.[25]

> (to catechize those who, disturbed in our Sacred Religion, wished to reconcile themselves with our Holy Catholic Apostolic Roman Church, an activity that proved successful among many coming from the country of Holland and elsewhere, who through conversion achieved at the same time the economic support of their nationals.)

In other words, ever since their foundation, one of the main objectives of Saint Andrew's pious house and chapel had been to convert heretics from the north of Europe. This was precisely the best card the Flemings could play, because hospitality and welfare, as well as commercial and legal advice, were activities that could be transferred to other institutions. But the 'innumerables obras de Piedad, y conversiones, que se han conseguido' (innumerable works of charity and conversions achieved) justified the maintenance of the nation's privileges, which would attract (following the above-mentioned reasoning of Torres) other Flemings who were already under Vienna's rule and who would thus lend continuity to its activities.[26] In addition to striving for the recognition of their privileges, steward Luis Doye litigated against Saint Thomas College to reduce the annual rent of 500 ducats paid for the nation's premises, 'no valiendo el tercio de ellos (y al presente ni aun la quinta parte)' (when they actually were not worth one third of that value [and presently not even one fifth of it]), if the devaluation of the currency implemented by the count of Oropesa in 1680, the terrible flood of 1684, and the decline in trade were considered.[27]

---

25 Seville, Biblioteca de la Universidad de Sevilla, A 111/124 (3).
26 Seville, Biblioteca de la Universidad de Sevilla, A 111/124 (3).
27 Seville, Biblioteca de la Universidad de Sevilla, A 109/101 (17) mentions it on fol. 10. The nation intended to pay an annual rent of 1230 *reales de vellón* 25 *maravedís*, corresponding to a principal of 30,622 *reales de vellón*.

Once the privileges were restored, the members of the nation,[28] whose numbers had dramatically decreased,[29] elected in July 1732 at the 'Capilla y Cassa pia del Glorioso Apostol señor San Andres, de la Nacion flamenca' (Chapel and Pious House of the Glorious Apostle our lord Saint Andrew of the Flemish Nation) their new chaplain, Pedro van de Sande, who until then had been the coadjutor of the late chaplain, Manuel José de Licht. In December of that year, steward Luis Doye and treasurer Juan Bautista van der Wilde drafted an inventory of all the 'bienes muebles ornamentos, plata, libreria y demas cosas pertenecientes a dicha Nacion en su Cassa pia, capilla y sachristia' (movable property, ornaments, silverware, library, and other belongings of this Nation kept in the pious house, chapel, and sacristy).[30]

Thanks to this document we know the objects that were housed in the chapel and those that decorated the walls of the pious house. Among them, we can count the vestments of the chaplain and his coadjutor, several altarpieces, fine furniture, sculptures, and many religious and profane paintings (including 'cinco lienzos quasi yguales, como de vara y media de alto, con marcos negros, retratos de administradores que han sido de la Nacion' [five paintings that are almost alike, about one hundred forty centimetres long, with black frames, portraits of the former administrators of the Nation]). This inventory is evidence of the wealth of the institution, and reveals for the first time the contents of the nation's library,[31] which was located in the pious house. The archives were also kept there, in 'un escaparate de pino pintado de mas de vara de ancho, con diez gavetas' (a wardrobe of painted pinewood almost one metre long, with ten drawers), the contents of which were not specified.[32] Up until now, the libraries of this kind of institutions, half welfare organizations devoted to religious and

---

28 In 1731, the nation had 26 members: Mr Luis Doye, steward; Mr Juan Bautista Vanderwilde, treasurer, born in or originally coming from Antwerp; Mr Carlos Davalos; Mr Luis Manteau; Mr Miguel de Lescart; Mr Luis Antonio Havet; Mr Livino Leyrens; Mr Livino Braquelman; Mr Francisco Steyautt; Mr Francisco Vanderwilde; Mr Carlos José Huneus; Mr Theodor Wynman; Mr Juan Bautista Mulier; Mr Pedro Jacobo Franchois; Mr Juan Franchois; Mr Jacobo Dumolini; Mr Francisco Daniel Mulier; Mr Guillermo Blommaert; Mr Pedro José Adriaensens; Mr Juan Carlos Vandercruyssen; Mr Francisco de Keyser; Mr Simon Obbes; Mr Nicolas Francisco Vandercruyssen; Mr Benito Vanhee; Mr Balthasar Praet; Mr Antonio Blommaert. See Seville, Arch. Hist. Prov. Prot. de Sev., file 14673, fol. 485^r.
29 Gamero Rojas, 'Flamencos en la Sevilla del siglo XVII', pp. 1029–30.
30 Seville, Arch. Hist. Prov. Prot. de Sev., file 14674, fols 656^r–64^v.
31 Seville, Arch. Hist. Prov. Prot. de Sev., file 14674, fols 662^r–64^v.
32 Seville, Arch. Hist. Prov. Prot. de Sev., file 14674, fols 662^r–64^v. This can be explained by the fact that it was in that place that the medical and religious assistance tasks were performed. For reasons of space, the contents of the chapel and the pious house will be studied in a later publication.

social matters, half corporate representations of the different nations in Spanish cities, have been unknown. This is why this library represents a unique and important example for bibliographical and historical analysis.[33]

Composition of the Library and Analysis

The small building annexed to Saint Thomas College was divided into three premises: a chapel, the pious house where an oratory, the archive, the meeting room, and the library were located, and, finally, the hospital.

The books in the library were organized by format in a bookcase that had two 'columns', each of them two metres and a half high. The first column or 'body' contained folio books, followed by quarto books, both 'large and small', and octavo books. The second column also contained folio books, followed by large and small quarto books, and octavo and medium octavo books.

The inventory does not specify places or dates of publication; it gives only the titles and authors, and sometimes just the title. This has made it almost impossible to ascertain any details, for in most cases several editions of the same book are known. Even if most books have been identified, it is not possible to analyse the pace at which the library was formed, or to determine the printing houses that provided its contents.

It is possible that many books found in the library came from the Plantinian printing press in Antwerp, given the commercial exchange between the members of the nation in Seville and this Flemish city.[34] We have opted to identify the author and the work when this was possible, and have added other data, such as the place of publication, printer, format, and catalogue number, when the book had only been edited once. Apart from the title and the author's name, only the format and the books' presentation

---

[33] There are no data available regarding the case of Cadiz, and the detailed and thorough inventory of Saint Andrew's pious house and hospital in Madrid, which was published by García García, 'La Nación Flamenca en la corte española', pp. 425–34, does not reflect the existence of those books.

[34] This is not the place to analyse the activity of the Flemish printers in the city; on this issue, see Wagner, 'Flamencos en el comercio del libro en España'. In the eighteenth century, the Flemings Leefdael and Dherve were active in the city as, respectively, printer and book merchant; cf. Palmiste, 'Los mercaderes de libros e impresores flamencos en Sevilla'. In relation to the Hospital de Saint Andrew of the Flemings in Madrid, we know that the representative of Baltasar Moretus in Madrid, Jan van Vucht, left in his will a painting by Rubens depicting the martyrdom of Saint Andrew, together with other bequests, to the hospital a fact that proves the good relations between that printing house and the foundation. Vidal Galache and Vidal Galache, *Fundación Carlos de Amberes*, pp. 40–44. Intellectual figures such as Arias Montano were essential for the development of that relation. See Bécares Botas, ed., *Arias Montano y Plantino*.

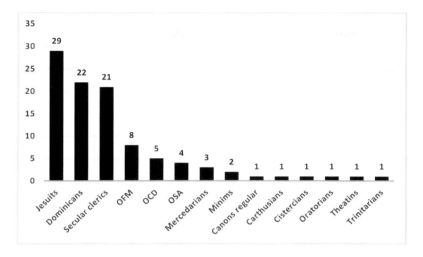

Figure 7.1. Number of books by religious authors (%). Source: Seville, Arch. Hist. Prov. Prot. de Sev., Notarial Protocols of Seville, file 14674, fols 662ʳ–64ᵛ.

in one or two volumes have helped us make a safe identification. In most cases, it was not possible to establish the exact publication data.

The shelves in the chapel housed 159 works, consisting of 235 volumes. Of the total number of books, 101 (63.5 per cent) were by religious authors, while only twenty-three (14 per cent) were the work of secular authors. There was a small number of books (six titles, 3.7 per cent) by Latin classical authors,[35] while the authors of the remaining thirty books (18.8 per cent) have not been identified. Among the religious authors, Dominican and Jesuit writers were highly represented (Fig. 7.1). Their prominence was due to the fact that many of their books dealt with religious controversies, an aspect that will be analysed later.[36] The prevailing language was Latin, with ninety-seven titles (61 per cent), followed by Spanish (twenty-eight books, 17 per cent of the total), and Flemish (twelve, 7.5 per cent), to which were added two books in Italian

---

35 Martial's epigrams commented by the Austrian Jesuit and teacher of Jeremias Drexel Mattheus Rader; Quintus Curtius Rufus, *De la vida y acciones de Alexandro el Grande*; Plutarch, *Libellus de fluviorum et montium*; Horace, *Poemata* (according to our attribution); Xenophon, *Obras*; Cicero, *Volumina tria*, in addition to Horace's emblems (entries 15, 20, 45, 62, 82, 155). We have included the latter in the political theory section, because they were commented and illustrated by Otto van Veen; Quintus Curtius and Plutarch have been filed under History and Geography, and the rest are found in the Latin Literature section.

36 There is only one religious author whose affiliation is unknown to us and who, consequently, is not reflected in the graph. This author figures in entry 4 as Reverend Father Masart.

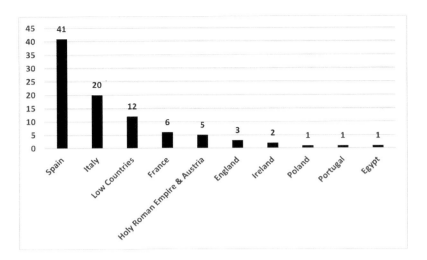

Figure 7.2. Origin of the religious authors (%). Source: Seville, Arch. Hist. Prov. Prot. de Sev., Notarial Protocols of Seville, file 14674, fols 662^r–664^v.

(1.2 per cent, entries 26 and 47), several bilingual Latin–French editions of King David's Psalms (1.2 per cent, entries 123 and 124), and five bilingual dictionaries (3.1 per cent). The latter must have proved very useful to those of the nation's members whose command of Spanish was not good and to those Flemish and German speakers recently arrived in the city. The lack of a Flemish–Spanish dictionary probably forced them to employ their knowledge of other languages to translate what they needed. The nation's interpreter also must have made good use of those dictionaries,[37] which include a French–Flemish dictionary and a grammar book on both languages (entries 97 and 49), a French–Italian dictionary, a German–Latin dictionary, and a Flemish–Latin dictionary, which was considered a classical work in the Low Countries (entries 22, 112, and 126). The remaining books (fifteen titles, 9 per cent) and the language in which they were written have not been identified.

Among the religious authors (Fig. 7.2), 37 were Castilian, and the Jesuit Rodrigo de Arriaga was represented twice (entries 5 and 6). Four of the authors were natives of the kingdom of Aragon, and, consequently, authors born in Iberia were the majority, being responsible for 45 per cent of the books. Among the Aragonese authors, the Capuchin Jaime de Corella

---

37 We are informed about the existence of a translator through references such as the lawsuit that took place between the public prosecutor of the Council of Castile and the Fleming Tobias Buq concerning the appointment of a consul and interpreter of the Flemish and German nations in 1604; cf. Madrid, Archivo Histórico Nacional, file 25438/1.

was represented with two books on moral theology (entries 11 and 36). Italian authors followed in importance, with twenty-one representatives, the most prominent of whom was the Jesuit cardinal Saint Robert Bellarmine, with four books in the library of Saint Andrew's pious house: one on dying well (*De bene arte moriendi*, entry 146), two on demonstrative theology and spiritual theology (*Explanatio in psalmos* and *De septem verbis a Christo in cruce prolatis*, entries 3 and 147), and the last one on political theory (*De officio principis Christiani*, entry 141). There were two copies of *Basis totius Theologiae* by the Dominican Julius Mercorum (entries 59 and 152). Far behind on the list, we find twelve authors from the Low Countries, among whom Franciscus Sonnius or Van de Velde has two books, one on dogmatic theology (*In religionem Christianam*, entry 12), and another one on the sacraments (*Demostratium ex verbo Dei de septem sacramentis*, entry 43). Carolus Scribani, a Jesuit from Brussels, is also represented in the library, with two titles (*Adolescens prodigus* and *Medicus religious*, entries 145 and 151). The confessor of Maximilian I of Bavaria, who was also a famous preacher in Munich, the Jesuit Jeremias Drexel, is included also with two titles (entries 157 and 158).

As for the secular authors, in most cases their profile is that of a humanist, man of science (three medical doctors), lawyer, or politician. There are five Castilian authors, followed by four Italian ones, and then by Flemish, Dutch, and German authors (three of each nationality), as well as Swiss, French, English, and Austrian (one author each).

Table 7.1. Secular authors and their books at the library

Origin	Profession	book
Castile		
de Vera y Zúñiga, Juan Antonio	Nobleman and diplomat	*El embaxador*
Fabro Bremudán, José*	Bibliographer, writer on a wide variety of subjects	*Floro historico de la guerra movida por el sultan de los turcos Mehemet IV contra ... Leopoldo primero*
Mantuano, Pedro	Historian, writer on a wide variety of subjects	*Advertencias a la Historia de Mariana*
Murcia de la Llana, Francisco	Medical doctor, proof-reader	*Selecta circa octo libros Physicorum Aristotelis*
Tamayo de Vargas, Tomás	Bibliographer, writer on a wide variety of subjects	*Historia general de España del P. D. Iuan de Mariana defendida por el Doctor Don Thomas Tamaio de Vargas*

Origin	Profession	Book
Southern Low Countries		
Lipsius, Justus	Philosopher, writer	*Diva Virgo Hallensis*
Van Kiel, Cornelis	Humanist, writer, proof-reader	*Etymologicum Teutonicae linguae: sive Dictionarium Teutonico-Latinum*
Van Veen, Otto	Humanist, writer	*Emblemata*
Holland		
Cats, Jacob	Poet, politician, writer	–
Junius, Hadrianus	Medical doctor and writer	*Batavia*
Van Egmont, Arnold	Nobleman	–
Holy Roman Empire		
Arnisaeus, Henning	Philosopher, medical doctor	*Doctrina politica in genuinam methodum Aristoteli*
De Chokier, Jean	Nobleman and writer	*Epimetron siue auctarium thesauri aphorismorum politicorum*
Omphalius, Jakob	Humanist	*De elocutionis imitatione ac apparatu liber unus*
Italy		
Coccio, Marco Antonio (Sabellico)	Humanist	*Rapsodiae Historia*
Manuzio, Aldo	Humanist	*Purae elegantes et copiosiae latinae linguae phrases*
Gamurini, Giuseppe	Engineer, writer	*Bellum Belgicum, sive Belgicarum rerum*
Guicciardini, Luigi	Nobleman, writer	*Pars prima sive Belgicae descriptio generalis*
Austria		
Honorius, Philippus	Humanist, secretary	*Thesauri Politici*
France		
Bugnot, Gabriel	Writer, humanist	*Archombrotus et Theopompus*

Origin	Profession	Book
England		
Sandys, George	Stateman, traveller, writer	*Voyagien in het Turkische rijk, Egypte enz., Amsterdam*
Switzerland		
Faber, Johannes Rodolphus	Philosopher	*Totius logicae peripateticae corpus*

Source: Seville, Arch. Hist. Prov. Prot. de Sev., Notarial Protocols of Seville, file 14674, fols 662ʳ–64ᵛ.

* Despite his (disputed) origin in Flanders or the Franche-Comté, we have decided to include this author in this category due to the fact that he developed most of his career in Spain.

The first title recorded in the inventory is formed by the *opera omnia* of Saint Thomas Aquinas (entry 1), which clearly indicates the interest of those who created the library in including the most important references in scholastic theology and, in general, the foundations of the formative and university thinking of the Jesuit and Dominican Orders. As we have already seen, the Dominicans were very well represented in the library with various authors. This is not surprising, given the fact that the nation's chapel and pious house had been built in a plot that had belonged to Saint Thomas Dominican College. Some titles discuss the organization and history of the Order in general terms, like *Summarium constitutionum declarationum et ordinationum* or, even more clearly, *Epitome de statu religionis et de priuilegijs, quibus a Summis Pontificibus est decorates*,[38] while others are more specific, for instance, *Calendario perpetuo conforme al instituto de la orden de nuestro glorioso P. S. Domingo*, which was specifically addressed to the Castilian Dominican monks (entries 37, 150, and 142). Obviously, there was also a history of the Dominican Order, its convents and activities in the province of Belgium: *Sancti Belgi Ordinis Praedicatorum*, as well as one collection of the lives of the martyrs of the order, *Palma fidei* (entries 39 and 116). The rest of the Dominican titles were concerned with various topics: there was a classical work of the fifteenth century on the reform of religious orders (by Nider, entry 98), several books on moral theology, as well as books on Saint Thomas, including essential titles like the comments by Francisco de Vitoria or those by the archbishop of Avignon, Dominicus de Marinis (entries 153 and 76).

---

38 The library of the Flemish Nation included one work about the Franciscan and other orders that was equivalent to these other works about the Dominican Order, the *Privilegia omnium religiosorum ordinum mendicantium et non mendicantium*, by Agustín de la Virgen María (entry 88).

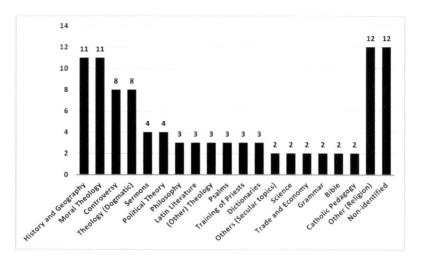

Figure 7.3. Classification by subject (%). Source: Seville, Arch. Hist. Prov. Prot. de Sev., Notarial Protocols of Seville, file 14674, fols 662^r–64^v.

The nature of the relationship between the library of the pious house and that of Saint Thomas College is unknown to us. There are only a few overlaps between the two, because the library at Saint Thomas College, of which 185 volumes are known,[39] seems to resemble that of a centre for theological studies, where books on dogmatic and demonstrative theology are basic. However, the library of the college included also famous works on moral theology like *Basis totius moralis theologiae* by Julius Mercorum (Order of the Preachers) or *Summula de peccatis* by Tomasso de Vio[40] (in the inventory of the pious house, entries 59, 152, and 127). As for the authors, the absence in the library of the Flemish pious house of Juan Eusebio Nieremberg (Society of Jesus), Domingo Báñez (Order of the Preachers), or Franciscus Titelmans (Order of the Friars Minors) is quite shocking, to mention one case only of books belonging to each of the orders that are best represented in the library of Saint Thomas College. Only the works by Julius Mercorum (Order of the Preachers), Domingo de Soto (Order of the Preachers), and, maybe (the identification is unclear), Enrique Villalobos (Order of the Friars Minors) are to be found in both libraries.[41]

According to the subject of the books, 56 per cent (eighty-nine titles) of those that have been identified deal with religious topics, while the

---

39 Sánchez Herrero, 'Colegio de Santo Tomás', pp. 205–08.
40 Sánchez Herrero, 'Colegio de Santo Tomás', pp. 206–07.
41 Sánchez Herrero, 'Colegio de Santo Tomás', p. 207.

rest (fifty-one works, 32 per cent) are about non-religious matters, and in nineteen of them (12 per cent) the topic has not been established (Fig. 7.3). The library encompasses three large fields of knowledge: theology, sermons, and training for religious people; Catholic controversies; and history, geography, and politics of the Low Countries, in addition to some other subjects with a small representation. Within the first group, the books on moral theology (seventeen titles) need to be highlighted. Those books were necessary, because confession was a basic pillar of the functioning of the institution, as the Flemings themselves acknowledged:

> Que se debía tener presente, que el principal destino de los Capellanes, era para la conversion de Hereges, en que tanto se servia a la Divina Magestad, y continuadas confesiones de los Nacionales que transitan, y vienen de assiento a esta Ciudad, a los quales no era facil comprehender el lenguage, y solo pudiera ocurrirse a esto por medio de dichos Capellanes, que han sido, y son, de la misma Nacion, e inteligentes en las lenguas Alemana, y Francesa.[42]

> (We must take into account that the main task of the chaplains was the conversion of heretics, because it served the Divine Majesty, as well as the continuous confession of transient nationals and nationals who settled in this city, whose language was not easily understood and who could not be assisted were it not by these chaplains, who have been and are of the same nation and understood in the German and French languages.)

A Bible in Latin could not be absent from the library (a 'very old and battered' volume), and there was also a Bible in Flemish (entries 44 and 65), both of them required for the preaching and pastoral work of the chaplains with Spanish- and Flemish-speaking people. Among other books that were frequently used by the chaplain, who had to be 'Docto, así en lo Escolástico, como en lo Dogmático, ha de poseer con perfeccion las lenguas Latina, Francesa, Flamenca y Alemana, y ha de ser natural de Flandes' (well-versed in Scholastics as well as in Dogmatics, and be perfectly familiar with the Latin, French, Flemish, and German languages, apart from being a native of Flanders),[43] we find a 'very old' manual for confessors printed in Antwerp (entry 159) and two classical books by Jaime de Corella (*Práctica del confesionario* and *Suma de la Theologia Moral*, entries 11 and 36), whose style much differed from that of *Fuero de la conciencia* (entry 35) by the Carmelite Valentín de la Madre de Dios.[44]

---

42 Seville, Biblioteca de la Universidad de Sevilla, A 111/124 (61). It was written by the nation's solicitor for the lawsuit, the attorney Francisco Gonzálvez Príncipe.
43 Seville, Biblioteca de la Universidad de Sevilla, A 111/124 (61), fol. 50. At certain moments there were two, as indicated on fol. 12.
44 Morgado García, 'Los manuales de confesores', p. 129.

There were many books on practical and doubtful cases that may arise in the confessional (entries 7, 55, 67, 102, 154), among which the great classic *Medulla theologiae moralis* (entry 125) by the Jesuit and rector of the Hildesheim and Münster Colleges, Hermann Busembaum, which saw forty editions despite papal objections to the solutions given to some of the cases analysed.[45] The Jesuit Egidius (or Gillis) de Coninck, professor at the University of Leuven during the first half of the seventeenth century and author of *De moralitate, natura e effectivus actuum supernaturalium*, is also represented (entry 81). There were also seven books of sermons, very helpful for the preparation of preaching, from the classical book by the Trinitarian Hortensio Paravicino *Oraciones evangelicas*, via *Sermones de las dominicas de Pentecostes* by the Mercedarian Juan Pérez de Rojas, to *Cento discorsi* by the Jesuit Gregorio Mastrilli (entries 72, 99, 26; the other four are entries 14, 93, 105, 118). The chaplains also had five books of Psalms, one of them a bilingual Latin–French edition by the Oratorian Fathers Julien Loriot and Pasquier Quesnel (entries 123, 124, and 148). Chaplain Manuel José de Licht and his coadjutor Pedro van de Sande brought about the conversion of seven Lutherans (a fact verified by the ministers of the Inquisition in Seville)[46] by using these works. They were a solid complement of the seven missals that were in the chapel, four 'misales romanos, las dos de a folio vien tratados y los otros dos en quarto mayor' (Roman missals, two well preserved folio volumes, and another two in large quarto), plus another three 'viexos, del Orden de Predicadores, los dos forrados en terciopelo Carmesi, y el otro en vadana' (old ones, of the Order of Preachers, two of them lined in crimson velvet and the other one in *vadana*).[47]

With regard to the writings on religious controversy, there were up to thirteen books on these issues, in line with the above-mentioned commitment to conversion, which was very much in tune with the vocation of many religious establishments located in port cities where a great number of nations met and where study and pastoral work was partly organized to be further developed in other latitudes. In addition to the English College, the Irish College, or Saint Francis convent, which was important in training and sending missionaries to America, there were prestigious educational institutions such as Saint Mary of Jesus College, the Jesuit Saint Gregory College, or Saint Thomas College itself, to which the chapel and hospital of Saint Andrew of the Flemish were attached.[48]

---

45 *Diccionario Histórico de la Compañía de Jesús*, I, p. 578.
46 Seville, Biblioteca de la Universidad de Sevilla, A 111/124 (61), fols 31–32.
47 Seville, Arch. Hist. Prov. Prot. de Sev., file 14674, fol. 656ʳ. 'Badana' is, according to the Dictionary of the Spanish Language Academy, the fine and tanned hide of a ram or sheep.
48 On the university, see Ollero Pina, *La Universidad de Sevilla*. On the English and Irish colleges, see Medina, 'El colegio inglés de San Gregorio Magno de Sevilla'; Murphy,

For this reason, the staff supervised by the chaplain and administrator of the institution needed to have at hand a good number of reference books on religious controversy, both in Latin and in Flemish and French, as well as various dictionaries. Luis Doye and Manuel José de Licht expressed it this way:

> Que tambien tiene por Constitucion [...] la conversion de los hereges, a que concurria con muchos gastos en su manutención, y despues de convertidos, los proporciona con ayuda de costa correspondiente, remitiendolos a parages donde no comuniquen con personas tocadas de la heregia, para evitar el daño, de que vuelvan a sus antiguos errores. Y esta especie de gasto acaece muchas vezes, como sucedio el año passado de mil seteciento y veinte, y siete, que huvo dos conversiones, y despues han continuado, con el motivo de hallarse la Corte en esta Ciudad, y concurrir tantas naciones Septentrionales [...] y en especial por las minas de Guadalcanal, Rio-Tinto y Galaroza.[49]

> (Which is also committed through its Constitution [...] to the conversion of heretics, the sustenance of whom required many expenses, and after they are converted, they are provided with economic support, and sent to places where they can avoid all contact with people touched by heresy, and thus prevent the damage of again making the same mistakes. And this kind of expenses occurs very often, as it happened last year, in 1727, when there were two conversions, and they have continued afterwards, given that the Royal Court has settled in this city and many northern nations are gathering here [...] but most especially because of the Guadalcanal, Río-Tinto, and Galaroza mines being near.)

The books on religious controversy in the library were in many cases written by important Jesuit authors and, as expected, were strongly linked to the *missio hollandica* and its main houses. In fact, the Antwerp College had a Jesuit chair on controversy.[50] However, none of the books on controversy by the most represented author in the library, the Jesuit cardinal

---

'Irish students and merchants in Seville'; Murphy, *Ingleses de Sevilla*. On other educational institutions, see *Fondos y procedencias*, ed. by Peñalver Gómez.

49 Seville, Biblioteca de la Universidad de Sevilla, A 111/124 (61), fols 7, 31. The constitution of the nation has not been found yet. On the conversion of Protestants at the different courts of Inquisition in the peninsula and the reasons that led these individuals to convert, see Thomas, *Los protestantes y la Inquisición en España*. On the court of Inquisition of Seville and the Protestants in the city, see, among others, Boeglin, *L'Inquisition espagnole au lendemain du Concile de Trente*.

50 On the indefatigable activity of the Jesuits in the Southern Low Countries from the last quarter of the sixteenth century onwards, see *Diccionario Histórico de la Compañía de Jesús*.

and writer on a wide variety of subjects Robert Bellarmine, who studied and was a professor at the University of Leuven for several years (1569–1576) and wrote several books on the matter,[51] was included in the library. In contrast, the works of the Jesuit and active preacher Oudenaarde are present in it, as well as those of the 'mayor controversista de la reforma catolica en los Países Bajos del Sur durante la segunda mitad del siglo XVII' (greatest controversialist of the Catholic Reform in the Southern Low Countries during the second half of the seventeenth century),[52] Cornelius Hazart (*Controvercias del Padre Hazart*, entry 121). We do not know exactly which of his books the inventory made reference to, although most of them discussed the religious controversy with the Calvinists, the main subject of his oeuvre. The Provincial of the Jesuits in the Flemish–Belgian province, a great promoter of the Jesuit apostolic work in that area, Carolus Scribani,[53] was also represented (although not with his works on controversy), just like other Jesuits of the Flemish–Belgian province such as the above-mentioned Egidius de Coninck.

The subject of some books can only be deduced from the titles, for instance *Olla de los herejes* (entry 140). Other books, like *Theomachia calvinistica* by the Franciscan Feuardant, *Assertiones Lutheranae* by Saint John Fisher, *Clypeus militantis ecclesiae* by Ludovico Maiorano, *Veritates de auxilio gratiae* by the Dominican Pierre Jammy, or the two works by Thomas Stapleton, *Principiorum fidei doctrinalium* and *Universa iustificationis doctrina hodie controversa* (entries 79, 27, 28, 58, 78, and 80) must have been a great support for the activity of the people responsible for religious matters at the institution.[54] They most probably resorted as well to the work by the Flemish Dominican Van den Bosche, *Den Katholyken pedagoge*,[55] and to *Instrucción Cristiana* (entries 120 and 134). In the library there was one work that we believe was concerned with Protestant religious controversy and which probably helped improve knowledge of the arguments used by the opposing party: *Legenda* (entry 70). In relation to the training of religious people, four titles (2.5 per cent) are registered in entries 42, 119, 143, and 144.

In contrast with theology, philosophy was scarcely represented in the library. There are only five books (3.1 per cent) within this category: two *Summa Philosophiae* that have not been identified, one *Cursus philosophicus* by the Jesuit Rodrigo de Arriaga, *Dignitas philosophiae acclamata* by the

---

51 *Diccionario Histórico de la Compañía de Jesús*, I, pp. 387–88.
52 *Diccionario Histórico de la Compañía de Jesús*, II, p. 1892.
53 *Diccionario Histórico de la Compañía de Jesús*, IV, p. 3541.
54 There is also a copy of the *Confutatio*, together with the classical work by Constanzo Boccafuoco, *Conciliatio dilucida omnium controversiarum*, and others (entries 21, 32, and entries 83, 84, 87, 107).
55 He was also in the first line of the dialectical discussion with the Protestants; see Quetif and Echard, eds, *Scriptores ordinis Praedicatorum*, II, p. 727.

Dominican José de Muñana, and one work on logic (entries 64, 115, 6, 109, and 86).

As for books on history and geography, their number is modest compared to that of the theology section (fifteen books on history, 9.4 per cent, and three works on geography, 1.8 per cent). There are interesting titles that deal with aspects of the history of Spain, the Southern Low Countries, and even Holland. We can mention the *Historia del Emperador Carlos Quinto* by Prudencio de Sandoval, *De rebus hispaniae* by the Jesuit Mariana, the critical work about this last book written by Pedro Mantuano, and the book defending Mariana's position authored by Tamayo de Vargas (entries 8, 3, 92, 130). A copy of the exemplary *Conquista de las islas Molucas* by Argensola (entry 74) also reached the library. Among titles about the history of the Low Countries, we can find the book by Pontanus de Huyter, *Veteris ac novi Belgi historia* (entry 132), and an interesting work on the wars in Flanders, *Bellum Belgicum* by Giovanni Gamurino, who was one of the engineers in charge of the siege of Ostend (entry 90).[56] There is a copy of *Pars prima sive Belgicae descriptio generalis* ..., and a manuscript describing its seventeen provinces (entries 63 and 69). The 'official' history of Holland is represented by classical works such as *Historia Bataviae* by Hadrianus Junius (entry 103).

The military feats of Emperor Leopold and his generals made a great impact in Spain. The evidence of the interest of Spanish readers in news pamphlets is found in works like *Admirables efectos de la providencia sucedidos en la vida e imperio de Leopoldo Primero* or *Floro histórico de la Guerra movida por el sultán de los turcos Mehemet IV contra ... Leopoldo primero* by Fabro Bremudán (entries 66 and 110). The classic *De la vida y acciones de Alexandro el Grande* by Quintus Curtius Rufus, a model for historians of all times, is certainly not missing (entry 20). World history is represented by the work of the Italian humanist Sabellico (*Rapsodiae Historia*) and world geography by the old classic by Plutarch *Plutarchi Libellus de fluviorum et montium nominibus et de his quae in illis inveniuntur* (entries 71 and 45). The history of the Church is covered by Cardinal Baronio and his *Epitome Annalium Ecclesiasticorum*, and the monumental *Concilia generalia et provincialia* (entries 24 and 68), to which we can add, given the affinity of their subjects, the *Compendium Constitutionum Summorum Pontificum*, and the constitution of the Provincial Synod of Cremona (entries 37 and 108). Finally, we find the miscellaneous travel book *Voyagien in het Turkische rijk Egypte*, in Flemish, a translation from the original in English by George Sandys (entry 94).

The rest of the subjects are only incidentally represented. We can highlight the books on political theory (seven titles, 4.4 per cent), which

---

56 On the interest, publication, and dissemination of works on the War of Flanders and military treatises, see Lombaerde, 'Los tratados de artillería', pp. 339–49.

include a champion of heterodoxy like *De officio principis Christiani* by Bellarmine, as well as *Thesaurus politicus* (entry 23) by Philippus Honorius (pseudonym of Giulio Belli), who appeared on the Spanish Index of forbidden books in 1667 with his work *Praxis Prudentiae Politicae*,[57] or the critical Tacitist work about Jean Bodin, *Doctrina politica in genuinam methodum Aristotelis* by the German philosopher Henning Arnisaeus, who was a Protestant and the medical doctor of Christian IV of Denmark. There is also one book that follows the tradition of the 'political treasures', the *Epimetron* by Jean de Chokier, and the book of emblems by the painter and humanist Otto van Veen, master of Rubens and member of Lipsius's Tacitist circle, which was much celebrated at the time.[58] This is perhaps the perfect book of emblems for this library, taking into consideration that, in addition to contributing to the fertile ground of neo-Stoic thinking that linked the Southern Low Countries with Spain, each emblem was presented in Latin, Castilian, Flemish, Italian, and French (entries 89, 156, and 75). In addition, we have included in this category the political satire *Archombrotus et Theopompus* by John Barclay, a solid defence of the prerogatives of royal power. We believed it was appropriate to also count in this category the work *El embajador* by Juan Antonio de Vera y Zúñiga (entry 104), one of the most respected diplomats in Spain during the Golden Age: his book served as inspiration for the renewal and progress of diplomacy in his time.

Apart from Protestant authors of political theory books, other authors of the same confession are also represented in other sections. Some of them are well known, like the man appointed as the Great Pensioner of Holland between 1629 and 1631, and then again between 1636 and 1651, considered the prince of Flemish literature, Jacob Cats. Unfortunately, we do not know to which of his books the entry (no. 51) in the inventory corresponds, and whether it was a poetic or a legal work. The German jurist and humanist (and correspondent of Erasmus) Jakob Omphal, who would much later convert to Protestantism,[59] is present with a work on rhetoric that was not forbidden by the Index, *De elocutionis imitatione ac apparatu liber unus* (entry 52). As a complement to this book, we find a *Gramatica franzeza y flamenca* (entry 49). It is very possible that both works were used by members of the nation to improve their ability in writing letters, a very common and frequent activity. The library also

---

57 De Sotomayor, *Index librorum prohibitorum*, p. 850. Belli translated the Italian book, *Thesaurus politicus*, which gathered several discourses, fragments of works on political matters, and advice on the same issues. Under that same title, several books supporting political ideas of various ideological persuasions circulated throughout Europe; see Testa, 'From the "Bibliographical Nightmare" to a Critical Bibliography'.

58 Van Veen, *Quinti Horatii Flacci Emblemata*.

59 On Omphal, see Bietenholz and Deutscher, eds, *Contemporaries of Erasmus*, III, pp. 32–33. On this work, see Baños, ed., *El arte epistolar en el Renacimiento europeo*, pp. 385–87.

preserved a volume of 'letters in Flemish' (entry 60). To improve the art of writing in Latin the library offered the work by Schoro, *Phrases linguae latinae e diversis Ciceronis operibus collectae* (entry 138).

As for the scientific books (three works, 1.8 per cent), there was one on surgery, the treatise on the sphere by Sacrobosco de Clavius, and a book on Aristotle's Physics by the medical doctor Francisco Murcia de la Llana (entries 136, 29, and 34). There is one work on arithmetic in Flemish, very useful in an institution where most members were merchants (entry 56), as was the copy of a treatise on trade with Spain written in Flemish (entry 113). To these we can add the classical work *Suma de tratos y contratos* by Friar Tomás de Mercado (entry 96).

Within the category Other (Religion), we have placed the books on the religious orders, the Dominican Order, meditations and spirituality (entries 57, 61), the Sacred Scriptures (entry 40), edifying literature on the Christian life (entries 128 and 157), the lives of saints (entries 16 and 25), the Virgin (entries 85 and 91), and a 'mirror for bishops' (entry 31). We include as well the rules of the Hermandad de la Santa Caridad (Brotherhood of the Holy Charity), refounded by Miguel de Mañara,[60] one book on canon law, another one on ecclesiastical benefits in America, a memorial sent by the canons of the cathedral of Seville to Philip V (entries 101, 18, 95, 73), and a few other books.

All of this informs us about a very singular library, which belonged to a religious institution founded by secular people of foreign origin. The members of this institution sought not only social and confessional prestige, but also tried to demonstrate the clarity and purity of their Catholic faith. After the hospital and pious house were created, many Protestants of Flemish, German, and other origins arrived at their doors, as is proven by the exorbitant petition to Philip III made in 1611 by the administrator of the hospital, Enrique Conde, to be granted an episcopate to better carry out the work of conversion and spiritual and physical assistance

> para catetizar [*sic*] alli por mano de este religioso tan religioso a los holandeses, alemanes y flamencos luteranos que vienen allí a quien su dotrina, costumbres y persuasión va reduziendo cada dia a nuestra santa fe y da baptismo a muchos y muchos que le tienen va reduziendo a verdadero conozimiento hasta sacallos de sus tinieblas y errores.[61]

---

60 Its members, belonging to the upper class in most cases, often encountered the Flemings at the many political and cultural spaces in the city. On the figure of Mañara and the Hospital de la Caridad (Charity Hospital), see Piveteau, *El burlador y el santo*.

61 García García, 'La Nación Flamenca en la corte española', p. 394. The Archbishop of Seville, Pedro de Castro, was absolutely against the granting of such dignity, and had a poor opinion of the assistance and pastoral work of the administrator and the institution. See on other controversies that developed around Conde: García García, 'La Nación Flamenca en la corte española', pp. 395–97.

(so that this very religious man can catechize the Dutch, German, and Flemish Lutherans that come here, whose doctrine, habits, and persuasion he will reduce and lead towards our holy Faith every day, and he will baptize many of them, and thus many will be carried towards the true knowledge until they are saved from their darkness and mistakes.)

This fact and the existence of the library tell us about a special function of this institution that has not been considered until now: the pastoral work and conversion of the non-Catholic members of the community, whether residents or transients. This gave prestige to the activities and existence of the nation and removed suspicion from its members and their alleged heterodoxy.

Even if the number of conversions achieved by the ministers of this foundation may have been exaggerated, their success must have been substantial and this apostolic activity was underlined by the Flemings in the eighteenth century as a primordial objective of their nation. They insisted that, according to the constitutions[62] of the hospital and pious house, the activity was both contemplative and committed:

> En la primera ponen la Capilla, y el culto divino en Sacrificios, Festividades y Sufragios: y en la segunda la Hospitalidad en la Casapía, donde se havian de exercitar las Obras de Misericordia con los proximos. Pero lo que mas se lleva la atencion de los Nacionales es la segunda, que mira a la Hospitalidad y limosnas, y conversion de Hereges, a cuyo fin se dirigen las mas de las Constituciones y Acuerdos.[63]

> (The former has to do with the chapel and the divine cult, with the celebration of sacrifices, festivities and intercessions; while the latter is concerned with the hospitality of the pious house, where the charity work with its close ones is developed. But the focus of the nationals is on the latter, providing hospitality and alms and converting heretics, which is the purpose of most constitutions and agreements.)

There were similar well-known institutions belonging to Flemish nations in other Spanish cities, but sources about the contents of their libraries, which they must surely have possessed, have not yet been found. These libraries and the pastoral activity they supported shed new light on the

---

62 We are quoting here an eighteenth-century document which selects some of the constitutions. We can find the original ones from 1615 analysed in Díaz Blanco, 'La construcción de una institución comercial', pp. 127–31. These considerations about the conversion of Protestants are not indicated in that article.
63 Seville, Biblioteca de la Universidad de Sevilla, A 111/124 (61), fol. 5.

presence of the Flemish nations in Spain. However, in a period when the nation's members in Seville struggled to secure its survival and that of its institutions and privileges, this library reflects interests that are very close to those of the Counter-Reformation of the seventeenth century, and most of the authors represented in it were born during the sixteenth century, mainly between 1570 and 1660, and only a few after 1700 (the lack of dates of publication hinders accuracy). In other words, in 1732 the ideas and the intellectual atmosphere that the books gathered in the pious house of the Flemish Nation exuded corresponded, beyond the presence of some classics, to a different world, that of the more glorious days enjoyed by the nation during the seventeenth century.

Appendix: Edition of the Catalogue of the Library of the Pious House and chapel of Saint Andrew in Seville (1732), with Identification of the Works Mentioned

Seville, Archivo Histórico Provincial de Sevilla, Notarial Protocols of Seville, file 14674, fols 662ʳ–64ᵛ.

[fol. 662ʳ]

Librería (Library)

Yten un estante de pino antiguo de dos cuerpos como de dos varas y media de largo, con los Libros siguientes. (Idem a two-part bookcase made of antique pinewood whose measurement is about two and a half *varas*, with the following books.)

Primer cuerpo: tomos de a folio (First body: books in folio)

1 *Todas las obras de Santo Thomas de Aquino en Veynte y un tomos.*[64]
2 *Joannes de Dicastillo Disputationes Scholasticee un tomo.*
   Dicastillo, Juan de (S.I.) (1585–1643): *De sacramentis disputationes scholasticae et morales...*, unidentified edition.
3 *Mariani de Rebus hispaniee en pasta, un tomo.*
   De Mariana, Juan (S.I.) (1536–1624): *De Rebus Hispaniae...*, unidentified edition.[65]
4 *Las obras del Reverendo Padre Masart en pasta, en ocho tomos...* unidentified work.
5 *Obras del Reverendo Padre Roderico de Arriaga en ocho tomos.*
   Arriaga, Rodrigo de (S.I.) (1592–1667).[66]
6 *Cursus Philosophicus, del mismo autor, un tomo.*
   Arriaga, Rodrigo de (S.I.): *Cursus philosophicus*, unidentified edition.
7 *Diana Summa, un tomo.*
   Diana, Antonino (CC.RR.MM.) (1585–1663): *Summa Diana: in qua R. P. D. Antonini Diana ... Clerici Regul ... Opera omnia, Diana ipso committente [et]*

---

64 Unidentified edition; it could be: *Sancti Thomae Aquinatis ex Ordine Praedicatorum ... Opera Omnia: ad fidem vetutissimorum Codicum M. SS. et Editorum emendata, aucta & cum Exemplaribus Romano, Veneto, & Antuerpiensi accurate collata: Omnia XXII Volum. Comprehensa...*, Paris, apud Societatem Bibliopolarum, via Iacobea, 1660, folio. CCPB000048703–1.
65 It might be: *Historiae de rebus Hispaniae libri XXV*, Toledo, typis Pedro Rodríguez, 1592, folio. USTC No. 339781.
66 Unidentified edition; it could possibly be: *Disputationes Theologicae* in which Arriaga glosses *Summa Theologica* (Saint Thomas Aquinas), because it was published in eight volumes in Lyons and Antwerp.

approbante, Ansonio verò Noctinot siculo Tertii Ordinis S. Francisci operam dante, in unicum volumen, duabus partibus distinctum, arctantur, unidentified edition.

8   *Historia del Señor Carlos Quinto, dos tomos.*

a) de Sandoval, Fray Prudencio (O.S.B.) (1552–1620): *Primera parte de la vida y hechos del emperador Carlos Quinto ... por el maestro fray Prudencio de Sandoval ... de la Orden de San Benito; tratanse en esta primera parte los hechos desde el año 1500 hasta el de 1528*, unidentified edition.

b) *Segunda parte de la vida y hechos del emperador Carlos Quinto ... por el maestro fray Prudencio de Sandoual ... de la Orden de San Benito; tratase en esta segunda parte los hechos desde el año 1528 hasta el de 1557 en que el emperador se fue al cielo*, unidentified edition.[67]

9   *Divi Atanasi opera, un tomo.*
Atanasio, Santo, Patriarca de Alejandría (295–373): *Athanasij Magni alexandrini episcopi ... Opera in quatuor tomos distributa quorum tres sunt ...*, unidentified edition.

10 *Castro de Meereses, un tomo.*
Unidentified work.

11 *Corrella practica del Confesionario, un tomo.*
Jaime de Corella (O.F.M. Cap.) (1657–1699): *Practica de el Confessonario y explicacion de las LXV. proposiciones condenadas por ... Inocencio XI: su materia los casos mas selectos de la theologia moral, su forma, un diálogo entre el confessor y penitente...*, unidentified edition.

12 *Sonnio in Religionem Christianam, un tomo.*
Sonnius, Franciscus (1506–1576): *Demonstratiunum religionis christianae liber secundus*, Antwerpen, apud Philippus Nutius, 1570, folio.
USTC No. 411507; Short-Title Netherlands, 690. g. 9, p. 189.

13 *Villalovos, Dos Tomos.*
Unidentified work.[68]

14 *El Predicador Apostolico, un tomo.*
de Santa María, Gabriel (O. de M.): *El predicador apostolico y obligaciones de su sagrado ministerio: parte primera [-segunda] / por ... fr. Gabriel de Santa Maria ... de Descalços de N. Señora de la Merced, Redencion de Cautivos*, Sevilla, por Thomas Lopez de Haro 'impressor y mercader de libros', 1684, folio.
CCPB000120018-6.

15 *Matthei Raderi Epigrammaton, un tomo.*

---

67 Considering that the work consists of two volumes, its first volume could be attributed to the following edition: Valladolid, por Sebastián de Cañas, 1604, folio, CCPB000040775-5; and the second volume to: Valladolid, por Sebastián de Cañas, 1606, folio, CCPB000040776-3.

68 Considering the prominence of works on moral theology in this period, it might be: *Summa de Theologia Moral y Canonica* from the Franciscan friar Enrique de Villalobos, Salamanca, Diego Cusio, 1620, CCPB000049271-X.

Rader, Matthäus (S.I.) (1561–1634): *Matthaei Raderi de Societate Iesv, Ad M. valerii Martialis Epigrammaton Libros Omnes...*, unidentified edition.

16 *Vida de San Ygnacio de Loyola, un tomo.*
Unidentified work.[69]

17 *Soto, Cinco tomos.*
de Soto, Domingo (O.P.) (1494–1560), unidentified work.

18 *Questiones Regulares et Canonicee, un tomo.*
Rodrigues, Manoel (O.F.M.): *Questiones regulares et canonicae, in quibus utriusque juris, et privilegiorum regularium, et apostolicarum constitutionum, novae, et veteres difficultates dispersae, et confusae, miro ordine scholastico per quaestiones et articulos elucidantur, praelatis ecclesiasticis, et regularibus, nec non judicibus cujuscumque tribunalis, et utriusque juris peritis, et quibuscumque ecclesiasticis regularibus maxime necessariae*, Antwerpen, P. et J. Bellerus, 1628.
Barbosa, III, p. 354.

19 *Disputationes Theologicee, un tomo.*
Unidentified work.[70]

20 *Quinto Curcio de Alexandro Magno, un tomo.*
Curcio Rufo, Quinto: *Quinto Curcio Rufo, De la vida y acciones de Alexandro el Grande; traducido de la lengua latina en española por Don Matheo Ibañez de Segovia y Orellana...*, unidentified edition.

21 *Confutatio, un tomo.*
Unidentified work.[71]

Libros en quarto mayor y menor (Books in quarto, large and small)

22 *El Grand Dictionario frances y Ytaliano, un tomo.*
It might be USTC No. 37617: Fenice, Giovanni Antonio, *Dictionnaire françois et italien*, Morges, et vendu à Paris, chez Jacques du Puys, 1584, 8°. Many later editions.

[fol. 662ᵛ]

23 *Philipe honorij Thesuari politici Continuatio, dos tomos.*
a) Honorius, Philippus (pseud. de Belli, Giulio): *Philippi Honorii I.V.D. Thesavrvs politicvs, hoc est, Selectiores tractatvs, monita, acta, relationes, et discvrsvs...: Opvs collectvm ex Italicis ... discursibus ... & ... nunc Latine simul & Italice*

---

69 It might be: Ribadeneira, Pedro de (S.I.) (1526–1611): *Vida del padre Ignacio de Loyola, fundador de la Compañía de Jesús y de los padres*, Madrid, por Pedro Madrigal, 1594, folio. USTC No. 337778.
70 There are several works with this title. We have already discussed *Disputationes Theologicae*, which probably can be attributed to the Jesuit Rodrigo de Arriaga, in the entry number 5.
71 There are several works with this title.

editum, Francofvrti, typis Nicolai Hoffmanni, impensis hæredum Iacobi Fischeri, 1617.

Zentralbibiothek Solothurn (Switzerland), ZBSO H 1203/1 // USTC No. 2030436 (this is the 1617 edition in USTC, there are more editions).

b) Honorius, Philippus: *Philippi Honorii ... Thesauri politici continuaio, hic est Selectiores tractatus, monita, acta, relationes et discursus pluriuariam...*, Francofurti, typis Nicolai Hoffmanni, impensis haeredum Iacobi Fischeri, 1618, 4º.

CCPB000233322-8

24 *Epitome Annalium Ecclesiaticorum Cesaris Baronij, Dos tomos.*

a) Baronio, Cesare, Cardenal (1538–1607): *Epitome Annalium Ecclesiasticorum Caesaris Baronii S.R.E. Card. Biblioth. Apost. / ab Ioanne Gabriele Bisciola Mutinen. Societ. Iesu confecta et eiusdem auctoris concessione nunc primum in lucem edita...*, unidentified edition.

b) *Epitome annalium ecclesiasticorum Caesaris Baronii ... / ab Ioan. Gabriele Bisciola ... confecta et eiusdem auctoris concessione nunc primum in lucem edita; tomus secundus...*, unidentified edition.

25 *Vida de San Laureano, un tomo.*

Tello Lasso de la Vega, Diego (O. de M.) (1686–1763): *Vida, milagros, y martyrio, del ... Arzobispo de Sevilla San Laureano con dissertaciones Chronologico-Historicas, en que se reducen à examen los puntos dudosos*, Roma, en la imprenta de Cayetano Zenobio, 1722, 4º.

CCPB000413077-4

26 *Cient Discursos sobre la Pacion de Nuestro Señor en Ytaliano, un tomo.*

Mastrilli, Gregorio (S.I.): *Cento discorsi del P. Gregorio Mastrilli della Compagnia di Giesu intorno alla sacra passione e morte del nostro redentore & al sacrosanto sacramento dell' eucharistia distinti in tre parti...*, unidentified edition.

27 *Assertionis Lutheranee confutatio, un tomo.*

Fisher, Santo John (1469–1535): *Assertionis Lutheranae confutatio iuxta verum ac originalem archetypum nunc ad vnguen diligentissime recognita...*, unidentified edition.

28 *Clypeus militantis Ecclesiee, un tomo.*

Maiorano, Ludovico (m. 1591): *Clypeus militantis Ecclesiae, seu De vero Dei cultu libri tres ... / Ludouico Maiorano ... authore; eiusdem De opt. Reip. statu oratio quam misit ad Patres in Concilio Tridentino...*, unidentified edition.

29 *Christophori Clavij in spheram vsa. un tomo.*

Clavius, Christophorus (S.I.) (1538–1612): *In sphaeram Ioannis de Sacro Bosco commentarius...*, unidentified edition.

30 *Explenatio in psalmos Bellarminij, un tomo.*

Bellarmino, Santo Roberto (1542–1621): *Explanatio in Psalmos...*, unidentified edition.

31 *Episcopus Regularis, un tomo.*

Lucarini, Reginaldo (O.P.) (d. 1671): *Episcopus regularis seu Tractatus de regulari assumendo et assumpto ad Episcopatum: in quo Episcopi regularis mores, vota,*

obseruantiae, ritus, habitus, privilegia et poenae expendetur..., Roma, ex officina typographica Caballina, 1659.
CCPB000617155-9

32 *Consiliatio omnium controversiarum, un tomo.*
Boccadifuoco, Costanzo (1531-1595): *Conciliatio dilucida omnium controversiarum: quae in doctrina ... addito non sine maxima accessione in universam theologicam...*, unidentified edition.

33 *Desiciones fidei Caholicee et Apostolicee, un tomo.*
Grisaldi, Paolo (O.P.) (d. 1614): *Decisiones fidei catholicae et apostolicae: ex sanctarum Scripturarum ... Romanorum Pontificum Diplomatum, sacrorum Conciliorum, fontibus ... et in uno alphabetico ordine collectae ...*, unidentified edition.

34 *Murcia in phisicam, un tomo.*
Murcia de la Llana, Francisco: *Selecta circa octo libros Physicorum Aristotelis, subtilioris doctrinae, quae in Complutensi Academia versatur...*, unidentified edition.

35 *Fuero de la Conciencia, un tomo.*
de la Madre de Dios, Valentín (O.C.D.): *Fuero de la conciencia: obra utilissima para los ministros, y ministerio del Santo Sacramento de la Penitencia...: contiene seis tratados...*, unidentified edition.

36 *Conferencias de Corella, Dos tomos.*
a) de Corella, Jaime (O.F.M. Cap.) (1657-1699): *Suma de la theologia moral: su materia, los tratados mas principales de casos de conciencia: su forma unas conferencias practicas; parte primera...*, unidentified edition.
b) *Suma de la Teologia moral: su materia, los tratados principales de los casos de conciencia: su forma, unas conferencias practicas: segunda parte...*, unidentified edition.

37 *Summarium Constitutionum ord. predicatorum, un tomo.*
Mártir, Pedro (O.P.): *Summarium constitutionum declarationum et ordinationum quae ad hanc usquè diem pro bono regimine sacri Ordinis Praedicatorum emanarunt...*, unidentified edition.

38 *Philippi a Santissima Trinitate, quatro tomos.*
de la Santísima Trinidad, Felipe (O.C.D.) (1603-1671), unidentified work.

<u>Libros en octavo</u> (Books in octavo)

39 *Sancti Belgi ordinis predicatorum, un tomo.*
Choquetus, Hyacinthus (O.P.): *Sancti Belgi Ordinis Praedicatorum*, Douai, Typis B. Balleri, 1618, 8º.
CCPB000214676-2; USTC No. 1507926.

40 *Concordantiee Bibliorum, un tomo.*
[*Sacrorum Bibliorum Concordiantae*], unidentified edition.

41 *Sciutum Dives Mariee Aspricollis, un tomo.*
   Dausque, Claude (S.I.) (1566–1647): *B. Mariae Aspricollis ... Scutum / a CL. Dausqueio Sanctomario ... alterum item I. Lipsi Scutum ab eodem Cl. Dausqueio; utrumq. adversus Agricolae Thracii satyricas petitiones.* Antwerpen, apud Haeredes Martini Mutij et Ioannem Meursium, 1617, 8º.
   CCPB000493701-5; USTC No. 1035928.

42 *Francisco Toleti Pistructio* [sic, for *Instructio*] *Sacerdotum, un tomo.*[72]
   Toledo, Francisco de (S.I.) (1532–1596): *Francisci Toleti e Societate Iesu ... Instructio sacerdotum...*
   USTC No. 6811304.

43 *Sonnio de Sacramentis, un tomo.*
   Sonnius, Franciscus (1506–1576): *Demonstrationum ex verbo Dei de septem Sacramentis ecclesiae...*
   USTC No. 406323.

44 *Biblia Sacra, en latin, muy viejo y maltratado, un tomo.*
   'Very old and damaged, in one volume'. Identification not possible.

45 *Plutarchis de fluviorum nominibus, un tomo.*
   Plutarch: *Plutarchi Libellus de fluviorum et montium nominibus et de his quae in illis inueniuntur / Philip. Iacob. Maussacus recensuit, latine vertit et notis illustrauit...*, Toulouse, apud Dominique Bosc, 1615, 8º.
   CCPB000369061-X.

46 *Binsfeldius, un tomo.*
   Binsfeld, Peter (1540–1603): unidentified work.

47 *Meditationes de Alessio en Ytaliano, tres tomos.*
   Segala, Alessio (O.F.M.) (1558–1628): *Corona celeste ornata di pretiosissime considerationi, overo meditationi accomodate per tutti li giorni dell'anno per contemplare i misterii della acerbissima passione del nostro salvatore...*, unidentified edition.
   It might be: USTC No. 4028948.

48 *Annales ab anno mill seiscientos y seis, iusque ad mill seiscientos y quinze, un tomo.*
   Unidentified work.

49 *Gramatica franzeza y flamenca, un tomo.*
   Unidentified work. It might be *Vocabulaire françois-flameng*, often reprinted.

50 *Aldi manutij Pharses* [sic, for *Phrases*], *un tomo.*
   Manuzio, Aldo (1547–1597): *Purae elegantes et copiosiae latinae linguae phrases...*, Cologne, apud Ioannem Gymnicum ..., 1579.
   CCPB000564396-1.

51 *Cats libro flamenco, un tomo.*
   Cats, Jacob (1577–1660): unidentified work.

52 *De Elocutionis mutatione de omphalio, un tomo.*

---

72 Unidentified edition; it could be: *De Instructione sacerdotum et peccatis mortalibus lib. VIII. Quibus suis locis interiectae accesserunt annotationes & additiones Andreae Victorelli*, Douai, ex typ. Balthazar I Bellère, 1617, 8º; USTC No. 1117561.

Omphalius, Jacobus (1500–1567): *De elocutionis imitatione ac apparatu liber unus*, unidentified edition.
It might be USTC No. 147222: Paris, apud Simon de Colines, 1537.

53 *De Sacro Adorationis cultu de Bernardo Puiol, un tomo.*
Pujol, Bernat: *De sacro adorationis cultu disputationes quatuor*, unidentified edition.

54 *El Camino del cielo allanado, un tomo.*
Pinamonti, Giovanni Pietro (S.I.) (1632–1703): *El camino del cielo allanado: obra sacada del Libro de los exercicios de San Ignacio*, Sevilla, imprenta castellana y latina de Diego Lopez de Haro, 1730.
CCPB000320234-8.

55 *Promptuario de materias morales, un tomo.*
de Salazar, Simón (O.P.): *Promptuario de materias morales: en principios y reglas para examen y sucinta noticia de los que en breve se dessean exponer para confessores...*[73]
It could be: USTC No. 5110640.

56 *Aritmetica en flamenco, Dos tomos.*
It could be USTC No. 425112: Schuere, Jacob van der, *Arithmetica, oft rekenconst, verchiert met veel schoone exempelen*, Haarlem, Gillis Rooman, 1600, 8°.

57 *Verdades eternas, un tomo.*
Rosignoli, Carlo Gregorio (S.I.) (1631–1707): *Verdades eternas: explicadas en lecciones ordenadas principalmente para los dias de los Exercicios Espirituales...*; Tomo I, Sevilla, Juan de la Puerta: A costa de Jacobo Dherve mercader de libros, [s.a.]. Fecha de la Licencia, 1714.
CCPB000492851-2.

58 *Veritatis de auxilio Gratiee, Dos tomos.*
Jammy, Pierre (O.P.): *Veritates de auxilio gratiae, ab erroribus et falsis opinionibus vindicatae, quas defendunt theologiae gratianopolitanae candidati ... praeside R. P. F. Petro Jammy,...*, Gratianopoli [Grenoble], P. Fremon, 1658–1659.
Paris, Bibliothèque Nationale de France, shelfmark D-12144.

59 *Basis totius moralis, un tomo.*
Mercorum, Jules (O.P.): *Basis totius moralis theologiae: hoc est praxis opinionum limitata...*, unidentified edition.[74]

[fol. 663ʳ]

60 *Cartas en flamenco, un tomo.*
61 *Recetas de Espiritu para enfermos del Cuerpo, un tomo.*
Recetas de espiritu para enfermos del cuerpo, Sevilla, by Iuan Cabeças, 1680, 8°.

---

[73] There is an edition published in Seville by the heirs of Thomás Lopez **de** Haro in 1696, but it is in 12°. See Escudero, 1917.

[74] Based on the title, we have attributed this work to the Italian Dominican Julium Mercorum. Another copy is in entry number 152.

CCPB000492688-9.
62 *Quinti horatij, un tomo.*
   Quinto Horacio Curcio: unidentified work.[75]
63 *Guiciardini Belgium, un tomo.*
   Guicciardini, Luigi: *Pars prima sive Belgicae descriptio generalis*, unidentified edition.
   It might be: USTC No. 1031389.
   Two copies in BUS B Rector Machado y Núñez (A 102/145 – A 025/061): Amsterdam, Willem Janszoon, 1613.
64 *Summa philosophiee, un tomo.*
   Unidentified work.
   It could be: Fr. Eustachio a Sancto Paulo: *Summa Philosophiae Quadripartita, De Rebus Dialecticis, Moralibus, Physicis, [et] Metaphysicis*, unidentified edition; possibly: USTC No. 2095236.

Segundo Cuerpo: tomos de a folio (Second body: Folio volumes)

65 *Biblia sacra, en flamenco, un tomo.*[76]
66 *Vida del Emperador Leopoldo, tres tomos.*
   a) *Admirables efectos de la providencia sucedidos en la vida, e imperio de Leopoldo Primero ... Emperador de los romanos: tomo primero en que se trata de los sucessos del año 1657 asta [sic] el de 1671*, unidentified edition.
   b) *Admirables efectos de la providencia sucedidos en la vida e imperio de Leopoldo Primero ... Emperador de romanos...: tomo segundo en que se trata de los sucesos del año 1672 asta el de 1681*, unidentified edition.
   c) *Admirables efectos de la providencia sucedidos en la vida, e imperio de Leopoldo Primero ... Emperador de los romanos...: tomo tercero en que se trata de los sucessos del año 1682 asta [sic] el de 1687*, unidentified edition.
67 *Summa de San Antonino, Dos tomos.*
   Antonino, Santo (1389–1459): *Summa Theologiae*, unidentified edition.
68 *Concilia Generalia et provincialia, Cinco tomos.*
   Bini, Severino (1573–1641): *Concilia Generalia, et Provincialia, graeca et latina quecunque reperiri potuerunt: item Epistolae decretales et romanor. pontific. vitae...*, unidentified edition.
69 *Description de las Diez y siete provincias, un tomo.*[77]

---

75 It is very probable that these are the *Poemata* edited in several occasions all over Europe.
76 There are many editions of the Bible in Flemish. For example, between 1597 and 1621 there were at least fourteen editions, as Simoni, *Catalogue of Books of the Low Countries*, pp. 60–62 states. On the website *Biblia Sacra*, http://www.bibliasacra.nl/ we can find one *Biblia Sacra dat is De geheele Heylighe Schrifture bedeylt int oudt ende nieu Testament*, Antwerpen, Joannes Moretus, 1599. Reference: 1599.B.dut.JM1.a. Consulted 10/8/2018.
77 It is probably the manuscript with the same name in the Biblioteca Nacional de Madrid: *Descripción de las diecisiete provincias de Flandes*, (dated to the 16th century), signature MSS/4489.

70 *Legenda en flamenco, un tomo.*
Unidentified work.[78]

71 [R]*Apsodiee historia, un tomo.*
Sabellico, Marco Antonio Coccio (1436–1506): *Rapsodiae historiarum Enneadum Marci Antonii Coccii Sabellici ab orbe condito...*, unidentified edition.

72 *Oraciones Evangelicas de Ortencio, un tomo.*
Paravicino y Arteaga, Hortensio Felix (O.SS.T.) (1580–1633): *Oraciones evangelicas que en las festividades de Christo nuestro Señor y su Santisima Madre predicò ... Fray Hortensio Felix Parauicino ... del Orden de la Santissima Trinidad...*, unidentified edition.
It might be USTC No. 5041618: Madrid, Imprenta del Reino a costa de Alonso Pérez, 1639, folio.

73 *Memorial al Rey Phelipe Quinto, por la santa Yglesia de Sevilla, un tomo.*
Cañas, José de (S.I.): *Memorial que con la mayor veneracion, y confianza pone a las reales plantas de la catolica magestad del rey nuestro señor D. Felipe V que Dios guarde la Santa Iglesias Metropolitana y Patriarcal de Sevilla. [s.l.: s.n., s.a.].*[79]
CCPB000068359-0.

74 *Conquista de las Yslas Malucas, un tomo.*
de Argensola, Bartolomé Leonardo (1592–1631): *Conquista de las Yslas Malucas*, Madrid, Alonso Martín, 1609.
CCPB000033982-2; USTC No. 5024466.

75 *Quinti Horatii emblemata, un tomo.*
van Veen, Otto, conocido como *Vaenius* (1556–1629): *Quinti Horatii Flacci Emblemata: Imaginibus in aes incisis, Notis'q illustrata...*, unidentified edition.[80]
It could be USTC No. 1435909: Antwerpen, apud Philippus Lisaert, 1612, folio.

---

[78] There is a book entitled *Legende véritable de Jean le Blanc*, whose author was Simon Goulart; it was published in 1575: USTC, No. 56428. But the one in the library is written in Dutch, and may be referred to a a controversial anti-Catholic work entitled, *Vvaerachtighe LEGENDE van Ian de Vvite. In Françoysche Tale ghenaemt Iean le Blancq. Waerinne ... vervatet wordt de afkoemste het op-wassen den voort ganc de kracht ... staet ende ... gheleghentheyt van der Papisten Broot-God overghezet wt de fransoysche rijme door IAN FRVITERS, s'Graven-Haghe, Aert Meuris, 1609 (Simoni, *Catalogue of Books of the Low Countries*, p. 333, L55).
If so, it is possible that this text, which circulated widely in the Low Countries, might have arrived in the library through the hands of some Flemish merchant, in order to make the chaplains familiar with it, and it would have allowed the chaplains to understand the ideas the text defended.

[79] Aguilar Piñal considers it to be from 1722, Aguilar Piñal, *Bibliografía de autores españoles*, II, p. 1137.

[80] In addition, we have found an edition in 4° published in Antwerpen, by Philippum Lisaert in 1612, CCPB000335373-7.

76 *Dominicus de marinis, Dos tomos.*
    Dominicus de Marinis (O.P.) (1599–1699): unidentified work.[81]
77 *Disputationum forensium, dos tomos.*[82]
78 *Principiorum fidei Doctrinalium Demonstratio, un tomo.*
    Stapleton, Thomas (1535–1598): *Principiorum fidei doctrinalium demonstratio methodica, per controuersias septem in libris duodecim tradita...*, unidentified edition.
    There are several editions. It might be USTC No. 170461: Paris, apud Michel Sonnius, 1578, folio.
79 *Theomachia Calvinistica, un tomo.*
    Feuardent, François (O.F.M.) (1539–1610): *Theomachia calvinistica: sedecim libris profligata: quibus mille et quadringenti huius sectae nouissimae errores ... refelluntur...*, unidentified edition.
    It could be USTC No. 6015917: Paris, apud Sébastien Nivelle, 1604, folio.
80 *Universa justificationis Doctrina, un tomo.*
    Stapleton, Thomas (1535–1598): *Universa iustificationis doctrina hodie controuersa libris duodecim tradita...*, unidentified edition.
    It could be: USTC No. 170596 or 170642. Both editions were published in Paris, apud Michel Sonnius, 1581–1582, folio.
81 *Egidus de Connink de actibus Supernaturalibus, un tomo.*
    de Coninck, Egidius (S.I.) (1571–1633): *De moralitate natura et effectibus actuum supernaturalium in genere et Fide Spe ac Caritate specitim: libri quatuor...*, unidentified edition.
    It could be USTC No. 6903376: Lyons, sumbtibus Jacques Cardon et Pierre Cavellat, 1623, folio.
82 *Las obras de xenophon, un tomo.*
    Xenophon, unidentified work.

Libros en quarto mayor y menor (Books in quarto, large and small)

83 *Henrici Seduli Apologeticus, un tomo.*
    Sedulius, Henricus (O.F.M.) (1547–1621): *F. Henrici Seduli[i] ex Ordine Minorum Apologeticus aduersus Alcoranum Franciscanorum, pro Libro Conformitatum Libri Tres*, unidentified edition.
    It could be USTC No. 1009767: Antwerpen, ex officina Plantiniana apud Joannem Moretum, 1607, 4°.[83]
84 *Disputationum libri duo, un tomo.*
    Hay, John (S.I.) (1546–1607): *Disputationum libri duo, in quibus calumniae et captiones ministri anonymi Nemausensis, contra assertiones theologicas &*

---

81 We think that this is possibly a work with commentaries on Saint Thomas Aquinas: *Expositio commentaria in primam [-tertiam] partem Angelici doctoris sancti Thomae*, unidentified edition.
82 There are several works with this title, with a wide variety of authors and topics.
83 One copy in BUS, A Biblioteca Palatina D142/D144, Antwerpen, Moretus, 1607, 4°.

philosophicas in Academia Turnonia, anno M.D. LXXXII propositas, discutiuntur..., unidentified edition.

It could be USTC No. 142101: Lyons, excudebat Jacques Roussin apud Jean Pillehotte, 1584, 4°.

85 *Justi Lipsij Diva Virgo hallensis, un tomo.*

Lipsio, Justo (1547–1606): *I. Lipsii Diva Virgo Hallensis Beneficia eius & Miracula...*, unidentified edition.

It could be several editions: USTC Nos 1004718, 1003260, 1540698, 1003191.

86 *Totius Logiceé paripateticee cursus* [sic, for *corpus*], *un tomo.*

Faber, Johannes Rodolphus (1580–1650): *Totius logicae peripateticae corpus ... nec-non totius organi Aristotelico-Ramaei compendium, perspicuis quaestionibus et exemplis methodicé expositum, et exacté ac fideliter conciliatum*, Geneuae [Geneva], apud viudam et haeredes Petri de la Rouiere, 1623.

CCPB000949682-3.

87 *Joannis de Roias, un tomo.*

Unidentified work.

88 *Privilegia mendicantium, un tomo.*

a Virgine Maria, Augustino (O.C.D.): *Privilegia omnium religiosorum ordinum mendicantium et non Mendicantium, in quibus ipsi communicant...*, unidentified edition.

89 *Epimetron aphoris morum politicorum, un tomo.*

de Chokier, Jean (1571–c. 1650): *Epimetron sive auctarium thesauri aphorismorum politicorum, hoc est quaestionum politicarum seu de administrandae Reipublicae ratione libri tres...*, unidentified edition.

90 *Bellum Belgicum de Gamurino, un tomo.*

Gamurini, Giuseppe: *Bellum Belgicum, siue Belgicarum rerum, e commentariis Pompei Iustiniani peditatus Italici tribuni, e confilijs Bellicis Regis Catholici libri sex, supplemento auctoris aucti*, Coloninæ Agrippinæ [Cologne], Apud Joannem Kinckium, 1611.

CUL, P.5.63

91 *Granatus de mimaculata* [sic] *Conceptione, un tomo.*

Granado, Diego o Jacobo (S.I.) (1572–1632): *De Immaculata B. V. Dei Genitricis M. Conceptione sive De singulari illius immunitate ab originali peccato, per Iesu Christi filii eius cumulatisimam Redemptionem: liber unus*, Sevilla, apud Franciscum de Lyra..., 1617.

CCPB000036946-2; USTC No. 5007813.

92 *Advertencia a la Historia de mañana* [sic, instead of *Mariana*], *un tomo.*

Mantuano, Pedro (1585–1656): *Advertencias a la Historia del Padre Iuan de Mariana de la Compañia de Iesus...: impressa en Toledo en latin, año de 1592 y en romance el de 1601, en que se enmienda gran parte de la Historia de España...*, unidentified edition.

It might be USTC No. 5022777: Madrid, Imprenta Real, 1613, 4°.

93 *Pedro de Valderrama, exercicios espirituales, dos tomos.*

Valderrama, Pedro de (O.S.A.) (1550–1611): *Primera parte de los ejercicios espirituales para todos los dias de la quaresma...*, unidentified edition.[84]

94 *Sandijs voage en flamenco, un tomo.*
It could possibly be: *Sandijs, Voyagien in het Turkische rijk, Egypte enz.*, Amsterdam, 1653.
Veilingcatalogus, register 251.[85]

95 *Capata de Justicia Distributiva, un tomo.*
Fratris Ioannis Capata [sic] *y Sandoual augustiniani ... De iustitia distributiua & acceptione personarum ei opposita disceptatio: pro noui indiarum orbis rerum moderatoribus summisque & regalibus consiliarijs elaborata...*, Valladolid, excudebat Christophorus Lasso Vaca, 1609.
CCPB000042823-X.

[fol. 663ᵛ]

96 *Summa de tratos y Contratos, un tomo.*
de Mercado, Fray Tomás (O.P.) (1523–1575): *Summa de tratos y contratos compuesta por ... Fray Thomas de Mercado de la Orden de los Predicadores...; diuidida en seys libros...*, unidentified edition.

97 *Dictionario flamenco y franzes, un tomo.*[86]

98 *J: nider de Reformatione Religiosorum, un tomo.*
Nider, Johannes (O.P.) (c. 1380–1438): *R. P. F. Ioannis Nider Ordinis Praedicatorum Theologi De reformatione religiosorum libri tres*, unidentified edition.

99 *Sermones del Padre Roxas, un tomo.*
Pérez de Rojas, Juan (O.Merced.): *Sermones de las dominicas de pentecostes. / Por ... Iuan Perez de Rojas ... del ordè de nuestra señora de la Merced redeciò de cautivos...; con elenco para predicar todos los demas euangelicos del año*, Ecija, por Simon Faxardo, 1624.
CCPB000211058-X; USTC No. 5008959.

---

84 We know of one edition of this collection of sermons which was printed in the Saint Augustine convent in Seville in 1602 by Francisco Pérez; it was so successful that the first and second parts were republished in 1604 (Francisco Pérez, Sevilla, 1604, CCPB000049024–5, 4º; Luis Sanchez, Madrid, año 1604) and then the third part was published in 1605 in Madrid by the printer Juan Flamenco (Palau, *Manual del librero hispanoamericano*, pp. 479–80).

85 The first edition in English: *A relation of a journey begun An: Dom: 1610. Foure bookes. Containing a description of the Turkish empire, of AEgypt, etc.*, W. Barrett, 1615, Short-title England, reg. 21726.

86 There are at least two possible identifications: *Dictionario. Coloquios, o dialogos en quatro lenguas, Flamenco, Frances, Español y Italiano ... En Anvers, Chez Iean Coesmans, sus le Cimetiere de nostre Dame, 1582, 16º*, CCPB000770313–9, and: *Diccionario coloquios o dialogos en quatro lenguas, latyn flamenco, francés y español: con las conjugaçiones, y insteuccions* [sic]*, en que se contiene la manera de ... pronunciar y leer las dichas lenguas ... A Bruxelles, chez Iean Mommaert, 1624, 16º*, CCPB000046365–5.

100 *Epitome de la nueva recopilacion y practica del fuero Ynterior del Padre Alonso de Vega, un tomo.*
de la Vega, Fray Alonso (Mínimos): *Epitome o compendio de la suma: llamada nueva recopilacion y pratica del fuero interior del P. F. Alonso de Vega, de la sagrada religion de los Minimos...*, Madrid, por Luis Sanchez, 1610.
CCPB000048988-3; USTC No. 5005545.

101 *Reglas de la Santa Charidad, un tomo.*
Regla de la insigne Hermandad de la Santa Caridad de N. Señor Jesu Christo, Sevilla, por Juan Francisco de Blas..., 1671.
CCPB000034206-8.

102 *Questiones practicas de casos morales, un tomo.*
Enríquez, Juan (O.S.A.): *Questiones practicas de casos morales*, unidentified edition.[87]

103 *Historia Bataviee, un tomo.*
Junius, Hadrianus, o de Jonge, Adriaen (1511-1575): *Batavia. In qua praeter gentis et insulae antiquitatem, originem ... aliaque ad eam historiam pertinentia, declaratur quae fuerit vetus Batavia...quae item genuina inclytae Francorum natonis fuerit sedes ... [Historia Bataviae]*, unidentified edition.
It might be: USTC No. 422668.

104 *El embaxador, por Don Juan Antonio Vera y Zuñiga, un tomo.*
Vera y Zúñiga, Juan Antonio (1583-1658): *El enbaxador: dividido en cuatro discursos*, Sevilla, Francisco de Lyra, 1620.
CCPB000042768-3.

105 *Laurea Evangelica, un tomo.*
Manrique, Ángel (O. Císter.): *Laurea evangelica: hecha de varios discursos predicables: con tabla para todos los Sanctos, y Dominicas de entre año...*, unidentified edition.
It might be USTC No. 5006898.

106 *Ludovici molina, un tomo.*
de Molina, Luis (S.I.) (1535-1600): unidentified work.

107 *Palinodia Religionis preetensee Reformatee, un tomo.*
Porter, Francis (O.F.M.) (1650-1702): *Palinodia religionis praetensae reformatae suam reformationem per propria principia reprobantis, & ex eisdem prpincipijs fatentis ... opus in duas partes diuisum*, Roma, typis, & sumptib. Nicolai Angeli Tinassij, 1679.
CCPB000479890-2.

108 *Compendium Constitutionum Summorum Pontificum, un tomo.*
Castellani, Giacomo: *Compendium Constitutionum Summorum Pontificum quae extant a Gregorio VII usque ad Clementem VIII...*, unidentified edition.[88]

---

[87] It might be USTC No. 5039571: Córdoba, por Salvador Cea Tesa, 1646.
[88] There is one edition from Turin, by Dominicum Tarinum, 1604 (USTC No. 4034495; CCPB000053965-1), and another from Venice in the same year by Franciscum Bolzettam (USTC No. 4036730; CCPB000122810-2).

109 *Dignitas Philosophie acclamata, un tomo.*
Muñana, José de (O.P.): *Dignitas philosophiae acclamata et vindicata / a Reverendo Patre lectore Iosepho de Muñana, hispalensi sacri ordinis praedicatorum...; opusculum omnibus, & singulis sapientiae cultoribus utilissimum...*, Sevilla, apud Ioannem de la Puerta..., 1702.
CCPB000944606-0.

110 *Floro Historico, Cinco tomos.*
Fabro Bremundán, Francisco (1621–1698):[89]
a) *Floro historico de la guerra movida por el sultan de los turcos Mehemet IV contra ... Leopoldo primero ... el año MDCLXXXIII*, Madrid, Imprenta de Bernardo de Villadiego, 1684.
CCPB000035449-X.
b) *Floro historico de la guerra sagrada contra turcos: segunda parte, que contiene los sucessos de los años MDCLXXXIV y MDCLXXXV*, Madrid, en la imprenta de Antonio Roman: a expensas de Sebastian de Armendariz ..., 1686.
CCPB000035451-1.
c) *Floro historico de la guerra sagrada contra turcos: tercera parte, que contiene los sucesos del año MDCLXXXVI*, Madrid, en la imprenta de Antonio Román: a expensas de Sebastián de Armendáriz..., 1687.
CCPB000035452-X.
d) *Floro historico de la guerra sagrada contra turcos: quarta parte, que contiene los sucessos del año MDCLXXXVII*, Madrid, Antonio Roman, 1688.
CCPB000035453-8.
e) *Floro historico de la guerra sagrada contra turcos: quinta parte que contiene los sucessos del año MDCLXXXVIII*, Madrid, Antonio Roman, 1690.
CCPB000035454-6.

111 *Arnooldo Van Gelve* [sic, for *Gelre*], *en flamenco, un tomo.*
van Egmont, Arnold, Hertog van Gelre en Graaf van Zutphen (1410–1473): unidentified work.[90]

112 *Dictionario Latin y aleman, un tomo.*
Unidentified work.

113 *Tratado de comercio de España, en flamenco, dos tomos.*[91]
Unidentified work.

---

89 Fabro translated the work in Italian and published it in five volumes between 1684 and 1690, changing its name in the second volume into *Floro historico de la guerra sagrada contra turcos*.
90 Arnold van Gelre made a pilgrimage to the Holy Land in 1450. The Koninklijke Bibliotheek in The Hague has a manuscript with the account, *Vanden gestant des Heiligen Landes*, written by Jan van Egmond (The Hague, Koninklijke Bibliotheek, KW 75 H 36).
91 Maybe this is the work *Handelsverdrag met Spanje* (Trade agreement with Spain), c. 1700. Amsterdam, Nederlandsch Economisch-Historisch Archief (NEHA), Bijzondere Collecties: 593.

114 *R. P. Fr. Thomaee a Ojesu Carmelita, quatro tomos.*
   de Jesús, Fray Tomás (O.C.D.) (1523–1627): unidentified work.[92]
115 *Summa Philosophiee, Dos tomos.*
   Unidentified work.
116 *Palma fiedei, un tomo.*
   Malpoeus, J. Petrus (O.P.): *Palma fidei S. Ordinis predicatorum / descriptore F. Petro Malpaeo eiusdem ordinis quondam priore Bruxell.*, Antwerpen, ex typographia Ioannis Cnobbari, 1635.
   CCPB000309552–5.
117 *R. P. Ricardus Archdekin, un tomo.*
   Archdeacon, Richard (S.I.) (1620–1693): unidentified work.[93]
118 *Parayso de la Gloria de los Santos, dos tomos.*
   de la Vega, Diego (O.F.M.): *Parayso de la gloria de los santos: donde se trata de sus prerrogativas y excelencias*, unidentified edition.
119 *Ynstruction de Saserdotes por fr. Antonio de Molina, un tomo.*
   de Molina, Antonio (O. Cart.): *Instruccion de sacerdotes: en que se les da doctrina ... para conocer la alteza del ... oficio sacerdotal y para exercitarles debidamente...*, unidentified edition.
120 *Catholiken pedagoge, en flamenco, un tomo.*
   vanden Bossche, Petrus (O.P.) (1634–1690): *Den katholyken pedagoge, ofte Christelyken onderwyzer in den catechismus...*, unidentified edition.[94]
121 *Controvercias del Padre Hasart, Cinco tomos.*
   Hazart, Cornelius (S.I.) (1617–1690): unidentified work.
122 *Theologia de la Rat. siete tomos.*

---

92 There is no work written by Fray Tomás de Jesús in four volumes; his *opera omnia* only has two volumes. Therefore, maybe this entry is related to several separate works by this author. He wrote about the conversion of schismatics, heretics, Jews and Muslims, and these books (published in Antwerp) are very much related to the other works of controversy and about heretics contained in this library. They are: *De procuranda salute omnium gentium, schismaticorum, haereticorum, Iudaeorum ... libri XII...: accedit pro laborantibus inter infideles breuis casuum resolutio, gratiarum ac priuilegiorum compendium & pro conversis catechismus*, Antwerpen, sumptibus viduae & haeredum Petri Belleri..., 1613, 4º, CCPB000234338-X; and the *Thesaurus sapientiae diuinae, in gentium omnium salute procuranda: Schimasticorum, haereticorum, iudaeorum, sarracenorum, caeterorumq[ue], infidelium errores demonstrans*, Antwerpen, sumptibus Viduae & haeredum Petri Belleri..., 1613, 4º, CCPB000253957–8.

93 This author wrote books about different topics, and we can note between them one about religious controversy: *R.P. Richardi Arsdekin Soc. Iesu ... Theologiae Tripartitae tomus tertius: qui est Apparatus doctrinae sacrae: complectens materiam & formam expeditam, pro quavis dictione, concione, & tota catechesi, per exquisitam expositionem, & selectissima exempla: cum praxi solida assistendi per omnia aegris, & sanis ...* Cologne, sumptibus Henrici Rommerskirchen, 1730, 4º, CCPB000206719–6.

94 One copy is today in the Erfgoedbibliotheek Hendrik Conscience, in Antwerpen, c:lvd:13275181. One version of this book was published in Latin, and this was widely used: *Paedagogus Catholicus in quinque partes distributus*, Antwerpen, Henrici van Dunwalt, 1690, 4º, in *Scriptores ordinis Praedicatorum recensiti*, ed. by Quetif & Echard, II, p. 727.

Unidentified work.
123 *Los Sphalmos en latin y frances, un tomo.*
Loriot, Julien (1633–1715) (Cong. Oratorio); Quesnel, Pasquier (1634–1719) (Cong. Oratorio): *Les Pseaumes de David: en latin & en françois avec des reflexions morales sur chaque verset …*, unidentified edition.
124 *Otros tres, quasi la misma materia.*[95]
125 *Theologia Buscembaum, un tomo.*
Busembaum, Hermann (S.I.) (1600–1668): *Medulla theologiae moralis…*, unidentified work.
126 *Dictionarium teutonico = latinum, un tomo.*
van Kiel, Cornelis; also Kiliaan, Cornelis (1528–1607): *Etymologicum Teutonicae linguae: sive Dictionarium Teutonico-Latinum, praecipuas Teutonicae linguae dictiones et phrases Latine interpretatas, & cum aliis nonnullis linguis obiter collatas complectens …*, unidentified edition.[96]
127 *Summula de Peccatis Cardinalis Cayetani, un tomo.*
De Vio, Tommaso (1469–1534): *Summula Caietani Summula de peccatis Reverendissimi Domini Thomae de Vio Caietani Cardinalis*, unidentified edition.
128 *Arte dada del miso Dios a Abraham, un tomo.*
Solís, Rodrigo de (O.S.A.) (1583): *Arte dada del mismo Dios a Abraham para le servir perfectamente*, unidentified edition.

[fol. 664ʳ]

129 *Archombrotus et Theopompus, un tomo.*
Bugnot, Gabriel: *Archombrotus et Theopompus sive Argenidis … secunda & tertia pars, ubi de institutione principis*, unidentified edition.[97]
130 *Defensa de la Historia de mañana [sic, for Mariana], un tomo.*
Tamayo de Vargas, Tomás (1589–1641): *Historia general de España del P. D. Iuan de Mariana defendida por el Doctor Don Thomas Tamaio de Vargas contra las aduertencias de Pedro Mantuano*, unidentified edition.
It might be USTC No. 5025586: Toledo, s.n., 1616.
131 *Apologia perfectionis, un tomo.*

---

95 The book cited in the preceding reference has three volumes, and besides there is another one with a very similar title to the work written by Macé, (*Les psaumes de David et les cantiques de l'église en latin et en françois* [Paris: André Palard, 1706]). For these reasons, it is very difficult to identify this work.

96 In this reference the title referred to in the third edition from 1599 on appears, although the first edition's title in 1574 was *Dictionarium Teutonicum Latinum*. With every new edition, Kiliaan enlarged the dictionary, and this makes it very difficult to identify exactly which edition we have in the library.

97 The first edition is: Lugd. Batau. et Roterod [Leiden and Rotterdam], ex officina Hackiana, 1669, 8°, CCPB000045285-8. It is the continuation of a political satire about religious events in the reigns of Henry III and Henry IV of France, whose original title is *Argenis*; its author is the Franco-Scottish John Barclay (1582–1621), who stands up for royal power (Archombrotus is Louis XIV) against the traps and interests of the nobility.

Nicolaus a Iesu Maria (O.C.D.): *Apologia perfectionis vitae spiritualis siuè Propugnaculum religionum omnium, sed maxime' mendicantium contrà Epistolam theologi cuisdam...*, unidentified edition.
It might be USTC No. 5019113: Barcelona, imprenta Pedro de Lacavallería, 1629.

132 *Vetus et novi Belgi historia, un tomo.*
Heuterus (de Huyter), Pontus (1535–1602): *Veteris ac novi Belgi[i] historia. In qua antiquarum Prouinciarum eius nomina, Flumina, Fontes, Decurssus, ac Ostia describuntur / Per Pontum Heuterum Delphium*, unidentified edition.
It might be USTC No. 1005503: Antwerpen, apud Jan I van Keerberghen [typ. Hendrik Swingen], 1605.

133 *Homildee fratris Hironimi Sabonarolee, un tomo.*
Savonarola, Jerónimo (O.P.) (1452–1498): unidentified work.

Libros en octavo y en medio (Books in octavo and in 'medium')

134 *Ynstruction Christiana en flamenco, un tomo.*
It could be USTC No. 1022680: Dionysius Spranckhuysen, *Christelycke instructie voor de nieuw-ghehoudene N.N*, Delft, Felix van Sambix, 1635, 12°.

135 *Decreta promulgata in sinodo Cremonensi prima, un tomo.*
Decreta et acta edita et promulgata In Synodo Diocesana Cremonensi, prima, quam Caesar Specianus Episcopus Cremonensis habuit: Additis nonnullis constitutionibus, & decretis Apostolicis, & Edictis Episcopalibus, unidentified edition.

136 *Libro de Sirugia en Latin, un tomo.*
Unidentified work.

137 *Onomastica onzena, un tomo.*
Unidentified work.

138 *Phrase linguee latinee, un tomo.*
Schoro, Antonio (S.I.): *Phrases linguae latinae e diversis ciceronis operibus collectae* ... unidentified edition.

139 *Timanno a Kuijck, un tomo.*
Tilleman Kuyck: unidentified work.[98]

140 *Olla de los herejes en flamenco, un tomo.*

141 *de Oficio principis de Belarminio, un tomo.*
Belarmino, Santo Roberto (S.I.) (1542–1621): *De officio principis christiani: libri tres* ... unidentified edition.
It might be USTC No. 4026747: Rome, typis Bartolomeo Zannetti, 1619

142 *Calendario perpetuo de la Orden de Santo Domingo, un tomo.*
Gutierrez, Juan (O.P.): *Calendario perpetuo conforme al instituto de la orden de nuestro glorioso P. S. Domingo, segun la costumbre desta provincia de Andaluzia: en el qual se añaden todos los santos de quien en particular la dicha prouincia reza en el discurso del año*, Sevilla, en casa de Iuan de Leon, 1598.

---

98 This author published several works on legal subjects.

USTC No. 335256; CCPB000302430-X.

143 *Ynterrogationes Clericorum, un tomo.*
Mena, Pedro de (O.Minim.): *Interrogationes clericorum primae tonsurae, &, promovendorum ad sacros ordines, & curam animaru & ad audienda, confessiones...*, unidentified edition.
It might be USTC No. 5006003: Burgos, apud Juan Bautista Varesio, 1602.

144 *Regula Cleri de jacobo Planat, un tomo.*
Planat, Jacques: *Regula cleri seu magisterium clerici*, unidentified edition.
It might be CCPB000211130-6: Sevilla, ex typograph. Lucae Martini da Hermosilla, [s.a.].

145 *Adolesens prodigus, un tomo.*
Scribani, Carolus (S.I.) (1561–1629): *Caroli Scribani e Societate Iesu adolescens prodigus*, unidentified edition.
It might be USTC No. 1003751: Antwerpen, apud Martinus III Nutius and fratres, 1621.

146 *de Arte Bene moriendi de Belarminio, un tomo.*
Bellarmino, Santo Roberto (S.I.) (1542–1621): *De arte bene moriendi libri duo*, unidentified edition.
It might be USTC No. 1009377: Antwerpen, ex officina Plantiniana apud Balthasar I Moretus and Jan II Moretus and Jan van Meurs, 1623.

147 *de Septem vervis a xristo in cruse prolatis de Belarminio, un tomo.*
Bellarmino, Santo Roberto (S.I.) (1542–1621): *De septem verbis a christo in cruce prolatis: libri duo*, unidentified edition.
It might be USTC No. 1005146: Antwerpen, ex officina Plantiniana apud Balthasar I Moretus, 1618.

148 *Davidicum gloriosissimi nominis Dei oficiolum, un tomo.*
Dominicus Janssenius Boy [Boij] (O.P.): *Davidicum gloriosissimi nominis Dei officiolum: ex ejusdem psalterio in exercitium Sodalitij Jesu apud ff. ordinis Prædicatorum collectum...*, unidentified edition.

149 *Padre fr. Ysidoro Lopez, versos sobre la passion de Nuestro Señor, un tomo.*
López, Isidoro (O.P.): *Passio Domini nostri Jesu Christi: de sacrorum quatuor evangelistarum dictis deprompta & elegiaci carminis numeris accommodata...*, unidentified edition.
It might be CCPB000669161-7: Sevilla, apud Franciscum Sanchez..., 1721.

150 *Epitome de Statu Religionis, un tomo.*
de la Cruz, San Juan (O.P.): *Epitome de statu religionis, et de priuilegijs, quibus a summis Pontificibus est decoratus...*, unidentified edition.
It might be USTC No. 5014851: Madrid, ex officina Cosme Delgado, 1613.

151 *Medicus Religiosus Caroli Scribani, un tomo.*
Scribani, Carolus (S.I.) (1561–1629): *Caroli Scribani e Societate Iesu Medicus religiosus de animorum morbis et curationibus...*, unidentified edition.
It might be USTC No. 1003684: Antwerpen, apud heirs of Martinus II Nutius, 1618.

152 *Basis totius moralis Theologiae, un tomo.*

Mercorum, Jules (O.P.): *Basis totius moralis theologiae: hoc est praxis opinionum limitata*... unidentified edition.[99]

153 *Summa Sacramentorum, un tomo.*
Vitoria, Francisco de (O.P.) (1483–1546): *Summa Sacramentorum Ecclesiae, ex doctrina R.P.F. Francisci a Victoria...*, unidentified edition.

154 *Tractatus de oficio peenitentis, un tomo.*
Reginaldus, Valerius [Valère Regnault] (S.I.) (1545–1623): *Tractatus de officio poenitentis in usu Sacramenti Poenitentia...*, multiple editions.

155 *M: Tullij Ciceronis volumina, tres tomos.*
Marco Tullius Cicero: unidentified work.[100]

156 *Henningi Doctrina politica, un tomo.*
Arnisaeus, Henning (1580–1636): *Arnisaei Henningi Doctrina politica in genuinam methodum Aristotelis*, unidentified edition.[101]

157 *Gimnasium patientiee, un tomo.*
Drexel, Jeremia (S.I.) (1581–1638): *Gymnasium patientiae*, unidentified edition.

158 *Hieremias Drexelio e Societate Ojesu, quatro tomos.*
Drexel, Jeremia (S.I.) (1581–1638): unidentified edition.[102]

159 *Manual de Confesores, Ympreso en Am*[fol. 664ᵛ]*berez, muy antiguo, un tomo.*
Unidentified work.

Abbreviations:

BUS: Biblioteca de la Universidad de Sevilla.
CCPB: Catálogo Colectivo del Patrimonio Bibliográfico Español.
CUL: Cambridge University Library.

Works Cited

Manuscripts and Archival Sources

Madrid, Archivo Histórico Nacional, State Section, file 610/21
——, Consejos Section, file 25438/1

---

99 The same author and book appear in the reference 59.
100 Adding the word 'voluminá' the first edition that we find is *M. T. Ciceronis, volumina tria*, divided in three volumes, all of which were printed by Johannes Sturm, Argentorati, Rihelius, 1540.
101 The first edition is from Johann Eichorn, Frankfurt am Oder, 1606, 4°.
102 It is not possible to determine which of Drexel's works there are, although his *opera omnia* is composed precisely by four volumes, but is *in folio*.

Seville, Archivo Histórico Provincial de Sevilla, Notarial Protocols of Seville, file 14673
―――, Notarial Protocols of Seville, file 14674

Primary Sources

Seville, Biblioteca de la Universidad de Sevilla, A 109/101 (17): Francisco Gonzálvez Príncipe, *Manifiesto jurídico que hace la nación flamenca que reside en esta ciudad para el pleyto que con ella sigue el Colegio Mayor de Santo Tomás* (n.p. n.d. [c. 1705?])
―――, A 111/124 (61): *Nueva defensa jurídica, que hace la Nación Flamenca, que reside en esta ciudad para el pleito que se si gue con el Colegio Mayor de Santo Thomas*
―――, A 111/124 (3): *D. LUIS DOYE, VEZINO DE / esta Ciudad* (printed c. 1731)
Veen, Otto van, *Quinti Horatii Flacci Emblemata*, ed. by Paloma Fanconi Villar (Villaviciosa de Odón: Universidad Europea de Madrid, 1996)

Secondary Studies

Abadía Flores, Carolina, 'La comunidad flamenca en Sevilla en el siglo XVI', *Archivo Hispalense*, 282–84 (2010), 173–92
Álvarez de Toledo y Pineda, Guillermo, 'Un linaje de origen flamenco afincado en Sevilla: los Licht', *Tavira*, 8 (1991), 69–82
Aguilar Piñal, Francisco, *Bibliografía de autores españoles del siglo XVIII: tomo IX* (Madrid: CSIC, 1999)
Baños, Pedro M., ed., *El arte epistolar en el Renacimiento europeo, 1400–1600* (Bilbao: Universidad de Deusto, 2005)
Barbosa Machado, Diogo, *Bibliotheca Lusitana* (Coimbra: Atlântida editora, 1966)
Bécares Botas, Vicente, ed., *Arias Montano y Plantino. El libro flamenco en la España de Felipe II* (León: Universidad de León, 1999)
Bietenholz, Peter T., and Thomas D. Deutscher, eds, *Contemporaries of Erasmus: A Biographical Register of the Renaissance and Reformation*, III (Toronto: University of Toronto, 1987)
Boeglin, Michel, *L'Inquisition espagnole au lendemain du Concile de Trente: le tribunal du Saint-Office de Séville (1560–1700)* (Montpellier: Université de Montpellier, 2003)
Bustos Rodríguez, Manuel, 'Le consulat des Flamands à Cadix après la Paix d'Utrecht (1713–1730): Jacques Vermolen', in *Orbis in Orbem. Liber amicorum John Everaert*, ed. by Jan Parmentier and Sander Spanhoge (Ghent: Universiteit Gent Academia Press, 2001), pp. 109–32
Crailsheim, Eberhard, *The Spanish Connection: French and Flemish Networks in Seville (1570–1650)* (Cologne: Böhlau, 2016)

Crespo Solana, Ana, *Entre Cádiz y los Países Bajos. Una comunidad mercantil en la ciudad de la Ilustración* (Cádiz: Ayuntamiento de Cádiz, 2001)

——, 'El patronato de la nación flamenca gaditana en los siglos XVII y XVIII: trasfondo social y económico de una institución piadosa', *Studia Historica. Historia Moderna*, 24 (2002), 297–329

——, 'Nación extranjera y cofradía de mercaderes: el rostro piadoso de la integración social' in *Los extranjeros en la España Moderna*, II, ed. by María Begoña Villar García and Pilar Pezzi Cristóbal (Málaga: Universidad de Málaga, 2003), pp. 175–87

——, ed., *Comunidades transnacionales: colonias de mercaderes extranjeros en el mundo atlántico (1500–1830)* (Madrid: Doce Calles, 2010)

——, 'El juez conservador ¿Una alternativa al cónsul de la nación?', in *Los cónsules de extranjeros en la Edad Moderna y principios de la Edad Contemporánea*, ed. by Marcella Aglietti, Manuel Herrero Sánchez, and Francisco J. Zamora Rodríguez (Madrid: Doce Calles, 2013), pp. 23–33

Crespo Solana, Ana, and Vicente Montojo Montojo, 'La Junta de Dependencias de Extranjeros (1714–1800): Trasfondo socio-político de una historia institucional', *Hispania*, 69.232 (2009), 363–94

De Sotomayor, Antonio, *Index librorum prohibitorum et expurgandorum novissimvs* (Madrid: Diego Díaz, 1667)

Díaz Blanco, José Manuel, 'La familia del bibliógrafo sevillano Nicolás Antonio', in *Testigo del tiempo, memoria del universo*, ed. by Manuel F. Fernández Chaves, Carlos A. González Sánchez, and Natalia Maillard Álvarez (Barcelona: Rubeo, 2009), pp. 223–49

——, 'La construcción de una institución comercial: el consulado de las naciones flamenca y alemana en la Sevilla moderna', *Revista de Historia Moderna*, 33 (2015), 123–45

Díaz Blanco, José Manuel, and Manuel Fernández Chaves, 'Una élite en la sombra: los comerciantes extranjeros en la Sevilla de Felipe III', in *Las élites en la Época Moderna: la monarquía española*, ed. by Enrique Soria Mesa, Juan Jesús Bravo Caro, and José Miguel Delgado Barrado, III (Córdoba: Universidad de Córdoba, 2009), pp. 35–50

Diccionario Histórico de la Compañía de Jesús. Biográfico-temático, ed. by Charles E. O'Neill and Joaquín María Domínguez (Madrid: Universidad Pontificia de Comillas, 2001)

Domínguez Ortiz, Antonio, *Los extranjeros en la vida española y otros artículos* (Seville: Diputación de Sevilla, 1996)

——, 'Documentos sobre los mercaderes flamencos establecidos en Sevilla a comienzos del siglo XVIII', in *Homenaje a Antonio Matilla Tascón*, ed. by José A. Casquero Fernández (Zamora: Diputación Provincial de Zamora, 2002), pp. 151–60

Escudero y Perosso, Francisco, *Tipografía Hispalense. Anales bibliográficos de la ciudad de Sevilla* (Seville: Ayuntamiento de Sevilla, 1999)

Everaert, John G., 'Infraction au monopole? Cargadores-navegantes flamands sur la Carrera de Indias (XVII siècle)', in *La Casa de Contratación y la navegación entre España y las Indias*, ed. by Enriqueta Vila Vilar, Antonio Acosta Rodríguez, and Antonio L. González Rodríguez (Seville: Universidad de Sevilla/CSIC, 2004), pp. 761–75

Fernández Chaves, Manuel F., Rafael M. Pérez García, and Béatrice Perez, eds, *Mercaderes y redes mercantiles en la Península Ibérica. Siglos XV–XVIII* (Seville: Editorial Universidad de Sevilla, 2019)

Fondos y procedencias en la Biblioteca de la Universidad de Sevilla, ed. by Eduardo Peñalver Gómez (Seville: Universidad de Sevilla, 2013)

Gamero Rojas, Mercedes, 'La mujer flamenca del mundo de los negocios en la Sevilla del siglo XVIII', in *Agentes e identidades en movimiento. España y los Países Bajos, siglos XVI–XVIII*, ed. by René Vermeir, Maurits Ebben, and Raymond Fagel (Madrid: Sílex, 2011), pp. 351–71

——, 'Flamencos en la Sevilla del siglo XVII. La capilla y el Hospital de San Andrés', in *Comercio y cultura en la Edad Moderna. Actas de la XIII Reunión Científica de la Fundación Española de Historia Moderna*, ed. by Juan José Iglesias Rodríguez, Rafael M. Pérez García, and Manuel F. Fernández Chaves (Seville: Editorial de la Universidad de Sevilla, 2015), pp. 1025–40

——, 'Flamencos en el siglo XVII. Actividades económicas entre Europa y América', in *Andalucía en el mundo atlántico moderno. Agentes y escenarios*, ed. by Juan J. Iglesias Rodríguez and J. Jaime García Bernal (Madrid: Sílex, 2016), pp. 287–310

——, 'Los hombres de negocios flamencos ante la guerra de Sucesión y el cambio de dinastía, 1680–1730', in *Andalucía en el mundo atlántico moderno. Ciudades y redes*, ed. by Juan J. Iglesias Rodríguez, J. Jaime García Bernal, and José M. Díaz Blanco (Madrid: Sílex, 2018), pp. 369–95

Gamero Rojas, Mercedes, and Fernández Chaves, Manuel F., 'Flamencos en la Sevilla del siglo XVIII: entre el Norte de Europa y América', in *Orbis Incognitvs. Avisos y legajos del Nuevo Mundo*, ed. by Francisco Navarro Antolín, II (Huelva: Universidad de Huelva, 2009), pp. 211–20

García Bernal, Jaime, and Mercedes Gamero Rojas, 'Las corporaciones de nación en la Sevilla moderna. Fundaciones, redes asistenciales y formas de sociabilidad', in *Las corporaciones de nación en la monarquía hispánica (1580–1750). Identidad, patronazgo y redes de sociabilidad*, ed. by Bernardo J. García García and Óscar Recio Morales (Madrid: Fundación Carlos de Amberes, 2014), pp. 347–87

García García, Bernardo J., 'La Nación Flamenca en la corte española y el Real Hospital de San Andrés ante la crisis sucesoria (1606–1706)', in *La pérdida de Europa. La guerra de Sucesión por la Monarquía de España*, ed. by Antonio Álvarez-Ossorio, Bernardo J. García García, and Virginia León Sanz (Madrid: Fundación Carlos de Amberes, Ministerio de Cultura, 2007), pp. 379–442

Girard, Albert, *El comercio francés en Sevilla y Cádiz en tiempos de los Habsburgo. Contribución al estudio del comercio extranjero en la España de los siglos xvi al xviii* (Seville: Centro de Estudios Andaluces/Renacimiento, 2006)

Gutiérrez Nuñez, Francisco Javier, 'Nicolás de Omazur Ullens, de Amberes a Sevilla (1641–1698). El primer coleccionista de Murillo', *Anuario de Hespérides. Investigaciones científicas e innovaciones didácticas*, 23–24 (2017), 251–74

Iglesias Rodríguez, Juan J., J. Jaime García Bernal, and José M. Díaz Blanco, eds, *Andalucía en el mundo atlántico moderno. Ciudades y redes* (Madrid: Sílex, 2018)

Jiménez Montes, Germán 'La comunidad flamenca en Sevilla durante el reinado de Felipe II y su papel en las redes mercantiles antuerpienses', in *Comercio y cultura en la Edad Moderna. Actas de la XIII Reunión Científica de la Fundación Española de Historia Moderna*, ed. by Juan José Iglesias Rodríguez, Rafael M. Pérez García, and Manuel F. Fernández Chaves (Seville: Editorial de la Universidad de Sevilla, 2015), pp. 353–66

———, 'Los inicios de una nación. Mercaderes flamencos en Sevilla durante el reinado de Felipe II', in *Andalucía en el mundo atlántico moderno. Agentes y escenarios*, ed. by Juan J. Iglesias Rodríguez and J. Jaime García Bernal (Madrid: Sílex, 2016), pp. 215–41

———, 'Sevilla, puerto y puerta de Europa: la actividad de una compañía comercial flamenca en la segunda mitad del siglo xvi', *Studia Historica, Historia Moderna*, 38.2 (2016), 353–86

———, *A Dissimulated Trade: Northern European Timber Merchants in Seville (1574–1598)* (Leiden: Brill, 2022)

Lombaerde, Piet, 'Los tratados de artillería, guerra y fortificación realizados en los Países Bajos meridionales', in *Un mundo sobre papel. Libros y grabados flamencos en el imperio Hispanoportugués (siglos xvi–xviii)*, ed. by Werner Thomas and Eddy Stols (Leuven: Acco, 2009), pp. 339–49

Márquez Redondo, Ana Gloria, *Sevilla 'ciudad y Corte' (1729–1733)* (Seville: Ayuntamiento de Sevilla, 2013)

Medina, Francisco de Borja, 'El colegio inglés de San Gregorio Magno de Sevilla', *Archivo Teológico Granadino*, 62 (1999), 77–106

Morgado García, Arturo, 'Los manuales de confesores en la España del siglo xviii', *Cuadernos Dieciochistas*, 5 (2004), 123–45

Murphy, Martin, 'Irish Students and Merchants in Seville', in *Los extranjeros en la España Moderna*, ed. by María B. Villar García and María del Pilar Pezzi Cristóbal, ii (Málaga: Universidad de Málaga, 2003), pp. 175–87

———, *Ingleses de Sevilla. El Colegio de San Gregorio, 1596–1767* (Seville: Universidad de Sevilla, 2012)

Ollero Pina, José A., *La Universidad de Sevilla en los siglos xvi y xvii* (Seville: Universidad de Sevilla, 1993)

Otte, Enrique, *Sevilla, siglo XVI. Materiales para su historia económica* (Seville: Consejería de la Presidencia de la Junta de Andalucía, 2008)

Palmiste, Clara, 'Los mercaderes de libros e impresores flamencos en Sevilla: organización de las redes mercantiles en Europa y América (1680–1750)', in *Comunidades transnacionales. Colonias de mercaderes extranjeros en el mundo atlántico (1500–1830)*, ed. by Ana Crespo Solana (Madrid: Doce Calles, 2010), pp. 251–70

Palau y Dulcet, Antonio, *Manual del librero hispanoamericano* (Barcelona: Antonio Palau Dulcet, 1972)

Piveteau, Michel, *El burlador y el santo. D. Miguel de Mañara frente al mito de D. Juan* (Seville: Fundación Cajasol, 2007)

Recio Morales, Óscar, 'Los extranjeros y la historiografía modernista', *Cuadernos de Historia Moderna*, 10 (2011), 33–51

——, ed., *Redes de nación y espacios de poder: la comunidad irlandesa en España y la América española* (Valencia: Albatros, 2012)

Sánchez Herrero, José, 'Colegio de Santo Tomás de Sevilla', in *Fondos y procedencias en la Biblioteca de la Universidad de Sevilla*, ed. by Eduardo Peñalver Gómez (Seville: Universidad de Sevilla, 2013), pp. 205–08

Short-Title England, *A Short-Title Catalogue of Books Printed in England, Scotland & Ireland and of English Books Printed Abroad* (London: The Biographical Society, 1976)

Short-Title Netherlands, *A Short-Title Catalogue of Books Printed in the Netherlands and Belgium and of Ducth and Flemish Books Printed in Other Countries from 1470 to 1600* (London: Trustees of the British Museum, 1965)

Simoni, Anna E. C., *Catalogue of Books of the Low Countries, 1601–1621 in the British Library* (London: The British Library, 1990)

Quetif, Jacobus, and Jacobus Echard, eds, *Scriptores ordinis Praedicatorum recensiti* (Paris: Chr. Ballard et Nic. Simart, 1719–1721; facsimile Turin: Bottega d'Erasmo, 1961)

Stols, Eddy, 'La colonia flamenca de Sevilla y el comercio de los Países Bajos españoles en la primera mitad del siglo XVII', *Anuario de Historia Económica y Social*, 2 (1969), 364–81

——, 'Les marchands flamands dans la Péninsule Ibérique à la fin du seizième siècle et pendant la première moitié du dix-septième siècle', in *Fremde Kaufleute auf der Iberischen Halbinsel*, ed. by Herman Kellenbenz (Cologne: Böhlau, 1970), pp. 226–38

——, *De Spaanse Brabanders of de handelsbetrekkingen der Zuidelijke Nederlanden met de Iberische wereld 1598–1648* (Brussels: Paleis der Academiën, 1971)

Testa, Simone, 'From the "Bibliographical Nightmare" to a Critical Bibliography: *Tesori Politici* in the British Library, and Elsewhere in Britain', *Electronic British Library Journal*, 1 (2008), 1–33

Thomas, Werner, *Los protestantes y la Inquisición en España en tiempos de Reforma y Contrarreforma* (Leuven: Leuven University Press, 2001)

Veilingcatalogus, Boeken F. Beudt (The Hague: H. Meurs, 20–27 October, 1851)

Vidal Galache, Florentina, and Benicia Vidal Galache, *Fundación Carlos de Amberes: Historia del Hospital de San Andrés de los Flamencos, 1594–1994* (Madrid: Fundación Carlos de Amberes, 1996)

Villar García, María Begoña, 'Los extranjeros en la España Moderna: la expansión de un campo historiográfico a partir de la obra de Domínguez Ortiz', in *Homenaje a Don Antonio Domínguez Ortiz*, ed. by Juan Luis Castellano Castellano and José Luis López-Guadalupe Muñoz, II (Granada: Universidad de Granada, 2008), pp. 859–72

Wagner, Klaus, 'Flamencos en el comercio del libro en España: Juan Lippeo, mercader de libros agente de los Bellère de Amberes', in *El libro antiguo español*, ed. by Pedro M. Cátedra and María Luisa López-Vidriero (Salamanca: Universidad de Salamanca, 2002), pp. 431–97

Ybarra Hidalgo, Eduardo, *Notas genealógicas y biográficas sobre la familia Becquer* (Seville: Universidad de Sevilla, 1991)

Mobility and Merchants

NATALIA MAILLARD ÁLVAREZ

Business is Business

Book Merchants, Printers, and the Spanish Inquisition during the Sixteenth Century[*]

Introduction

In 1579 Alvar Gómez, professor of Greek at the University of Toledo,[1] wrote a letter to the Spanish Inquisition's headquarter in Madrid expressing his concern about the arrival of books that were entering the Spanish market from abroad:

> Porque me parece, según lo que me dicen, que en los puertos y en Medina del Campo no hay todo el recado necesario para la visita y examen de los libros que entran y vienen de reinos extraños.
>
> (Because it seems to me, that in the harbours and in Medina del Campo there is not as much diligence as would be desirable to examine the books being brought from foreign kingdoms.)

---

[*] This study has been written within the framework of the project 'Las redes internacionales del comercio de libros en la Monarquía Hispánica (1501–1648)', reference HAR2017-82362-P, funded by the Spanish Government. It was also possible thanks to the project 'Books Trade Networks between France, the Iberian Peninsula and the Americas', supported by the European Institute of Advanced Studies (EURIAS) Fellowship Programme, call 2015–2016, at the Collegium de Lyon. I would like to note my gratitude for the wise advice and inspiration provided by Professors Jean Pierre Dedieu and Clive Griffin.

[1] A respected humanist, Alvar Gómez taught Greek first at the University of Alcala de Henares, and later in Toledo. Vaquero Serrano, *El maestro Alvar Gómez*.

Natalia Maillard Álvarez is Associate Professor at the University Pablo de Olavide in Seville. Previously she was Ramón y Cajal Fellow at the same university and Marie Curie Fellow at the European University Institute (Florence). Her latest project is 'International Book Trade Networks in the Hispanic Monarchy (1501–1648)' (HAR2017–82362-P), funded by the Spanish Government.

Networking Europe and New Communities of Interpretation (1400–1600), ed. by Margriet Hoogvliet, Manuel F. Fernández Chaves, *and* Rafael M. Pérez García, New Communities of Interpretation, 4 (Turnhout: Brepols, 2023), pp. 171–200
BREPOLS PUBLISHERS 10.1484/M.NCI-EB.5.134314

In his letter, the professor tried to advise on the dangers that the lack of proper vigilance was causing Spain and on how this lack of vigilance was a threat to both the economy and religion:

> De pocos años a esta parte, cuatro o cinco extranjeros libreros que traen y venden libros en mucha suma y cantidad cada un año a estos reinos, han subido el precio de los dichos libros la mitad por medio, y en algunos mucho más de la mitad, y finalmente venden sin tasa ni moderación [...], y por tanto es justo y necesario que se tenga luego cuenta con ello, y se remedie tan notoria tiranía como en esto hacen contra nuestros naturales los dichos libreros extranjeros, los cuales se van riendo con los dineros del reino, y en mucha cantidad, y los naturales quedan llorando con pérdida notable de sus haciendas, y muchas veces con los libros sospechosos y de mala doctrina y de autores herejes, por no conocerse ni examinarse cuando llegan a los puertos del reino, ni tenerse noticia de ellos antes que los vendan los extranjeros.[2]

> (That, over the last few years, four or five foreigners who bring and sell a great quantity of books in this kingdom have increased the price of these books to half as much again, and sometimes much more than half; that, in short, they sell the books which they bring to the kingdom for as much as they like, with no sense of measure [...]. It is, in consequence, just and imperative that the appalling tyranny of the foreign booksellers over our citizens comes to an end, because these sellers go away laughing with great quantities of our money while our citizens remain, crying, with their wealth much diminished and books which are often suspicious and of bad doctrine, having been written by heretics, and this happens because these books are not duly examined in the harbour on arrival, and no information exists about the time when these foreigners sell them.)

Much has been written about the relationship between the Spanish Inquisition and books, focusing mainly on censorship. Thanks to that prolific historiography, we know how the Index was made,[3] we know well the strict standards which the Inquisition was supposed to apply in order to

---

2 Madrid, AHN, Inquisición, Leg. 4435, no. 5, received in Madrid 29 August 1579. The negative effects on the Spanish balance of trade caused by imported books had been an important concern from the beginning of the sixteenth century. Gonzalo Sánchez-Molero, 'Los impresores ante el Consejo Real', p. 23. I would like to thank the author for his clear comments about the Inquisition and books.
3 Martínez de Bujanda, *El Índice de libros prohibidos y expurgados*.

control the circulation and reading of books,[4] and we know that the actual implementation of these objectives was not always as strict as it was meant to be.[5] However, although there are some studies that have mainly focused on the cases with the most conflict, little has been written about the day-to-day relationship between the Inquisition and those professionals responsible for the production and distribution of books in the Hispanic monarchy during the sixteenth century. We believe that it is essential, if we want to know better the mechanism of book circulation in the early modern period and the agents who made it possible, to analyse that relationship in its quotidian dimension, and this is the objective of this chapter.

The Development of Book Control

In Spain, the Catholic Monarchs, Ferdinand and Isabella, started to legislate on printed books at the end of the fifteenth century. Their first actions aimed to guarantee the quality of books and to protect their trade, rather than controlling their content, but in 1502 the need to obtain a licence in order to print and sell books was introduced in Castile.[6] The running of the system was quite irregular during the first decades of the sixteenth century.[7] It was during Philip II's reign that legislation on books became tighter, while the Inquisition became more closely involved in the process.[8] The distribution of competences between different institutions allowed the Hispanic monarchy to create a more effective system, in which the Inquisition played a key role: this system was one of the most useful mechanisms used by the Spanish monarchs to control the circulation and reading of books, although its functioning was not always as effective as has been thought.

In relation to the organization of the Hispanic monarchy, which involved different territories that kept their own legislation, frontiers, and

---

[4] De los Reyes Gómez, *El libro en España y América*. A survey about the topic can be found in Martínez de Bujanda, *Censura de la Inquisición y de la Iglesia en España*.
[5] Peña Díaz, *Escribir y prohibir*. About the control of books and the work of censors in early modern Europe, see Infelise, *I libri proibiti*; Vega, Weiss, and Esteve, eds, *Reading and Censorship*; López Souto and Velázquez Puerto, eds, *Libros, imprenta y censura*. Regarding censorship in Spanish America, the viceroyalty of Peru has been studied by Guibovich Pérez, *Censura, libros e Inquisición*, while a complete survey about New Spain might be found in Ramos Soriano, *Los delincuentes de papel*.
[6] De los Reyes Gómez, *El libro en España y América*, I, pp. 96–98.
[7] Pérez García, *La imprenta y la literatura espiritual castellana*, pp. 127–49.
[8] For instance, the 1558 law on controlling book production and sales would remain valid until the end of the eighteenth century. A good treatment of how the license system worked in Castile can be found in Bouza, *Dásele licencia y privilegio*.

customs, the Catholic religion acted as an ideological framework that invested the Crown with a universal meaning.[9] The Spanish Inquisition, whose activities began in 1480,[10] helped to fix and maintain this ideology in those territories ruled by the Spanish Crown where it operated. This was especially relevant in the case of control over reading: Castilian legislation on books was not applied in the Crown of Aragon (including Aragon, Catalonia, Valencia, and the Balearic Islands) or the Kingdom of Navarre, whereas the Spanish Inquisition extended its jurisdiction over all those territories in the Iberian Peninsula, and the New World,[11] facilitating the standardization of the control of books in all of them. The Inquisition provided the necessary infrastructure for the prosecution of pernicious texts throughout an enormous territory. On 19 May 1572, for instance, the inquisitors from Cordoba (Spain) acknowledged the receipt of instructions to prohibit and collect all the copies of a Spanish translation of Petrarch's *Trionfi*, published in Valladolid in the year 1541.[12] Within the next two years, the same instructions arrived in Guatemala[13] and Peru.[14]

The participation of the Spanish Inquisition in the control of books was gradual: by the end of the fifteenth century, the newly created Inquisition had become involved in the control of religious books, although its actions against them were not yet systematic.[15] At this early stage, inquisitors were especially worried about Muslim, Hebrew, and superstitious books, and some of them were burnt in different cities.[16] At the end of the Middle Ages, it was relatively easy to find booksellers who were Jews or *conver-*

---

9 Palomo, 'Un catolicismo en plural'. See also Cardim and others, *Polycentric Monarchies*, p. 4.
10 García Cárcel and Moreno, *Inquisición. Historia Crítica*, pp. 132–33. By 1493 we can note twenty-three tribunals throughout the peninsula, each one with a territory or district that was reorganized over the following years in order to improve its efficiency. Contreras and Dedieu, 'Estructuras geográficas'.
11 After a period in which the prosecution of heresy in America depended on bishops, the tribunals of Lima and Mexico City were created in 1570 and 1571, each one controlling the total territory of its viceroyalty. Castañeda Delgado and Hernández Aparicio, *La Inquisición de Lima*; Alberro, *Inquisición y Sociedad en México*; Escandell Bonet and Huerga, 'Las adecuaciones estructurales'.
12 Madrid, AHN, Inquisición, Leg. 2392–2, s.n. The book was the *Translacion de los seys triumphos de Francisco Petrarca: de toscano en castellano: fecho por Antonio de obregon*, published in Valladolid in 1541 by the printer Juan de Villaquirán. Martínez de Bujanda, *El Índice de libros prohibidos y expurgados*, p. 887.
13 Mexico City, AGN, Inquisición, vol. 77, exp. 19. About the difficulties of implementing censorship in New Spain, see Nesvig, *Ideology and Inquisition*, pp. 226–46.
14 Guibovich Pérez, *Censura, libros e Inquisición*, p. 277.
15 Dedieu, 'Le modèle religieux', p. 292.
16 Lea, *A History of the Inquisition*, III, p. 480.

sos,[17] but despite some cases of *converso* booksellers being prosecuted,[18] the archival documents suggest that the main concern of the Inquisition regarding booksellers and printers during the sixteenth century was the threat posed by Protestantism. Indeed, everything started to change after 1517: the Spanish authorities became increasingly worried about books when the Reformation appeared in Europe, because books were considered a fundamental element in the diffusion of heresy (defined as *herejes mudos* or 'mute heretics'), and were thus much more harmful than the spoken word.[19] At the same time, the international book trade networks were becoming stronger, and the Spanish market increasingly depended on them.[20] In 1521 the Grand Inquisitor Adrian of Utrecht (the future Pope Hadrian VI) published an edict banning Lutheran books, but it was not enough: in the following years the inquisitors found Luther's books in different parts of Spain, and anxiety continued to grow.[21] In less than one century we can note the creation in Spain of a system that allowed the Inquisition to control the production, commercialization, and reading of books, always in close cooperation with the civil authorities;[22] this occurred especially after 1540, at which time they triumphed over some jurisdictional problems regarding the licenses for new books.[23]

The Inquisition was in charge, first of all, of the preparation of the Indexes of forbidden and expurgated books. The Spanish Inquisition wrote its own Indexes. Indeed, the coexistence of the Spanish and Roman Indexes generated some confusion, but the support of the monarchy reinforced the power of the Inquisition with regard to the compilation of Indexes.[24] Booksellers and printers were certainly not pleased with the situation generated by the Indexes. In May 1560, just one year after the first Spanish Index of forbidden books was published,[25] the printer and lawyer Pedro de Luján sent a petition to the Inquisition in the name of his fellows in Seville pointing out the problems that the Index posed for their profession and their doubts:

---

17 In Barcelona during the fourteenth century, for instance, most of the booksellers were Jewish; but in 1391, after the destruction of the Jewish quarter, many of them became Christians. Rubió i Balaguer, *Llibreters i impressors*, pp. 63–67.
18 At least six booksellers were accused by the Inquisition in Valencia between 1484 and 1530, five of whom were allegedly Jews. García Cárcel, *Orígenes de la Inquisición española*, pp. 251–314.
19 Pinto Crespo, *Inquisición y control ideológico*, p. 29; see also Gacto, 'Libros venenosos'.
20 Pettegree, 'Centre and Periphery in the European Book World'.
21 Dedieu, 'Le modèle religieux', pp. 270–71.
22 Dedieu, 'Le modèle religieux', p. 299.
23 Gonzalo Sánchez-Molero, 'Los impresores ante el Consejo Real', pp. 38–46.
24 The Spanish Inquisition forbade books that were included in the Roman Index, but also permitted the circulation of books that were prohibited by Rome. Defourneaux, *L'Inquisition espagnole et les livres français*, pp. 19–20.
25 Martínez de Bujanda, *Index de l'Inquisition Espagnole, 1551, 1554, 1559*.

> Hay algunos libros de romance buenos en que leen los niños, como Cid Ruy Díaz e Infante don Pedro y Abad don Juan, y otros semejantes, los cuales nunca tuvieron nombre de autor y por eso no osamos imprimirlos.[26]
>
> (There are some good books in Spanish for children, such as *Sid Rui Díaz*, *Infante don Pedro*, and *Abad don Juan*, and other similar ones, which we don't dare print, because their author is unknown.)

That same year, Andrea de Portonariis made a similar complaint on behalf of the booksellers and printers from Salamanca, one of the main centres for the production and distribution of books in Spain together with Seville:[27]

> Digo que lo dichos mis partes y yo teníamos impresos al tiempo que se publicó el Catálogo muchos libros de los que por él se prohíben, los cuales imprimimos con toda buena fe y guardando en todo la forma y orden de las leyes y pragmáticas de estos reinos, y precediendo licencia y examen necesario antes y primero que se imprimiesen, y de los más de ellos hay privilegio concedido por el Consejo Real, en el cual gastamos mucha parte de nuestras haciendas, y ahora entiendo que se prohibía por el Catálogo los dimos y entregamos al maestro Francisco Sancho catedrático de teología en la universidad de la dicha ciudad, lo cual hicimos en cumplimiento de los prohibido y mandado por vuestra señoría ilustrísima, y porque no es justo que habiendo mis partes e yo gastado nuestras haciendas en la impresión de los dichos libros con toda buena fe y por virtud de los privilegios y licencias que para ello tuvimos, perdamos lo que gastamos en la dicha impresión, suplico a vuestra señoría ilustrísima sea servido de dar alguna buena orden para que a lo menos se nos satisfaga y pague la costa y gasto que hicimos en la impresión de los dichos libros.[28]
>
> (When the catalogue was published, we had in stock many of the books which the said catalogue prohibited, books which had been printed in good faith, at all times following the letter and the spirit of the law of these kingdoms, and with all due permits and licences before and after printing, and most of these books were printed with the express permission of the Royal Council, on which [books] most of our money was spent. And now, seeing that these books have been forbidden by the catalogue, we handed them over

---

26 Madrid, AHN, Inquisición, Leg. 4442, no. 40. Griffin, *Los Cromberger*, p. 162.
27 Ruiz Fidalgo, *La imprenta en Salamanca*. See also Bécares Botas, *Librerías salmantinas del siglo XVI*.
28 Madrid, AHN, Inquisición, Leg. 4442, no. 36.

to Francisco Sancho,[29] Professor of Theology in the university of said city, in compliance with the order issued by your honour. And because it is not fair that my partners and I have spent all our money in printing these books, which was done in good faith and in the exercise of due privileges and licences, and now we lose it all, I beg your honour to issue an order, so we are reimbursed at least the costs incurred by us in the impression of said books.)

The pressures on book professionals and readers produced an effect, and in the next Spanish Index, published in 1583–1584, the complete condemnation of some works had been replaced by the expurgation of their problematic parts.[30]

The Inquisition also controlled the arrival of books into Spanish ports[31] and the circulation and reading of books within the various Spanish kingdoms, including the American territories. Although it was not its task in the beginning,[32] the Inquisition soon started to visit bookstores and printing offices. In September 1540, due to the limited attention paid by booksellers and merchants to the prohibitions of pernicious books,[33] several district courts received instructions to accomplish this mission, usually with the aid of some intermediaries such as the friars Domingo de Soto and Francisco del Castillo at Salamanca, who were given very precise orders to close all the bookstores unexpectedly and ask booksellers for a list of their books and clients.[34] The inquisitors also had to provide booksellers with a list of banned books, so they could display it in their shops. At least theoretically, this would become common practice once the inquisitorial Indexes started to appear, and booksellers (who were forced to have a copy of them) could not claim ignorance; at the same time, the Indexes began to receive more publicity. A visit to seventeen bookshops in Medina del Campo in 1551 discovered suspicious books in

---

29 This professor had a key role in the creation of the first Spanish Index. García Cárcel, *Herejía y sociedad en el siglo XVI*, p. 299.
30 Martínez de Bujanda, *Index de l'Inquisition Espagnole, 1583, 1584*; Martínez de Bujanda, 'Sguardo panoramico sugli indici dei libri proibiti'.
31 Maillard Álvarez, 'Puertas de *mala ventura*'.
32 By 1536 the Inquisition was still not in charge of visiting bookstores. García Oro, *La monarquía y los libros*, p. 74.
33 The inquisitor's diagnosis was repeated in the letters sent to Seville and Salamanca: 'cada día vienen libros reprobados a estos reinos, no teniendo temor los mercaderes y libreros a las censuras y prohibiciones del Santo Oficio, de que resulta cada día mayor perjuicio a nuestra religión cristiana, y así conviene hacer mayores diligencias y agravar las penas contra los transgresores' (forbidden books arrive in the kingdom on a daily basis, because booksellers are not scared of prohibitions and the punishment of the Holy Office, which is to the detriment of Christian religion, and more diligence and harsher punishments are therefore in order), Madrid, AHN, Inquisición, Lib. 574, fols 40^v–41^v, 19 September 1540.
34 Madrid, AHN, Inquisición, Lib. 574.

fifteen of them, including Sacrobosco's *Sphaera* with a preface by Philipp Melanchthon, proving how easy it was to introduce forbidden books into Spain at that time.[35] Visits were probably a common practice during the sixteenth century,[36] but we do not have a complete record of them, only news scattered throughout the archives. It is therefore difficult to judge the frequency with which they were undertaken within each district, and how often forbidden books were found. In the case of the New World, we can note some news about visits to Mexican libraries and bookshops as early as the sixteenth century,[37] while in Peru the first known order to visit the bookshops of Lima was given in 1605 and implemented in 1609.[38]

Book Professionals and the Spanish Inquisition

As we can see, early modern book merchants and printers in the Hispanic monarchy developed their tasks at a time of ideological and legal changes. We believe that dealing with the Inquisition increasingly became a crucial aspect of their everyday life and work. But how did they deal with the system of control established by the Spanish Inquisition?

The most critical moment seems to occur during the 1550s and 1560s,[39] when a crisis in the publishing industry coincided with the reinforcement of the legislation on books and the discovery of alleged Lutheran groups in Seville and Valladolid.[40] Philippe Berger attributed the crisis in the book trade in Valencia between 1550 and 1555[41] in part to the pressures of the Inquisition, and according to García Oro booksellers and printers from Seville could hardly breathe owing to Inquisition harassment starting in 1557–1558.[42] Some printers were judged: in an *auto-da-fé* in Seville in 1560, Antonio Inglés, defined in the sources as printer or typesetter ('ymprimidor o componedor'), neighbour of Granada, was absolved,[43] and a year later the French bookbinder Antón Martel was accused of being Lutheran and burnt in Toledo.[44]

---

[35] 'Visita a las librerías de Medina del Campo (1551)', Valladolid, AHPV, Leg. 7335, fols 499ʳ–506ᵛ.

[36] According to Anne Cayuela, inquisitors frequently visited the bookshops in order to control them actively. Cayuela, *Alonso Pérez de Montalbán*, p. 117.

[37] Fernández del Castillo, *Libros y libreros en el siglo XVI*. The activities of the Inquisition to control the circulation of books in New Spain, especially during the seventeenth and eighteenth centuries, have been studied by García, 'Before we are condemned'.

[38] Guibovich Pérez, *La inquisición y la censura de libros*, pp. 28–29.

[39] Vázquez de Prada, 'La Inquisición y los libros sospechosos'.

[40] Books would play a key role in those events. Gilmont, 'La propagande protestante'.

[41] Berger, *Libro y lectura*, p. 301.

[42] García Oro, *La monarquía y los libros*, p. 90.

[43] Madrid, AHN, Inquisición, Leg. 2075-I.

[44] Madrid, AHN, Inquisición, Leg. 3068, no. 8.

During the same period, the printer Gaspar Zapata, who worked in Seville before 1545, escaped from the Holy Office that had accused him of printing Lutheran books. His effigy was then burned in 1562.[45] Even worse was the fate of the clergyman and typesetter Sebastián Martínez, who during his youth was one of Zapata's employees. According to the Inquisition's sentence he 'compuso y escribió e imprimió y echo número de papeles y coplas heréticas y detestables en sevilla y Toledo y en otras partes' (wrote, copied out, printed, and distributed many abominable and heretical flysheets and verses in Seville, Toledo, and elsewhere), and therefore he was burnt in Seville in 1562.[46] The Inquisition records suggest that Sebastián Martínez may have been betrayed by a colleague, the printer Cristóbal Álvarez, who was also associated with people close to the Reformation in Seville.[47] If this suspicion is true, this would be just one more example of a role that we have noted as being played by booksellers and printers in different years and cities: that of the Inquisition's informant.

A similar misfortune awaited the French printers Benito Dulcet and Guillermo Herlin, as studied by Clive Griffin. Like many French humble printers and booksellers, they had migrated to Spain looking for better opportunities, but both were accused of heresy and imprisoned in 1569. Their trial revealed a network of foreign Protestants who were working on Spanish printing presses. At least seven of those men or their effigies were burnt in 1570 and 1572, and many others received different kinds of severe punishments, such as being sent to man galleys.[48]

However, in spite of these cases, the Spanish Inquisition did not always inflict the same level of severity on all book professionals who crossed its path. Indeed, we can note several cases where an inquisitorial process did not mean the end of a professional career or the demise of the defendant. For instance, the typographer Miguel de Eguía from Alcala de Henares, who printed many of Erasmus's texts in the first half of the sixteenth century, was accused of being Lutheran and imprisoned as early as 1531, but after two years in jail he was absolved and returned to his activities.[49] Bernart de Baquedano, a bookseller from Navarre, was accused in 1555 and 1568 of trading books with Lutheran people (probably from Lyons), but he continued working and importing books from the Low Countries

---

45 Moll, 'Gaspar Zapata, impresor sevillano condenado'.
46 Madrid, AHN, Leg. 2075-I, no. 2. Maillard Álvarez, 'Estrategias de los profesionales del libro sevillanos', p. 30.
47 Griffin, *Oficiales de imprenta, herejía e inquisición*, pp. 30–33.
48 Griffin, *Oficiales de imprenta, herejía e inquisición*, pp. 23–24. Most of the foreign printers and booksellers condemned by the Inquisition courts were indeed French. Werner, *Los protestantes y la Inquisición*, p. 241.
49 Kamen, *The Spanish Inquisition*, p. 90. The whole case can be found in Goñi Gaztámbide, 'El impresor Miguel de Eguía'.

and Lyons.[50] It appears that his biggest problems were with the royal authorities: in 1571–1572, while visiting the kingdom's libraries,[51] they confiscated some of his books and imprisoned him. However, he did not stop working and subsequently died in France on a business trip.

In 1564 a bookseller from Alcala, Gaspar de la Vega, was imprisoned. In his confession he mentioned at least fourteen colleagues, accusing many of them of being Lutherans.[52] Unfortunately we do not have all the documents from the trial, but we were able to identify most of those men, and sometimes also trace their very different ends after the Inquisition's inquiries. The majority of them were foreigners connected with France, such as the aforementioned Gaspar de la Vega, from Burgundy, who was burnt in 1565.[53] The effigies of two other French colleagues, a man called 'Juan Peruça'[54] and Juan Temporal,[55] from Lyons, were burnt in an *auto-da-fé* in Toledo in 1571.[56] But other men accused by De la Vega of being Lutheran, including Charles Pesnot, Symphorien Beraud, and Benito Boyer, kept working and developed brilliant careers in Spain and France. Gaspar de la Vega declared that the bookseller from Alcalá Luis Gutiérrez, known as 'el Rico' (The Rich), had a condemned book about the Old Testament in his shop and sold it to a Huguenot doctor. The Inquisition found further evidence against him when he was accused of blasphemy by other colleagues, but Gutiérrez escaped the trial by paying a fine, and kept working until his death in 1570.[57]

In other cases, the Inquisition behaved almost indulgently. The Flemish bookseller and printer Matias Gast was settled in Salamanca, but had

---

50 Ostolaza Elizondo, *Impresores y libreros en Navarra*, pp. 51–53.
51 García Oro and Portela Silva, *Felipe II y los libreros*.
52 Madrid, AHN, Inquisición, Leg. 3068–1, exp. 82. Griffin, *Oficiales de imprenta, herejía e inquisición*, pp. 169, 177–78.
53 Werner, *Los protestantes y la Inquisición*, p. 448.
54 A man called 'Juan Peruso' was working for Bartolomé de Robles in 1559. Morisse, 'Blas de Robles (1542–1592)', p. 299.
55 In 1560 the same Juan (i.e. Jean) Temporal from Lyons, together with a colleague from Bordeaux, wrote a letter to the Inquisition protesting because the commissaries from Bilbao had stopped for over three months 140 bales of books on different subjects that they carried for booksellers and other people to Salamanca, Valladolid, Medina del Campo, Alcala, and Toledo. They asked the Inquisition to hasten the visits to Bilbao or to undertake them in the destination cities, so that they could get the licenses to sell all the good books. Jean Temporal was a modest printer in Lyons from 1550 to 1571. He specialized in the production of poetic books in French, but he also worked as a factor for powerful booksellers of the city. Rissoan, 'Jean Temporal: libraire de la Renaissance Lyonnaise'. His production decreased notably after 1561, which coincides with the times we can place him in Spain.
56 Martín Abad, *La imprenta en Alcalá de Henares*, p. 146. Together with their effigies, another one representing the French printer Esteban Carniel was also burnt. De Horozco, *Relaciones Históricas Toledanas*, pp. 230–31.
57 Martín Abad, *La imprenta en Alcalá de Henares*, pp. 138–40.

important contacts in Antwerp and Lyons and was married to a member of the Spanish branch of the Giunti.[58] In 1554 he was accused of possessing and selling forbidden books and was exiled from Salamanca for three months. Four years later, he was accused of criticizing the sacrament of reconciliation in front of the bookseller Alessandro de Canova,[59] but apparently nothing happened. Finally, in 1572, heretical book covers were found in his house and shop, and he confessed to having listened to three Lutheran sermons and having read forbidden books in Germany. The accusation was serious, and he was imprisoned, but it seems that he was given a small penalty and continued working.[60]

In Mexico, the case of the French printer Pedro de Ocharte was more dramatic, but had a similar ending. Ocharte was the third printer to work in Mexico City.[61] Just after the arrival of the Inquisition in New Spain, and only three weeks after the Edict of Faith requiring all Catholics to report the presence of heretical texts in the city, Pedro Ocharte and his employee, the engraver Juan Ortiz (also French in spite of his name), were accused of reading a forbidden book. Ocharte was even tortured, but he was finally absolved.[62] Both trials have been studied by different scholars, who have usually argued that the Inquisition targeted Ocharte just after its arrival to Mexico in an attempt to control printed materials. A careful scrutiny of the trials against Pedro Ocharte and Juan Ortiz at the Archivo General de la Nación has allowed Kenneth Ward to undertake a different and stimulating reading of them, stressing the attempts of both defendants 'to contest or manipulate the Holy Office to their own ends'.[63]

---

58 Born in Antwerp, Matías Gast moved to Spain, started work as a bookseller in Medina del Campo, and later became a printer. He married Lucrecia Junta (or Giunti) and worked at his father-in-law's workshops in Salamanca and Burgos. From 1558 onwards, he had his own workshop, which he maintained until his death in 1577, although he never gave up the importation business, as proven by the letters that Christophe Plantin sent to him from Antwerp. Delgado Casado, *Diccionario de impresores españoles*, pp. 267–69. On his correspondence with Plantin, see Rosses, *Correspondance de Christophe Plantin*, I, pp. 103–05, 286.
59 Alessandro de Canova arrived in Spain as a factor of Luc'Antonio Giunti, and he was linked to at least one other printer accused by the Inquisition of being Lutheran, the Flemish Enrique Loc. Martín Abad, *La imprenta en Alcalá de Henares*, pp. 113–14. On Canova and his connection with the Giunti, see: De la Mano, *Mercaderes e impresores de libros*.
60 In 1572, the inquisitors from Valladolid wrote a short summary of the state of the case in a letter. Madrid, AHN, Inquisición, Leg. 3194, no. 54. A study of the whole trial can be found in Moreno Gallego, 'Matías Gast, preso inquisitorial'.
61 Stols, *Pedro Ocharte*.
62 The proceedings of both trials can be found in Fernández del Castillo, *Libros y libreros en el siglo XVI*, pp. 85–243.
63 Ward, '*Estas cuentas son si cuenta*', p. 4. I want to thank Kenneth Ward for generously sharing his work with me. Despite his unpleasant experience, a few years later Ocharte did not hesitate to turn to the Inquisition, asking for protection when, in the context of a lawsuit in civil justice, his former business partner, Jorge de Arando, accused Ocharte of spreading a

Were those men totally innocent, as they proclaimed? Or were they sympathetic to the new religion? It is difficult to say. Foreigner or not, they exhibited practical business sense, and did not flood the Spanish market with heretical books, as certain people were feared.[64] But it is likely that some of them moved in a kind of grey area, at least for a while, that allowed them to keep working in Spain and, sometimes, even allowed them to negotiate or take advantage of their relationship with the Inquisition. A good example of this is the bookseller from Alcalá Bartolomé de Robles: he could count on the intercession of Fray Pedro de Quintanilla, who was in charge of examining the books in Valladolid after the Index of 1559 was published. When many suspicious books were found in his shop, Fray Pedro wrote to the *Suprema* (the Inquisition's headquarter) asking them to allow Robles to recover those that were not prohibited, such as a good number of Erasmus's works, and also 'a book called Petrus Galatinus, containing a *trac[tatus] De Arte Cabalistica*, if this were removed'. He even recommended returning to Robles 'other books, which have prologues or annotations by heretics [...], if the name of such authors were blotted out'.[65] In 1564 Bartolomé de Robles was accused by Gaspar de la Vega of hanging a Protestant version of the Ten Commandments in French on a wall in his shop. The inquisitors went to visit it and, although they could not find the prayer, they found three copies of the *Explicatio Symboli sive Catechismus* by Erasmus,[66] bound with another book (*Icones Simboli Apostolici*). He claimed not to have known that the books were there, and highlighted that he had already delivered to the Inquisition all the forbidden books he had found, and had also expurgated the works by Erasmus that he had. I could not find any information of further action against him.[67]

At least two men mentioned in Gaspar de la Vega's deposition (Melchor Treschel, who was a neighbour of Toledo, and Antonio Ricardo, an Italian bookseller living in Alcalá, both connected with Lyons) seem to have been there as possible informers for the Inquisition. This likely became common practice among booksellers, publishers, and printers as the Inquisition tightened its net around offenders. A collaboration that might have produced good results: Antonio Ricardo moved to Mexico in 1570

---

defamatory letter against him, and brought about his trial and torture, after accusing him of having corresponded with some French Lutherans. Mexico City, AGN, Inquisición, vol. 89, exp. 25 bis. Jiménez, 'Cuentas fallidas, deudas omnipresentes'.

64 Even in Lyons, where many booksellers and printers openly joined the Reformation, it is not always possible to find a direct relationship between personal confession and editorial choice. Constantin, 'Les enjeux de la controverse religieuse'.

65 Lea, *A History of the Inquisition*, pp. 487–88.

66 Prohibited by the 1559 Index. Martínez de Bujanda, *Index de l'Inquisition Espagnole, 1551, 1554, 1559*, p. 349.

67 Madrid, AHN, Inquisición, Leg. 4519, no. 1, 12 July 1564.

where he worked as a printer and maintained a good relationship with the prosecutor of the Inquisition, Alonso Fernández de Bonilla, who seems to have been linked to his arrival to Peru, where Ricardo became the first person to run a printing press.[68] In those territories of the monarchy that the Inquisition could not reach, book professionals were still an important source of information in the fight against heresy. That was also the case of the Flemish Pierre Bellère, who in 1558 informed the archbishop of Toledo how and where heretic books were carried to Spain from Europe.[69]

Although some book professionals were persecuted by the Inquisition, a good number of these professionals collaborated with the tribunal in different ways. It seems that, as the Inquisition became more involved in the control of books, and especially after 1558–1559, collaboration with book professionals became more profitable and easier for both parties. In 1500 the bookseller from Trujillo (Extremadura) Pedro Tello had to ask the Catholic Monarchs for protection because his collaboration with the Holy Office had earned him the enmity of some powerful people.[70] In the second half of the same century, collaboration with the Inquisition was easily turned into personal security and business opportunities for book professionals, who, in exchange, offered better information to the Holy Office.

The early modern markets developed frequently in a reciprocal relationship with the authorities.[71] Booksellers needed to work with the Inquisition in everyday life, and thus a good relationship with the inquisitors (particularly local ones) was crucial. One of the most obvious ways to collaborate with the Inquisition was to become a *familiar*. These were laymen who assisted the Inquisition tribunals. Becoming a *familiar* meant benefitting from economic, judicial, and social privileges, and it served as proof of old-Christian Status (*limpieza de sangre*).[72] There is no doubt today that the relationships of some intellectuals with the Holy Office were close and even profitable,[73] and according to the archival documents the relationship between book professionals and the Inquisition was also frequently fruitful. I have found booksellers and printers who were *familiares* in six different cities during the sixteenth century: Seville, Salamanca,[74]

---

68 Tauro, 'Antonio Ricardo. Primer impresor', pp. xxi–xxxii.
69 Tellechea Idígoras, 'Bartolomé Carranza en Flandes'.
70 Simancas, AGS, Registro General del Sello, Leg. 150001, 57.
71 Herrero Sánchez and Kaps, 'Connectors, Networks and Commercial Systems'.
72 Cerrillo Cruz, *Los familiares de la Inquisición española*.
73 Márquez, *Literatura e Inquisición en España*, pp. 121–39. Márquez not only remarks on the existence of writers who collaborated with the Holy Office in different ways (for instance, the playwright and poet Lope de Vega was a 'familiar'), but also the large number of inquisitors who were writers.
74 In that city, the printer Alonso Rodríguez del Barrio was one of the witnesses against Matías Gast.

Toledo, Medina del Campo, Granada, and Valencia. It is highly credible that there were more.

A detail of Ocharte's trial warrants our attention: during his statement, the inquisitors asked him why he did not try to become a *familiar* of the Inquisition. The printer answered that he did not want to become a 'malsín' (slanderer or tell-tale) to anyone.[75] His case is more significant if, instead of taking it as an isolated case in Mexican book history, as is usually done, we situate him within the networks that carried out the business of book production and trade between Europe and the Americas. Ocharte's second wife was the daughter of a Seville bookseller, Diego de Sansorel. Another of Sansorel's son-in-laws, the bookseller Alonso Montero, was himself a *familiar* of the Seville Inquisition for several years, although the Inquisition had some suspicions about his *limpieza*.[76] We do not know whether this collaboration caused him any enmity within his profession, but in general it seems that it benefitted him: in 1575 he was in charge of the distribution and sale in the Sevillian archbishopric of the *Nuevo Rezado* (the liturgical books approved by the Council of Trent),[77] a privilege that in 1580 was extended to all Andalusia.[78] Theoretically, the Inquisition was not directly involved in the business of the *Nuevo Rezado*, but in Granada the bookseller in charge of this task in 1574 was also a *familiar*,[79] and in Murcia the secretary of the Inquisition, Andrés de Cisneros, was directly involved in the arrival of the *Nuevo Rezado* to the city. It was he who authorized the booksellers Luis and Juan Segura (father and son) to go to Madrid and collect the books addressed to Cartagena.[80]

---

75 'Que diciéndole a este el dicho Dr de la Fuente que cómo no procuraba ser familiar de este Santo Oficio, este le respondió estando a solas que no quería, porque no quería ser malsín de nadie' (On being asked by the said Dr de la Fuente why he did not become an agent of the Holy Office, he replied, when they were alone, that he did not want to be a snitch on anyone's behalf). González del Castillo, *Libros y libreros en México*, p. 116.

76 In 1580 he requested the position of 'nuncio' in the Inquisition of Seville. It required a new investigation into his 'limpieza' that produced some doubts about him and his wife (Madrid, AHN, Inquisición, Leg. 2947, 9 April 1580 and 17 March 1581). The inquisitors even recommended removing him from his position as 'familiar'. However, he might have been too valuable for the Inquisition, as many other testimonies prove that he was still acting as 'familiar' at least until 1589. Maillard Álvarez, 'Estrategias de los profesionales del libro sevillanos', p. 38. His connection with the local inquisitors was also reinforced by more personal events, for example, the baptism of his daughter Ana in 1555. One of Ana's godfathers was don Luis Sotelo, 'alguacil mayor' of the Inquisition in the city (Seville, APS, Lib. 5 of Baptisms, fol. 55^r). The same Luis Sotelo was also godfather to a daughter of the bookseller Juan de Medina in 1551 (Seville, APS, Lib. 4 of Baptisms, s.f.).

77 Julia, 'Lecturas y Contrarreforma'.

78 Seville, AHPSe, Leg. 12425, fols 284^r–86^v; Álvarez, *Impresores, libreros y mercaderes*, pp. 137–38. Seville, AHPSe, Leg. 10756, fols 400^r–11^r.

79 Osorio Pérez, Moreno Trujillo, and De la Obra, *Trastiendas de la cultura*, p. 110.

80 De Pascual Martínez, 'Libros y libreros en Murcia'. Despite the fact that the Inquisition was not directly involved in the distribution of the *Nuevo Rezado*, Pedro Velarde, member

At the end of the century another bookseller from Seville, who also had strong bonds with the New World, Diego Mexía, was in charge of the distribution of the *Nuevo Rezado* in Andalusia. We do not know whether he was also a *familiar* of the Inquisition, but one of his sons, the poet Diego Mexía de Fernangil, collaborated with the tribunal in Peru and was in charge of the visit to the libraries in Potosí, a city that the inquisitors considered particularly exposed to heresy.[81]

It is obvious that there were other advantages to being a *familiar*, or at least some cases suggest that book professionals received different treatment according to how close they were to the Inquisition. In 1553, Diego López, a bookseller and *familiar* from Toledo, was sent to the royal prison for wounding a silversmith (who was a relative of other booksellers). He used his position as *familiar* to get out of jail with a fine and recover his sword. To pay the fine, he offered to give a Missal that he was binding to the Inquisition for free.[82] But in 1591, in Valencia, a young bookseller, Juan Ortiz, was incarcerated in the Inquisition prison and accused of wounding the bookseller and *familiar* Baltasar Simón, his former employer.[83] The strategy of using booksellers as *familiares* may have helped to control the traffic of 'pernicious' books, but it could also provoke abuses. This was likely the reason that Professor Alvar Gómez, in the aforementioned letter addressed to the Inquisition in 1579, suggested forbidding the use of booksellers as *familiares*.[84] At the same time, he proposed adopting a system of controlling booksellers and printers that was similar to the Flemish one.[85]

In the American sources, too, the collaboration between book professionals and the Inquisition can be traced. During his torture, Ocharte

---

of the Council of the Inquisition was also appointed to control the *Nuevo Rezado* and its distribution in the 1570s; Bécares Botas, 'Aspectos de la producción y distribución'.
81 Guibovich Pérez, *Censura, libros e Inquisición*, p. 94.
82 Madrid, AHN, Inquisición, Leg. 58, no. 13. In 1562 we can also note the name of the bookseller Juan Vázquez in a list of 'familiares' from Toledo; Madrid, AHN, Inquisición, Leg. 3068 (28).
83 Madrid, AHN, Inquisición, Leg. 5312, no. 36. The defendant claimed that his former boss owed him money and that all his servants had complaints about him. A good part of the testimonies during the trial were devoted to proving that Baltasar Simón's position as 'familiar' was well known by everyone.
84 Madrid, AHN, Inquisición, Leg. 4435, no. 5.
85 'Que haya libreros e impresores, y aún encuadernadores, examinados y jurados como en Flandes, los cuales no solamente hagan consigo mismos lo que deben, más empero avisen al Santo Oficio luego de todo lo que supieren y a su noticia viniere de libros o autores prohibidos que otras personas tuvieren' (That, as it is done in Flanders, booksellers and even binders are examined and appointed, not only to do themselves what they ought to, but also to inform the Holy Office of everything they hear concerning forbidden books, and authors, which other people may have in their possession), Madrid, AHN, Inquisición, Leg. 4435, no. 5.

declared that another colleague in Mexico, Pedro Balli, was trying to become a *familiar*.[86] Although we do not know whether he succeeded, in September 1581 the same Pedro Balli, following the inquisitors' orders, wrote a report with a detailed list of all those who had been involved in the book trade in the city of Mexico over the previous twelve years, paying special attention to the links between Mexican booksellers and their suppliers in Spain.[87] He also served as a French translator for the Mexican Inquisition for many years.[88]

The collaboration of booksellers may also have been crucial for the control of readers, and those who were *familiares* may have played a special role in this. In 1577 the inquisitors from Valladolid received an order to look for some books, which they did, looking in all the bookstores of the city without finding anything. After that, the local inquisitors charged two booksellers, who were *familiares*, with the task of looking for the books within the private libraries of the city.[89]

As we have seen in the case of the bookseller from Toledo, Diego López, another way of collaborating and, at the same time, of taking advantage of the Inquisition was binding books, selling paper, and publishing or printing for the Inquisition.[90] For example, in 1503, the German printer Juan Luschner printed the *Directorium Inquisitorum* in Barcelona. The Inquisitor Diego de Deza, who also ordered all the Inquisition courts

---

86 'Y lo mismo dixo éste a Pedro Balli, librero, diciéndole que él mismo lo procuraba hacer [ser familiar], el cual le respondió que no había de ser malsín, porque todos, aunque no fuesen familiars, tienen obligación de decir lo que saben' (And he [Ocharte] said the same to Pedro Balli, bookseller, when he told him that he was trying to become a ['familiar'], to which Balli replied that he would not be a snitch, because everyone's duty is to say what they know, whether they are 'familiars' or not). Fernández del Castillo, *Libros y libreros en México*, p. 116. It seems that Balli started working for Pedro Ocharte and maintained a close relationship with him even after he opened his own workshop. Ymhoff Cabrera, *Los impresos mexicanos*, pp. 169–70.

87 Mexico City, AGN, Inquisición, vol. 90, exp. 45. The document is transcribed in Mena, 'El librero Pedro Bally'. See also Jiménez, 'Comerciantes de libros en la Nueva España'.

88 Toribio Medina, *La imprenta en México*, I, p. xc.

89 Madrid, AHN, Inquisición, 3193, exp. 136. Received in Madrid 14 July 1577. In 1568 the inquisitors of Salamanca received an order to take some of Petrus Ramus's books out of circulation. To do so, they published a list of those books for booksellers, schools, churches, and monasteries (Madrid, AHN, Inquisición, Leg. 3189, exp. 79). Many Spanish followers of the French philosopher Pierre de la Ramée (Petrus Ramus) were working at the University of Salamanca. About the inquisitorial persecution of his works and followers, see Martínez Jiménez, 'La persecución inquisitiorial del ramismo'.

90 We can find different examples of this: in 1589 Alonso Montero, bookseller and *familiar* in Seville, was paid by the inquisitors of Seville for binding some books and trials for them. Madrid, AHN, Inquisición, Leg. 2949, s.f. In 1616 the Mexican inquisitors paid nine *pesos* to the bookseller Diego de la Rivera for a Dominical Missal, see Chuchiak, ed., *The Inquisition in New Spain*, p. 192.

to buy this text, financed the edition.[91] The printing of the inquisitorial Indexes would have been good business, as would also have been the edicts with new prohibitions that were printed in large numbers; sometimes these were even reprinted by local typographers in their districts. In the case of Peru, for instance, the edicts were reprinted in Lima and sent to the rest of the Viceroyalty.[92]

On the other hand, several examples found in the archives indicate that local inquisitors sometimes played the role of mediator between book professionals of their communities and the central Inquisition. They informed the *Suprema* of the petitions made by booksellers and printers (usually to allow them to expurgate the prohibited books and keep selling them).[93] They commented, on different occasions, on the economic problems that the prohibitions and confiscation of books were causing local businessmen, and even on the necessity of books for children or learned people in their districts. Finally, they even testified in their favour after these people had committed a felony if they thought the sentence was too hard. In 1568, Friar Francisco Sancho (Professor of Theology), in charge of visiting the bookstores of Salamanca, inspected twenty-five boxes of books that had arrived from Venice. He found some high-quality copies ('buenas y bien obradas') of canon law books with some writings by Charles du Moulin that were forbidden. He immobilized the stock, but at the same time wrote on behalf of the owner of the books, who had (apparently) received them from Venice thinking that they were Catholic books because of their title. The friar implored that the owner, after cutting out the mistaken parts, be allowed to sell the books.[94] In 1577, the inquisitors from Toledo received an order to take some primers (*cartillas*) out of circulation. They obeyed, but at the same time the inquisitors served as a conduit through which printer's complaints could arrive at the *Suprema*.[95] The same instructions arrived in Valladolid, and again we can find local inquisitors acting as intermediaries in favour of the city printers and booksellers who, they

---

91 Gil Fernández, *Panorama social del humanismo español*, p. 571.
92 Guibovich Pérez, 'La Inquisición y los libros prohibidos'.
93 Berger provides an example of this: in 1551 the Inquisition started a campaign against forbidden books in Valencia, based on the Index of Louvain. Booksellers asked permission to expurgate or rectify the books found at their shop, so that they could continue selling them. The four theologians appointed by the inquisitors of Valencia to examine their petition gave quite a favourable report that was sent to the *Suprema*. Berger, *Libro y lectura*, pp. 281–83.
94 Madrid, AHN, Inquisición, Leg. 3189, nos 23 and 24. His petition was transferred by the inquisitors of Valladolid, in which the Salamanca district was included, to the *Suprema*, who ordered a further examination of the books.
95 Madrid, AHN, Inquisición, Leg. 3072, exp. 129. The petition was presented by the printer Francisco de Guzmán, from Toledo. He argued that to destroy all the *cartillas* that he had (more than one thousand) instead of amending them would cause much damage to his businesses.

argued, were losing money.[96] In both cases, the *Suprema* finally allowed them to keep the *cartillas* as long as they deleted the controversial parts.

To collaborate with the Inquisition may also have been a way to fight competitors. In the case against Pedro Ocharte and Juan Ortiz in Mexico, for instance, Kenneth Ward suggests that the first report of the former employer of Ortiz against him may have been, indeed, an attempt to protect his own position against a potential economic competitor, while Ocharte 'got caught in the crossfire'.[97] This might also have been the reason for the testimony offered by the Florentine Andrea Pescioni to the Inquisition in 1563. He arrived in Spain around 1550 in connection with the Lyons and Italian publishing firms established in the Iberian Peninsula.[98] In 1560 we can find him negotiating in Seville, where he was going to settle down and start his own business as bookseller and printer.[99] Three years later, Pescioni reported to the Seville Inquisition the way in which books were carried from La Rochelle,[100] in France, to Spain by the 'Lutheran' Peregrino del Baño, from Lucca. Of course, he could have been inspired by religious zeal, but the merchant he pointed out as Lutheran also used this route to bring paper (and maybe legal books):

> Ayer, día de la Concepción de Nuestra Señora, en la tarde, estando el inquisidor Pazos en su posada hablando con un Andrea Pescioni, mercader de libros que dice ser florentino, cerca de la manera que tenían en traer libros de Francia a España, el dicho Andrea Pescioni le dixo que de León de Francia enviaban mercaderes cargazones de libros a la Rochela, que es puerto de mar, a un Peregrino del Baño, que allí reside, que es el luqués de que vuestra señoría nos tiene escrito que es gran luterano [...]; y así mismo le dijo que el dicho Peregrino del Baño tiene aquí un hermano que se llama Andrea del Baño, a quien envía libros y otras mercaderías, y que trae en este mar dos o tres navetas

---

96 Madrid, AHN, Inquisición, Leg. 3193, exp. 181. The inquisitors put forward the same argument as the printer Francisco de Guzmán a few months earlier: the booksellers had a large quantity of 'cartillas', so they would lose a lot of money if they were not allowed to amend them; besides this, they were also necessary for children.

97 Ward, '*Estas cuentas son si cuenta*', pp. 39, 43–46.

98 Rojo Vega, 'Letras Humanas'. The oldest testimony of his presence in Spain dates back to 1550, when he acted as agent of the Italian book merchants Jácome de Liarcari and José María de Terranova, both settled in Salamanca. Salamanca, AHPSa, Leg. 3650, fol. 696.

99 González Sánchez and Maillard Álvarez, *Orbe Tipográfico*. See also Montero Delgado, 'Andrea Pescioni, librero, tipógrafo y traductor'.

100 La Rochelle was a Calvinist bastion, used by Huguenot pirates as a base to attack Spanish ships, and also to deliver Reformed books to Spain. Griffin, *Oficiales de imprenta, herejía e Inquisición*, p. 91. In 1590 a man called Jerónimo de Borja, accused by the Inquisition of Toledo, declared that he had met the prince of Bearne in La Rochelle, who told him his plan of introducing 2000 copies of a Lutheran version of the New Testament into Spain. Sierra, *Procesos de la Inquisición de Toledo*, pp. 372–74.

suyas con que envía diversas mercaderías a estos puertos de España; y que había pocos días que el dicho Peregrino del Baño había enviado aquí a Sevilla al dicho Andrea del Baño en una nao de ellos mucho papel blanco de Francia, y que enviaba ahora al presente al dicho su hermano una naveta cargada de libros que vendría en breve.[101]

> (Yesterday, the day that we celebrated the Immaculate Conception of our Lady, Inquisitor Pazos was in his lodgings talking with Andrea Pescioni, a book merchant who claims to be from Florence, about the way books were brought from France into Spain; Andrea Pescioni told him that merchants from Lyons, in France, send book cargos to La Rochelle, a sea port, and that these books are addressed to a Peregrino del Baño, who lives there and who is that Lucca-born Lutheran whom you have written to us about [...]; also, that Peregrino del Baño has a brother here, called Andrea del Baño, to whom he sends books and other goods, and has two or three small ships which he uses to bring goods into Spain, and that a few days ago Peregrino del Baño had sent Andrea del Baño in Seville a cargo of white paper from France, and that a small vessel would be shortly sent full of books.)

Despite the valuable information that Pescioni brought to the inquisitors, they did not seem to trust him totally: 'y el inquisidor no quiso tratar más este negocio por disimular y que no se tomase alguna sospecha' (and the inquisitor decided not to pursue this business, in order not to raise suspicions).

A series of petitions preserved in the National Archive in Madrid demonstrate the preferential treatment that was given to some important merchants by the Inquisition. Between 1563 and 1564, five booksellers received large numbers of books from the Low Countries and France that entered the Iberian Peninsula through the northern ports of Bilbao and Laredo: some of these booksellers were also printers, most of them were foreigners, and all of them had strong links outside Spain. According to the law, the boxes containing books had to be opened at the ports where they arrived before moving anywhere else. All the merchants begged to transport the closed boxes to their cities and for them to be inspected there, where they were probably expecting better treatment by local (and

---

101 Madrid, AHN, Inquisición, Leg. 2943, nos 122 and 124. The presence in Seville in 1564 of a merchant called Andrea del Baño is confirmed by the notarial archives of the city: Maillard Álvarez, 'Estrategias de los profesionales del libro sevillanos'. The brothers Del Baño or D'Albaigne, as they were known in France (Andrea, Peregrino, and Francesco), left much evidence of their activities in different places, such as Lyons, Navarre, Bordeaux, and even the French Court. Baudrier, *Bibliographie Lyonnaise*, I, p. 84; Brumont, 'Les foires du Poitou'; Allaire, *Crépuscules ultramontains*; Hamy, 'Francisque et Andrea d'Albaigne'. I would like to thank Oury Oldman for the information on this very interesting family.

better-known) inquisitors. More surprising than the petition is the answer given by the Inquisition: in all cases it seemed to agree to the requests.[102] Only six years later, the inquisitors from Valladolid warned that in those northern ports the inspectors allowed prohibited books to pass without checking them in exchange for money.[103] They were also worried about some prominent merchants (not booksellers, and again most of them foreigners) who were importing books inside the containers of other merchandise. The local inquisitors warned them not to do it.[104]

The Inquisition sometimes exhibited a sense of pragmatism that could create some space for tolerance.[105] Inquisitors could be, for example, quite permissive with fraud, as long as this did not involve heretical books. Fraud was quite widespread in early modern trade, and the *Carrera de Indias* was a perfect environment for it.[106] The case of Pedro Calderón, a merchant–bookseller from Seville involved in the trade with New Spain, is a good example of this. In July 1580 the Mexican Inquisition accused a Mexican merchant, Francisco Velasco, of selling books that were not legally registered.[107] He declared that Pedro Calderón and Diego Mexía, both settled in Seville, had sent him and the merchant Juan Pérez de Rivera[108] these books via Cape Verde, on a slave ship. Books could not be loaded onto this kind of ship outside of the seasonal Indias Fleet. The inquisitors, who wrote to Madrid in 1581 about the case, knew that this was a way of avoiding taxes and controls, but this was also a strategy used by booksellers to make more money by getting the books to New Spain before their competitors. Although the books were hidden in barrels and the fraud was obvious, the inquisitors insisted that Pedro Calderón had not acted in bad faith, and that his only motivation was greed.[109] In

---

102 Madrid, AHN, Inquisición, Leg. 4519, no. 1. The booksellers were Francisco del Canto, Benito Boyer, and Francisco de Nevrese, from Medina del Campo; Mathías Gast, from Salamanca; and Salvador Hernández, from Valladolid.
103 Madrid, AHN, Inquisición, Leg. 3191, no. 33.
104 Madrid, AHN, Inquisición, Leg. 3191, nos 33 and 49. The merchants were Dionisio Renao, Hilario de Bonafonte, Francisco Gallo, Gonzalo de Salazar, and Simón Ruiz. The last one complained to the Suprema, and it seems that he was influential enough to make them hear his protest. Apparently, that same year (1572) Simón Ruiz decided to stop importing books from France because of the corruption coming from that country. Maclean, 'Murder, Debt and Retribution', p. 249; Lapeyre, *Une Famille des Marchands*, p. 570.
105 García Cárcel, 'Estudio Preliminar'.
106 González Sánchez, *Atlantes de papel*, pp. 24–26.
107 Mexico City, AGN, Inquisición, vol. 89, exp. 24. Fernández del Castillo, *Libros y libreros en el siglo XVI*, pp. 250–54.
108 This Juan Pérez de Rivera is likely the same merchant from Seville who settled in Mexico City in 1560. His importation business prospered in New Spain, and he was also a tax collector and 'familiar' of the Holy Office, a position that would be kept by his son, the public notary Juan Pérez de Rivera. Mijares Ramírez, *Catálogo de Protocolos*, pp. 32–34.
109 Madrid, AHN, Inquisición, Lib. 597, fol. 182ᵛ.

March 1582 the inquisitors in Seville received a letter from Madrid warning them only to admonish Pedro Calderón seriously for his behaviour, and to be more careful with their controls.[110]

Conclusion

At the beginning of the sixteenth century, the Inquisition was not particularly concerned about printers and booksellers, but as the Protestant threat spread through Europe and books played a major role in the diffusion of the new ideas, the relationship between the Holy Office and book professionals became more intense, for better and for worse. Those relationships sometimes became a tragedy, but this chapter has tried to study those relationships in their entirety, not just the most dramatic parts. As we have seen, often the actors in this play chose a role that not only kept them away from danger but also allowed them to improve their situation. The collaboration between booksellers or printers on the one hand and the Inquisition on the other could be positive for both: for the Holy Office it was a very effective source of information and, in consequence, a better way to control the circulation and reading of books. In return, some booksellers and printers seem to have received better, even benevolent, treatment for their business (whether this was legal or not), and they could earn money working for the Inquisition, fight competitors, and use the local inquisitors as mediators to intercede between them and the *Suprema*. Their collaboration might have been caused by fear, by faith, or both, but we cannot deny the importance of such relationships in Hispanic cultural history.

---

110 Madrid, AHN, Inquisición, Lib. 328, fols 22ᵛ–23ʳ. It is worth remarking that in 1583 the control system of books sent to the Americas from Seville became stricter, and it is from this year onwards that we have a complete series of the titles carried by the Fleet. González Sánchez, *Los mundos del libro*.

Works Cited

Manuscripts and Archival Sources, and Other Unedited Material

Abbreviations used: Leg. (Legajo), Lib. (Libro), exp. (expediente), no. (número), fol. (folio), s.f. (sin folio)

Madrid, Archivo Histórico Nacional (AHN), Inquisición, Leg. 58, no. 13
———, Inquisición, Leg. 2075-I, no. 2
———, ———. 2943, no. 122, 124
———, ———. 2947
———, ———. 2949
———, ———. 2392–2
———, ———. 3068, no. 8
———, ———. 3068–1, exp. 82
———, ———. 3072, exp. 129
———, ———. 3189, no. 23, 24
———, ———. 3189, exp. 79, 136
———, ———. 3191, no. 33, 49
———, ———. 3193, exp. 136, 181
———, ———. 3194, no. 54
———, ———. 4435, no. 5
———, ———. 4442, no. 36, 40
———, ———. 4519, no. 1
———, ———. 5312, no. 36
———, Inquisición, Lib. 574
———, ———. 594
———, ———. 597
———, ———. 328
Mexico City, Archivo General de la Nación (AGN), Inquisición, vol. 77, exp. 19
———, Inquisición, vol. 89, exp. 24, 25
———, Inquisición, vol. 90, exp. 45
Salamanca, Archivo Histórico Provincial de Salamanca (AHPSa), Leg. 3650
Seville, Archivo Histórico Provincial de Sevilla (AHPSe), Leg. 10756
———, Leg. 12425
Seville, Archivo de la Parroquia del Sagrario (APS), Lib. 4 of Baptisms
———, Lib. 5 of Baptisms
Simancas, Archivo General de Simancas (AGS), Registro General del Sello, Leg. 150001, 57
Valladolid, Archivo Histórico Provincial de Valladolid (AHPV), Leg. 7335

Secondary Studies

Alberro, Solange, *Inquisición y Sociedad en México 1571–1700* (Mexico City: FCE, 1993)

Allaire, Bernard, *Crépuscules ultramontains: marchands italiens et grand commerce à Bordeaux au XVIe siècle* (Pessac: Presses universitaires de Bordeaux, 2008)

Álvarez, Carmen, *Impresores, libreros y mercaderes*, II (Zaragoza: Libros Pórtico, 2009)

Baudrier, Henri, *Bibliographie lyonnaise: recherches sur les imprimeurs, libraires, relieurs et fondeurs de lettres de Lyon au XVIe siècle*, I (Lyons: A la Libraire Ancienne D'Auguste Brun, 1895)

Bécares Botas, Vicente, 'Aspectos de la producción y distribución del Nuevo Rezado', in *Early Music Printing and Publishing in the Iberian World*, ed. by Iain Felon and Tess Knighton (Kassel: Reichenberger, 2006), pp. 1–22

——, *Librerías salmantinas del siglo XVI* (Segovia: Instituto Castellano y Leonés de la Lengua, 2007)

Berger, Philippe, *Libro y lectura en la Valencia del Renacimiento*, I (Valencia: Edicions Alfons el Magnànim, 1987)

Bouza, Fernando, *Dásele licencia y privilegio. Don Quijote y la aprobación de libros en el siglo de Oro* (Madrid: Akal, 2012)

Brumont, Francis, 'Les foires du Poitou et le commerce franco-espagnol au XVIe siècle', in *Le commerce atlantique franco–espagnol. Acteurs, négoces et ports (XVe–XVIIIe siècle)*, ed. by Jean-Philippe Priotti and Guy Saupin (Rennes: Presses Universitaires de Rennes, 2008), pp. 129–46

Cardim, Pedro, Tamar Herzog, José Javier Ruiz Ibáñez, and Gaetano Sabatini, *Polycentric Monarchies: How did Early Modern Spain and Portugal Achieve and Maintain a Global Hegemony?* (Brighton: Sussex Academic Press, 2012)

Castañeda Delgado, Paulino, and Pilar Hernández Aparicio, *La Inquisición de Lima*, I: *1570–1635* (Madrid: Deimos, 1989)

Cayuela, Anne, *Alonso Pérez de Montalbán. Un librero en el Madrid de los Austrias* (Madrid: Calambur, 2005)

Cerrillo Cruz, Gonzalo, *Los familiares de la Inquisición española* (Valladolid: Junta de Castilla y León, 2000)

Chuchiak IV, John F., ed., *The Inquisition in New Spain, 1536–1820: A Documentary History* (Baltimore: John Hopkins University Press, 2012)

Constantin, Léa, 'Les enjeux de la controverse religieuse dans l'imprimerie lyonnaise, 1560–1565' (unpublished Mémoire de recherche, June 2011, ENSSIB-Université Lumière Lyon 2)
<https://www.enssib.fr/bibliotheque-numerique/notices/56719-les-enjeux-de-la-controverse-religieuse-dans-l-imprimerie-lyonnaise-1560-1565> [accessed 14 August 2021]

Contreras, Jaime, and Jean P. Dedieu, 'Estructuras geográficas del Santo Oficio en España', in *Historia de la Inquisición en España y América*, ed. by Joaquín Pérez Villanueva and Bartolomé Escandell Bonet, II (Madrid: Biblioteca de Autores Cristianos, 1993), pp. 3–47

De los Reyes Gómez, Fermín, *El libro en España y América. Legislación y censura, siglos XV–XVIII* (Madrid: Arco/Libros, 2000)

Dedieu, Jean-Pierre, 'Le modèle religieux: le refus de la Réforme et le contrôle de la pensée', in *L'Inquisition Espagnole. XVe–XIXe siècle*, ed. by Bartolomé Bennassar (Paris: Hachette, 1979), pp. 263–303

Defourneaux, Martin, *L'Inquisition espagnole et les livres français au XVIIIe siècle* (Paris: Presses Universitaires de France, 1963)

Delgado Casado, Juan, *Diccionario de impresores españoles (siglos XV–XVII)* (Madrid: Arco/Libros, 1996)

Escandell Bonet, Bartolomé, and Álvaro Huerga, 'Las adecuaciones estructurales: establecimiento de la Inquisición en Indias', in *Historia de la Inquisición en España y América*, ed. by Joaquín Pérez Villanueva and Bartolomé Escandell Bonet, I (Madrid: Biblioteca de Autores Cristianos, 1993), pp. 713–30

Fernández del Castillo, Francisco, *Libros y libreros en el siglo XVI* (México: FCE, 1982)

Gacto, Enrique, 'Libros venenosos', *Revista de Inquisición*, 6 (1997), 7–44

García, Idalia, 'Before we are Condemned: Inquisitorial Fears and Private Libraries in New Spain', in *Books in the Catholic World during the Early Modern Period*, ed. by Natalia Maillard-Álvarez (Leiden: Brill, 2014), pp. 171–90

García Cárcel, Ricardo, *Orígenes de la Inquisición española. El tribunal de Valencia, 1478–1530* (Barcelona: Península, 1976)

——, *Herejía y sociedad en el siglo XVI. La Inquisición en Valencia. 1530–1609* (Barcelona: Ediciones Península, 1980)

——, 'Estudio Preliminar', in *Estudios de la Inquisición Española*, ed. by Antonio Domínguez Ortiz (Granada: Comares, 2010), pp. ix–xxxi

García Cárcel, Ricardo, and Doris Moreno, *Inquisición. Historia Crítica* (Madrid: Temás de Hoy, 2000)

García Oro, José, *La monarquía y los libros en el Siglo de Oro* (Alcalá de Henares: Centro de Estudios Cisneros, 1999)

García Oro, José, and María J. Portela Silva, *Felipe II y los libreros: actas de las visitas a las librerías del reino de Castilla en 1572* (Madrid: Cisneros, 1997)

Gil Fernández, Luis, *Panorama social del humanismo español (1500–1800)* (Madrid: Tecnos, 1997)

Gilmont, Jean-François, 'La propagande protestante de Genève vers l'Espagne au XVIe siècle', in *El libro antiguo español. VI. De libros, librerías, imprentas y lectores*, ed. by Pedro M. Cátedra and María Luisa López-Vidriero (Salamanca: Universidad de Salamanca, 2002), pp. 119–33

González del Castillo, Francisco, *Libros y libreros en México en el siglo XVI* (Mexico City: Guerrero, 1914)

González Sánchez, Carlos A., *Los mundos del libro. Medios de difusión de la cultura occidental en las Indias de los siglos XVI y XVII* (Seville: Universidad de Sevilla, 2001)
———, *Atlantes de papel. Adoctrinamiento, creación y tipografía en la Monarquía Hispánica de los siglos XVI y XVII* (Barcelona: Ediciones Rubeo, 2008)
González Sánchez, Carlos A., and Natalia Maillard Álvarez, *Orbe Tipográfico. El mercado del libro en la Sevilla de la segunda mitad del siglo XVI* (Gijón: Trea, 2003)
Gonzalo Sánchez-Molero, José Luis, 'Los impresores ante el Consejo Real: el problema de la licencia y del privilegio (1502–1540)', in *Actas XIII y XIV Jornadas bibliográficas Bartolomé J. Gallardo* (Badajoz: Unión de Bibliófilos Extremeños, 2009), pp. 119–84
Goñi Gaztámbide, J., 'El impresor Miguel de Eguía procesado por la Inquisición', *Hispania Sacra*, 1 (1948), 35–88
Griffin, Clive, *Los Cromberger: la historia de una imprenta en Sevilla y Méjico* (Madrid: Ediciones Cultura Hispana, 1991)
———, *Oficiales de imprenta, herejía e inquisición en la España del siglo XVI* (Madrid: Ollero y Ramos, 2009)
Guibovich Pérez, Pedro, *La inquisición y la censura de libros en el Perú virreinal (1570–1813)* (Lima: Ediciones del Congreso del Perú, 2000)
———, *Censura, libros e Inquisición en el Perú colonial, 1570–1754* (Seville: CSIC, 2003)
———, 'La Inquisición y los libros prohibidos en el virreinato del Perú (siglos XVI–XVII)', *Cultura Escrita y Sociedad*, 2 (2008), 60–75
Hamy, Eugéne T., 'Francisque et Andrea d'Albaigne. Cosmographes Lucquois au service du roy de France', *Études Historiques et Géographiques* (1896), 241–60
Herrero Sánchez, Manuel, and Klemens Kaps, 'Connectors, Networks and Commercial Systems: Approaches to the Study of Early Modern Maritime Commercial History', in *Merchants and Trade Networks in the Atlantic and the Mediterranean, 1550–1800*, ed. by Manuel Herrero Sánchez and Klemens Kaps (London: Routledge, 2017), pp. 1–36
de Horozco, Sebastián, *Relaciones Históricas Toledanas, introducción y transcripción de Jack Weiner* (Toledo: I.P.I.E.T., 1981)
Infelise, Mario, *I libri proibiti: Da Gutenberg all'Encyclopédie* (Rome: GLF editori Laterza, 1999)
Jiménez, Nora, 'Comerciantes de libros en la Nueva España en el siglo XVI. Perfiles y estrategias', in *Impresos y libros en la historia económica de México (siglos XVI–XIX)*, ed. by M. Pilar Gutiérrez (Guadalajara: Universidad de Guadalajara, 2007), pp. 17–40
———, 'Cuentas fallidas, deudas omnipresentes. Los difíciles comienzos del mercado del libro novohispano', *Anuario de Estudios Americanos*, 71.2 (2014), 423–46

Julia, Dominique, 'Lecturas y Contrarreforma', in *Historia de la lectura en el mundo occidental*, ed. by Guglielmo Cavallo and Roger Chartier (Madrid: Taurus, 1997), pp. 370–75

Kamen, Henry, *The Spanish Inquisition: A Historical Revision* (London: Weidenfeld & Nicolson, 1997)

Lapeyre, Henri, *Une Famille des Marchands: les Ruiz. Contribution à l'étude du commerce entre la France et l'Espagne au temps de Philippe II* (Paris: Armand Colin, 1955)

Lea, Henry C., *A History of the Inquisition of the Middle Ages* (London: Sampson Low, 1888)

López Souto, Noelia, and Inés Velázquez Puerto, eds, *Libros, imprenta y censura en la Europa Meridional del siglo XV al XVII* (Salamanca: IEMYRhd, 2020)

Maclean, Ian, 'Murder, Debt and Retribution in the Italic–Franco–Spanish Book Trade: The Beraud–Michel–Ruiz Affair, 1586–1591', in *Learning and the Market Place: Essays in the History of the Early Modern Book*, ed. by Ian Maclean (Leiden: Brill, 2009), pp. 227–72

Maillard Álvarez, Natalia, 'Puertas de *mala ventura*: el control inquisitorial de la entrada de libros en los puertos del distrito sevillano durante el Quinientos', in *El mar en los siglos modernos. Actas de la X Reunión Científica de la Fundación Española de Historia Moderna*, ed. by Manuel-Reyes García Hurtado, Domingo L. González Lopo, and Enrique Martínez Rodríguez, II (Santiago de Compostela: Junta de Galicia, 2009), pp. 279–91

——, 'Estrategias de los profesionales del libro sevillanos ante el Santo Oficio: entre la evasión y la colaboración', *Litterae*, 26 (2012), 25–44

De la Mano, Marta, *Mercaderes e impresores de libros en la Salamanca del Siglo XVI* (Salamanca: Universidad de Salamanca, 1998)

Márquez, Antonio, *Literatura e Inquisición en España 1478–1834* (Madrid: Taurus, 1980)

Martín Abad, Julián, *La imprenta en Alcalá de Henares (1502–1600)*, I (Madrid: Arco Libros, 1991)

Martínez de Bujanda, Jesús, *Index de l'Inquisition Espagnole, 1551, 1554, 1559* (Sherbrooke: Centre d'Études de la Renaissance, 1984)

——, *Index des Livres Interdits* (Sherbrooke: Centre d'Études de la Renaissance, 1985–2002)

——, *Index de l'Inquisition Espagnole, 1583, 1584* (Sherbrooke: Centre d'Études de la Renaissance, 1993)

——, 'Sguardo panoramico sugli indici dei libri proibiti del XVI secolo', in *La censura nell'Europa del secolo XVI*, ed. by Ugo Rozzo (Udine: Università di Udine, 1997), pp. 1–14

——, *El Índice de libros prohibidos y expurgados de la Inquisición española (1551–1819)* (Madrid: BAC, 2016)

——, *Censura de la Inquisición y de la Igleisa en España (1520–1966)* (Madrid: BAC, 2019)

Martínez Jiménez, Alfonso, 'La persecución inquisitorial del ramismo en la España de la segunda mitad del siglo XVI', in *Autour de Ramus. Le combat*, ed. by Kees Meerhoff and Jean-Claude Moisan (Paris: Honoré Champion, 2005), pp. 451–76

Mena, Ramón, 'El librero Pedro Bally en la Inquisición, 1581', *Boletín del Archivo General de la Nación*, 4.1 (1933), 71–73

Mijares Ramírez, Ivonne, *Catálogo de Protocolos del Archivo General de Notarías de la Ciudad de México. Introducción* (Mexico City: UNAM, 2002)

Moll, Jaime, 'Gaspar Zapata, impresor sevillano condenado por al Inquisición en 1562', *Pliegos de Bibliofilia*, 7 (1999), 5–10

Montero Delgado, Juan, 'Andrea Pescioni, librero, tipógrafo y traductor en Sevilla', in *Italie et Espagne entre Empire, cités et États. Constructions d'histoires communes (XVe–XVIe siècles)*, ed. by Alice Carette, Rafael M. Girón-Pascual, Raúl González Arévalo, and Cécile Terreaux-Scotto (Rome: Viella, 2017), pp. 87–99

Moreno Gallego, Valentín, 'Matías Gast, preso inquisitorial', in *La memoria de los libros: estudios sobre la historia del escrito y de la lectura en Europa y América*, ed. by Pedro M. Cátedra and María Luisa López-Vidriero, I (Salamanca: IHLL, 2004), pp. 851–68

Morisse, Gérard, 'Blas de Robles (1542–1592). Primer editor de Cervantes', in *El libro antiguo español. De libros, librerías, imprentas y lectores*, ed. by Pedro M. Cátedra and Maria Luisa López-Vidriero (Salamanca: Universidad de Salamanca, 2002), pp. 285–320

Nesvig, Martin A., *Ideology and Inquisition: The World of the Censors in Early Mexico* (New Haven: Yale University Press, 2009)

Osorio Pérez, María J., María A. Moreno Trujillo, and Juan M. de la Obra, *Trastiendas de la cultura: librerías y libreros en la Granada del siglo XVI* (Granada: Universidad de Granada, 2001)

Ostolaza Elizondo, María Isabel, *Impresores y libreros en Navarra durante los siglos XV–XVI* (Pamplona: Universidad Pública de Navarra, 2004)

Palomo, Federico, 'Un catolicismo en plural: identidades, disciplinamiento y cultura religiosa en los mundos ibéricos de la Edad Moderna', in *Poder, sociedad, religión y tolerancia en el mundo hispánico, de Fernando el Católico al siglo XVIII*, ed. by Eliseo Serrano Martín and Jesús Gascón Pérez (Zaragoza: Instituto Fernando el Católico, 2018), pp. 193–217

De Pascual Martínez, Lope, 'Libros y libreros en Murcia según los Protocolos del siglo XVII', in *El libro antiguo español. II. Actas del segundo coloquio internacional*, ed. by Pedro M. Cátedra and María Luisa López-Vidriero (Salamanca: Universidad de Salamanca, 1992), pp. 163–75

Peña Díaz, Manuel, *Escribir y prohibir. Inquisición y censura en los Siglos de Oro* (Madrid: Cátedra, 2015)

Pérez García, Rafael M., *La imprenta y la literatura espiritual castellana en la España del Renacimiento* (Gijón: Trea, 2006)

Pettegree, Andrew, 'Centre and Periphery in the European Book World', *Transactions of the Royal Historical Society, Sixth Series*, 18 (2008), 101–28

Pinto Crespo, Virgilio, *Inquisición y control ideológico en la España del siglo XVI* (Madrid: Taurus, 1983)

Ramos Soriano, José Abel, *Los delincuentes de papel. Inquisición y libros en la Nueva España (1571–1820)* (Mexico: FCE, 2011)

Rissoan, Bastien, 'Jean Temporal: libraire de la Renaissance Lyonnaise (1549–1571)' (unpublished Master thesis, Lyon, ENSSIB, June 2013)

Rojo Vega, Anastasio, 'Letras Humanas en una de las mejores librerías de la España de Carlos V: Liarcari-Terranova (Salamanca, 1557)', in *Bibliotecas y librerías en la España de Carlos V*, ed. by José Mª Díez Borque (Madrid: Calambur, 2015), pp. 251–75

Rosses, Max, *Correspondance de Christophe Plantin*, I (Nendeln: Kraus Reprint, 1968)

Rubió i Balaguer, Jordi, *Llibreters i impressors a la Corona d'Aragó* (Barcelona: Abadia de Montserrat, 1993)

Ruiz Fidalgo, Lorenzo, *La imprenta en Salamanca (1501–1600)* (Madrid: Arco/Libros, 1994)

Sierra, Julio, *Procesos de la Inquisición de Toledo (1575–1610). Manuscrito de Halle* (Madrid: Trotta, 2005)

Stols, Alexander A. M., *Pedro Ocharte. El tercer impresor mexicano* (Mexico City: Biblioteca Nacional, 1990)

Tauro, Alberto, 'Antonio Ricardo. Primer impresor', in *Incunables peruanos en la Biblioteca Nacional de Perú (1584–1619)*, ed. by Irma García Gayoso, Dionicia Morales de la Cruz, and Silvana Salazar Ayllón (Lima: Biblioteca Nacional del Perú, 1996), p. xxiv

Tellechea Idígoras, Ignacio, 'Bartolomé Carranza en Flandes. El clima religioso de los Países Bajos (1557–1558)', in *Reformata Reformanda*, ed. by Erwin Iserloh and Konrad Repgen, II (Münster: Aschendorff, 1965), pp. 317–43

Toribio Medina, José, *La imprenta en México (1539–1821)*, I (Mexico: UNAM, 1989)

Vázquez de Prada, Valentín, 'La Inquisición y los libros sospechosos en la época de Valdés-Salas (1547–1566)', in *Simposio Valdés-Salas conmemorativo del IV centenario de la muerte de su fundador D. Fernando de Valdés (1483–1568): su personalidad, su obra, su tiempo, Oviedo 8–11 Diciembre 1968* (Oviedo: Universidad de Oviedo, 1968), pp. 147–55

Vaquero Serrano, Carmen, *El maestro Alvar Gómez: biografía y prosa inédita* (Toledo: Caja de Castilla la Mancha, 1993)

Vega, María José, Julian Weiss, and Cesc Esteve, eds, *Reading and Censorship in Early Modern Europe* (Barcelona: Universidad de Barcelona, 2010)

Ward, Kenneth C., '*Estas cuentas son si cuenta*: The Inquisition Trials of Juan Ortiz and Pedro Ocharte, A Historical Revision' (unpublished report presented to the Faculty of the Graduate School of the University of Texas at Austin, 2001)

Werner, Thomas, *Los protestantes y la Inquisición en España en tiempos de la Reforma y al Contrarreforma* (Leuven: Leuven University Press, 2001)

Yhmoff Cabrera, Jesús, *Los impresos mexicanos del siglo XVI en la Biblioteca Nacional de México* (México: UNAM, 1990)

VLADIMIR ABRAMOVIĆ

The Colony of the Republic of Ragusa Merchants in Belgrade in the Sixteenth Century and their Printing Press[*]

Introduction: The Development of the Republic of Ragusa (Dubrovnik) from the Late Middle Ages until the Late Sixteenth Century

Since its founding in the seventh century and up to 1205, when it came under Venetian rule, Ragusa (Dubrovnik) was a relatively small settlement of fishermen, artisans, merchants, and sailors. Venetian suzerainty and the desire to rule the Adriatic Sea had forced the residents of Ragusa to look for different markets and trade opportunities. During the decades following 1205, they established a merchant network that was deeply rooted in the Balkan lands. Local feudal rulers were not always pleased with these developments and the accompanying Ragusan trade supremacy; however, none took action against them. The unwillingness (or inability) of Ragusa to exert political pressure in the wake of economic penetration was probably the reason for this, sometimes grudging, tolerance.[1]

---

[*] This paper has been written as a part of national project 'Modernisation of Western Balkans' (No. 177009), funded by The Ministry of Education, Science and Technology of Republic of Serbia. Translation of titles of publications in Serbian are given in the bibliography.

[1] Samardžić, *Veliki vek Dubrovnika*, pp. 7–8.

Vladimir Abramović is a Postdoctoral Researcher at the Department of History at the Faculty of Philosophy of the University of Belgrade. He was a member of the working groups on the international project COST Action IS1301 *New Communities of Interpretation: Contexts, Strategies and Processes of Religious Transformation in Late Medieval and Early Modern Europe*. He has been secretary of the academic journal *Acta historiae medicinae stomatologiae pharmaciae medicinae veterinariae* since 2013.

Networking Europe and New Communities of Interpretation (1400–1600), ed. by Margriet Hoogvliet, Manuel F. Fernández Chaves, *and* Rafael M. Pérez García, New Communities of Interpretation, 4 (Turnhout: Brepols, 2023), pp. 201–214
BREPOLS PUBLISHERS   10.1484/M.NCI-EB.5.134315

This deep-rooted network of trade posts and caravan routes was the reason for the even greater prosperity of Ragusa following the Ottoman conquest of the Balkans between the fourteenth and sixteenth centuries. The Ottoman state needed some sort of trade connection with the West, and this well-developed system was able to fulfil that role. Hence the Republic of Ragusa received its privileged position in trade from the Ottoman sultans, while at the same time the abolition of old feudal boundaries and the establishment of a single customs area caused Ragusan trade to boom. Its old overlord, Venice, was still more interested in commerce with the Levant, while the Western European states were oriented towards overseas trade. This vacuum opened the opportunity for Ragusa to collect enormous riches from trade with the Ottomans; it could be argued that their profits rose exponentially.[2] It is worth noting that the Ottoman conquests had also enabled the establishment of far-reaching trading connections with the Middle East, as the presence of Persian traders in Ragusa can be attested from 1522.[3]

This economic rise of the Republic of Ragusa in the sixteenth century was accompanied by increased political importance. Its diplomats succeeded in obtaining Ottoman protection and support in conflicts with Venice, which often tried to usurp Ragusan trade interests, and even its independence.[4] Furthermore, the emergence of Spain as a dominant power in the Christian part of the Mediterranean was seen as an opportunity to acquire another patron. Ragusa managed to convince the Spanish Crown to grant trading privileges to its merchants, as well as political protection from all others, but primarily from Venice. The strategic equilibrium enjoyed by the Republic of Ragusa was maintained without too much effort and lasted throughout the sixteenth century. However, the closing decade of that century saw a change in this dynamic. Venice managed to open the port of Split on the Dalmatian coast in 1592, thereby redirecting trade with the Ottoman Empire into their hands and becoming a direct competitor with Ragusa. Stimulated by this development, Sarajevo became a significant trading centre, with its merchants spreading through the Balkans, creating yet more competition for Ragusans. Around the same time, traders from the Ottoman realms, mainly Greeks, Armenians, and Jews, also started to spread through the Balkan Peninsula, creating even more competition for the merchants of the Republic of Ragusa. On top of that, France, England, and Netherlands have started to penetrate Mediterranean

---

2 Samardžić, *Veliki vek Dubrovnika*, pp. 8–9; Tadić, 'O društvenoj strukturi', p. 556.
3 Hrabak, 'Trgovina Persijanaca', pp. 257–58.
4 Vojnović, *Istorija Dubrovačke Republike*, pp. 98–101.

and especially the Levantine trade routes at the very end of sixteenth century. All this created an unfavourable conjuncture for Ragusans and inaugurated a period of decline for the Republic in the following century.[5]

The Ragusan Colony in Belgrade

One of the significant colonies of Ragusan merchants was found in Belgrade. They began trading there at the beginning of the fifteenth century, when the city became part of the Serbian Despotate, and when its ruler, Despot Stefan Lazarević, tried to develop Belgrade's economy and commerce. However, by the mid-fifteenth century the Serbian Despotate was conquered by the Ottomans, while the city and its surroundings became battlegrounds between the Hungarians and Turks. These turbulent events proved unfavourable for the Ragusans, so they withdrew from the area. Only when the Ottomans had finally conquered Belgrade (1521), did the merchants return. We can only loosely pinpoint the exact year of their establishment, but the earliest data point to 1532, the date of the testament of a Ragusan merchant permanently settled in Belgrade. The first association of Ragusan merchants, founded with the aim of settling and trading in Belgrade, was established on 31 October 1536.[6]

Not all of them, however, settled permanently in Belgrade. According to archival data, the majority of merchants resided there only temporarily; combinations of favourable circumstances for trade enabled the merchants to become rich very quickly, so after a few years they returned back to Ragusa. Their families had remained in Ragusa during their absence. The number of those permanently settled in Belgrade had increased in the last third of the century, primarily because of two reasons. Firstly, the volume of trade had increased, which meant a more permanent presence was desirable in order to better exploit the opportunities. Secondly, the composition of the merchant group had changed. In the beginning they had come from a noble background, or from the more affluent citizen families. Now, the majority of traders were from less well-off citizens, or former peasants turned traders, who adapted to the life abroad more easily.[7]

Regardless of whether they chose to settle permanently or not, or whether they rented or purchased a house or an estate, merchants from Ragusa aimed to reside in a single neighbourhood. They chose an area on the north-eastern slope of the city, oriented towards the Danube, and close

---

5 Samardžić, *Veliki vek Dubrovnika*, pp. 10–11.
6 Samardžić, 'Dubrovčani u Beogradu u XVI i XVII veku', pp. 425–26.
7 Samardžić, 'Dubrovčani u Beogradu u XVI i XVII veku', p. 426; Tadić, 'O društvenoj strukturi', p. 559.

to the *Bezistan* (or *Bedesten*), the trading heart of the city. It was called the Ragusan, Christian or Latin Quarter. The colony was compact and territorially unified. This was the result of a conscious policy of the Ragusan merchants and of support rendered by the Republic, so by the end of the sixteenth century there were no other residents in the Quarter except for them. The land on which their property was built remained in Ottoman ownership, but Ragusans could use it or sell it as undisputed owners, as long as the property tax was paid. The document proving their possession of property was issued by the Belgrade *kadi* (judge) who presided over contracts regarding changes in ownership. The Ragusan colony was to be destroyed in the sieges of Belgrade in 1688 and 1690, during the Great Turkish War (1683–1699).[8]

The Ragusan merchants had several names for their settlements in the Ottoman Empire. If they wanted to designate a settlement or business community, they used the term *plazza*; if they thought of a colony in legal terms, they used the word *collona* or municipality. The body which gathered the majority of merchants in a given settlement was called *skup* (assembly); it had a more layered meaning, as it was used to name a group of people taking part in the assembly, to name of the institution itself, and also the very act of gathering and deliberating on a given issue.[9] The *skup*'s tasks were twofold. It had, up to a point, judicial power over the colony, primarily in the fields of property, inheritance, marital, and civil-legal relations and issues. Cases that were deemed important were sent to Ragusa for inspection and confirmation by the authorities. The second task was to implement instructions arriving from Ragusa regarding to the organization of trade, price politics, tax collection, relations with the Ottoman authorities, and the management of the colony itself. The number of *skup* members was not predetermined: all merchants that were part of the colony were obliged to attend its meetings. Decisions were made by secret voting and by a simple majority. When a decision had been voted for, all present would take an oath on the Gospel, promising that they will honour the decision regardless of their personal opinion. Those that were absent from the meetings for various reasons (illness or business trips) were also subject to decisions being made at the *skup*.[10]

All the major Ragusan colonies in the Ottoman Empire had a supervisor (*capo di colona*), elected by the *skup* from among the oldest and most respected members. This decision always had to be confirmed by the Ragusan government. Once appointed, the supervisor had a wide range of duties. He organized *skup*'s sessions, presided over meetings, and kept the seal of the colony. He had the authority to conduct negotiations

---

8 Samardžić, 'Dubrovčani u Beogradu u XVI i XVII veku', pp. 427–28.
9 Samardžić, 'Dubrovčani u Beogradu u XVI i XVII veku', p. 430.
10 Samardžić, 'Dubrovčani u Beogradu u XVI i XVII veku', pp. 431–32.

with local Ottoman officials (albeit with permission from the Ragusan government), and he also enjoyed the privilege of secret and uncontrolled correspondence with the authorities in Ragusa. The administrative affairs of the colony were run by a chaplain, who kept the minute book, along with the colony's archive. However, he was in a peculiar position, as he was subject both to the Ragusan authorities and the *skup*, serving as a link between the two. He was not allowed to take part in any decision-making, according to long-established Ragusan rules. In order to function as municipalities, the Ragusan colonies had their own treasuries. The coffers were filled by taxes paid for every transaction, while the expenditure was in the hands of a supervisor, the chaplain, and an appointed merchant. They were held accountable by *skup*, and indirectly by the Ragusan authorities. The end of the sixteenth century was marked by a shift in Ragusan policy towards its colonies. This was the time of the greater influx of merchants originating from the lower classes, who were considered to be prone to local influences. Therefore, the Ragusan authorities increased the level of control. This was achieved by occasional visits of Ragusan ambassadors, who had sovereign rights and could intervene directly in the colony's affairs.[11]

Ragusan traders in Belgrade adapted their residences to local urban forms, i.e. their settlement was not divided in quarters that were intended for residence or storing their goods (as it was the case in Ragusan settlements in Italy, for example). Instead, in Belgrade their private and business spaces overlapped, which is a clear characteristic of Oriental urban framework. The size of the colony in sixteenth- and seventeenth-century Belgrade in is estimated to be around thirty or forty houses.[12]

The Social and Educational Backgrounds of Ragusan Merchants in Belgrade

The question of the literacy and the social origins of the Ragusan merchants settling in the Balkan colonies is interesting. As mentioned before, the first traders living in Belgrade belonged to noble families and therefore their education was on a comparatively high level, as was the case with the European nobility of the era generally. However, in the second half of sixteenth century there was an influx of merchants of more humble origins, namely originating from the lower classes of Ragusan citizens, or former peasants from the vicinity of the city of Ragusa. They did not show a particular interest in education, but nonetheless maintained the level of literacy needed for trading and for the management of the colony.

---
[11] Samardžić, 'Dubrovčani u Beogradu u XVI i XVII veku', pp. 433–34.
[12] Samardžić, 'Dubrovčani u Beogradu', pp. 55–56.

Although bookkeeping was done by merchants of noble origin personally, the increase in the volume of trade necessitated the hiring of scribes, whose task it was to keep business records in *il libro quaderno*, either for a particular trader or for a merchant association.[13]

While merchants from Ragusa had a sufficient level of literacy, what was the situation of those who were born in the colonies? They had access to adequate education, and parents had several options for schooling their children: some gave their offspring into the foster care of a renowned merchant, who promised to teach the child to read and write, as well as to instruct a son into the art of trade and bookkeeping. And those merchants who were well off would send their sons to Ragusa, where they could receive the best education possible. In the early seventeenth century, the Jesuits opened a school in Belgrade, which made becoming literate even easier.[14]

One of the side-effects of the Ragusan merchants' presence and literacy levels was their significant impact on trading customs in the European part of the Ottoman Empire. Written contracts suppressed the use of tally sticks and similar methods; they also had positive effects on the literacy of the domestic, Serbian (and other Slavonic) population. There were two reasons for this: merchants from Ragusa spoke, beside Italian, the Serbian language, so at least half of their letters to Ragusa were written in the Serbian language and in Cyrillic script. They themselves pointed out this fact in their letters: 'in carattere serviano' (in Serbian letters), 'nella lingua serviana' (in Serbian language), 'in serviano' (in Serbian), 'nella lingua nostra serviana' (in our Serbian language), etc. The official correspondence of a colony was conducted in Italian and Latin, but the authors of those letters and reports were mostly scribes. As for private letters, the Cyrillic script was used up until the very end of the seventeenth century, when Latin script took over due to Catholic propaganda aimed at Christians in the Ottoman Empire.[15] A good illustration of this is the fact that Ragusan merchants in Belgrade frequently converted books printed in the Latin language and script to Cyrillic letters. One of the best examples would be the *Hortulus animae* — Ортус аниме (*Ortus anime*) (Fig. 9.1).[16]

---

13 Samardžić, 'Dubrovčani u Beogradu u XVI i XVII veku', p. 452.
14 Samardžić, 'Dubrovčani u Beogradu u XVI i XVII veku', pp. 454–55; Samardžić, 'Podmladak dubrovačkih trgovaca', pp. 77–78.
15 Samardžić, 'Dubrovčani u Beogradu u XVI i XVII veku', p. 456.
16 Samardžić, 'Dubrovčani u Beogradu u XVI i XVII veku', pp. 456–57.

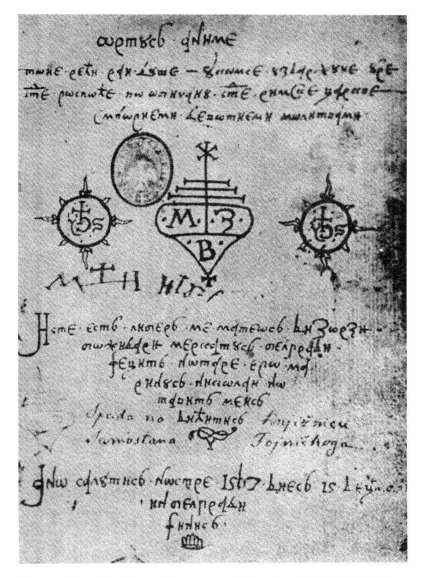

Figure 9.1. Hortulus animae — Ортус аниме (Belgrade, 1567). Archive HAZU, Zbirka kodeksa, sig. III a 25. Image taken from *Istorija Beograda*, I, p. 457, with permission from IP Prosveta AD. All rights reserved.

The Principal Activities of Ragusan Traders in Belgrade

Ragusan traders in the Balkans did not restrict themselves with regard to the types of merchandise they were interested in. If some endeavour was profitable, whether it was book publishing or the wheat trade, they would invest their money, hoping for a relatively quick profit. The spectrum of their activities was very broad, and there are indications that they were engaged in the insurance business in Belgrade (this was mostly ship insurance for river sailings).[17] Ragusan merchants were not conducting trade only for themselves: they formed a very important link which supplied the city of Ragusa with wheat in case of food scarcity or famine. The government of the Republic of Ragusa used its connections and the wealth of its merchants in order to procure foodstuffs. This practice was especially evident in the years of food crisis, such as 1564–1565, 1569–1570, and the 1590s.[18]

One of the Belgrade Ragusans' merchant activities was the book trade. They imported Cyrillic liturgical books printed in Venice or Ancona. Preserved data indicate that in October 1554 a trader from Ancona, Chiriacus de Gualteruciis, accepted a contract to deliver two hundred leather-bound liturgical books, printed in 'Serbian language and letters', in two months. The same merchant provided mediation in 1560 regarding another purchase order of Cyrillic liturgical books printed in Italy. In this way, Ragusan merchants fostered and improved the literacy of the Slavonic population of the Balkan Peninsula, and they also helped the propagation of printed books in the region.[19]

Trojan Gundulić and His Printing Press: The Publishing of the *Tetraevangelion* in 1552

All these traits and business habits were present in the person of Trojan Gundulić, a merchant credited with the establishment of the first printing press in Belgrade, who published the first book there in 1552: the *Tetraevangelion* (Figs 9.2 and 9.3). His early biography merits some attention, although there are some lacunae. He was an illegitimate son of the noble Federico Gundulić, who was a peculiar character himself, as he had children only with maids or servant girls (he had three sons with three different women). Trojan became a barber apprentice in 1523. He is mentioned as a merchant in 1529, and he issued bonds several years

---

17 Hrabak, 'Beograd kao pristanište i brodogradilište', pp. 35–36.
18 Hrabak, 'Beograd kao žitno tržište', pp. 63–64.
19 Samardžić, 'Dubrovčani u Beogradu u XVI i XVII veku', p. 457.

Figure 9.2. Tetraevangelion (Belgrade: Trojan Gundulić, 1552), the beginning of the Gospel of Matthew (frontispiece). Belgrade City Museum, inv. num. I1 1196. With permission from Belgrade City Museum. All rights reserved.

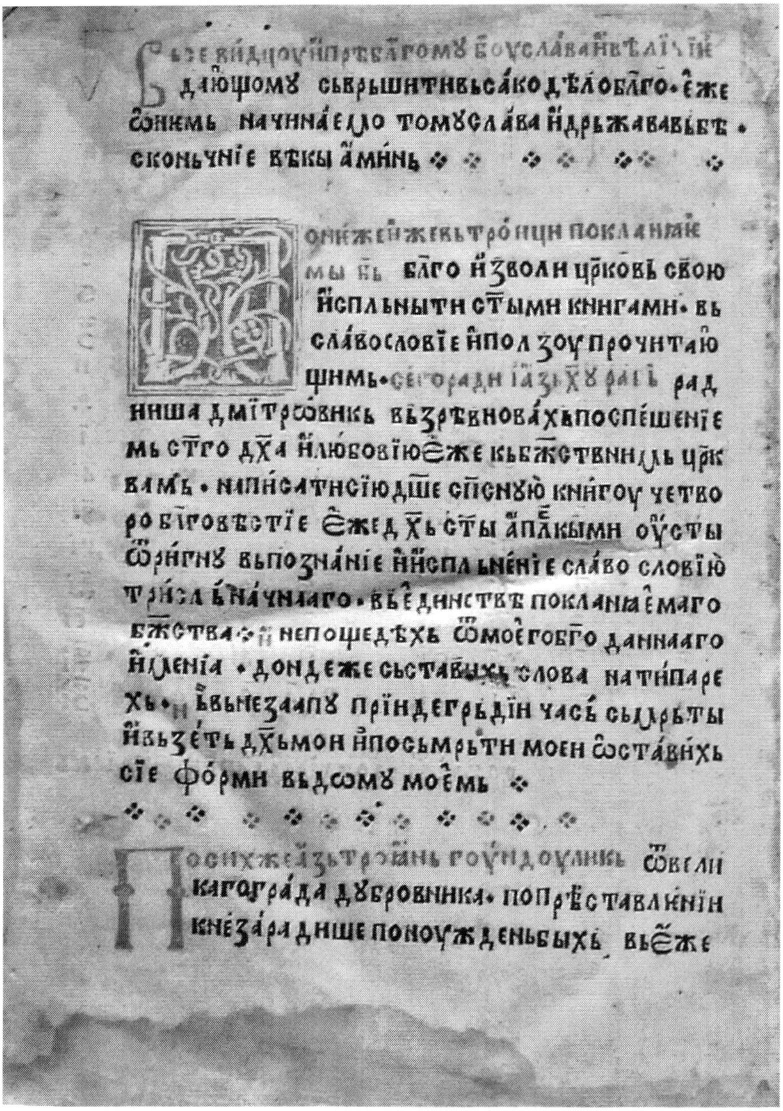

Figure 9.3. Tetraevangelion (Belgrade: Trojan Gundulić, 1552), afterword and colophon. Belgrade City Museum, inv. num. I1 1196. With permission from Belgrade City Museum. All rights reserved.

later. He probably moved to Belgrade around this time, although the exact year is unknown. Being an illegitimate son, he was excluded from the ranks of the nobility, but he nonetheless received a good education. Barbers in sixteenth-century Ragusan society enjoyed a high social status, as they had surgical skills. Besides that, it was possible to buy books in some barbershops, and it seems that trading in books was one of Trojan's main occupations when he settled in Belgrade. It is not surprising, therefore, that he extended his business to printing as well.[20]

He took over an already established publishing business, belonging to *knez* Radiša Dmitrović,[21] who understood printing activities as a form of endowment. Unfortunately, Dmitrović passed away before he was able to finish the *Tetraevangelion*, so Gundulić stepped in and took over the endeavour. He employed a monk named Mardarije to cast letters for the press from 'iron and bronze' and to act as the typographer.[22]

Unfortunately, the only information we have on this activity can be gleaned from the afterword of the *Tetraevangelion* itself. We have no other contemporary sources on the subject. The reader is addressed in the afterword by all three mentioned persons (Dmitrović, Gundulić, and Mardarije), who speak in the first person singular, and who describe the history of the publication process. It is assumed that the actual author of the afterword was Mardarije, who applied this narrative method to fully explain the genesis of this book. This concluding chapter is the only source of information on Dmitrović as well.[23] There has been some discussion in the literature regarding the origins of *knez* Dmitrović; however, the results are inconclusive. One claim from the 1860s asserted that he was from Herzegovina, and that he was Mardarije's feudal lord, but this was never substantiated by any evidence.[24]

When Gundulić died in 1554 (or 1555)[25] and his business in Belgrade ceased its operation, the monk Mardarije took the press to the Mrkšina crkva monastery, where he printed another *Tetraevangelion* (1562), along with *Pentecostarion* (1566).[26] Like the issue of Dmitrović's origins, the exact location of this monastery sparked a debate among historians. Data from the sources are scarce and potentially misleading. The printers of old Serbian books had a habit of letting their readers know where a particular book was printed. They noted the geographical location of the

---

20 Samardžić, 'Dubrovčani u Beogradu u XVI i XVII veku', pp. 457–58.
21 *Knez* was a medieval noble title that translates as a 'prince', but at this time it was used to denote a Serbian chieftain in the service of the Ottoman Empire.
22 Radojčić, 'Četvorojevanđelje iz 1552 god.', pp. 12–13; Zore, 'Dubrovčanin Trojan Gundulić', pp. 898–99.
23 Zore, 'Dubrovčanin Trojan Gundulić', p. 898; Kesterčanek, 'Inventar', p. 198.
24 Radojčić, 'Četvorojevanđelje iz 1552 god.', p. 13.
25 Samardžić, 'Dubrovčani u Beogradu u XVI i XVII veku', p. 460.
26 Radojčić, 'Četvorojevanđelje iz 1552 god.', p. 19.

printing press in the foreword or the concluding chapter of the publication. We have two such notes for Mrkšina crkva: one claims that it was located in Smederevo Metropolitanate, while the other mentions that it was located 'at the foothills of the Black Mountain'.[27] The problem is that the monastery ceased to exist during the seventeenth century, and not even ruins survive today. The territory of Smederevo Metropolitanate was relatively wide, while two toponyms called 'Black Mountain' existed (and still exist) in this region: *Skopska Crna Gora* (Black Mountain of Skopje) and *Užička Crna Gora* (Black Mountain of Užice). So, the issue is, under which 'Black Mountain' was the monastery located? The most plausible location is a locality in present-day western Serbia near the town of Užice, as Luko Zore has quite eloquently suggested.[28]

The Belgrade *Tetraevangelion* was not the first book printed in the Balkans;[29] however, it was the first book printed in Belgrade, and it remained the only book printed there until the nineteenth century.[30] Therefore it is a significant cultural monument. It should be noted that the closing of this press did not lead to the termination of the publication of books in the Serbian language, and that this activity continued in other centres, even outside the Balkans — in Italy for example. It is also noteworthy that the majority of these printing enterprises was short-lived, and that they usually closed after several years of activity. We have to bear in mind that these endeavours occurred sporadically, in the periphery of the Ottoman Empire, and therefore in the border region between the Islamic and Christian worlds, and that they had a limited, albeit not insignificant, impact on the proliferation of books, ideas, and knowledge in south-eastern Europe. The Ragusan trade network had helped this transfer, as we could see, and thus had aided the development of the 'Republic of Letters' in its early stages.

---

27 Radojčić, 'Četvorojevanđelje iz 1552 god.', pp. 18–19.
28 Zore, 'Dubrovčanin Trojan Gundulić', pp. 896–97.
29 That was *Oktoih prvoglasnik* (Octoechos of the First Tone), printed in 1494 in the monastery of Cetinje (present-day Montenegro).
30 Kesterčanek, 'Inventar', p. 197.

Works Cited

Secondary Studies

Hrabak, Bogumil, 'Beograd kao žitno tržište i žitarstvo šire beogradske okoline u XVI veku [Belgrade as a Wheat Market and Agriculture of Belgrade's Wider Area in the 16th Century]', *Godišnjak Muzeja grada Beograda* [Yearbook of Belgrade City Museum], 4 (1957), 59–70

——, 'Beograd kao pristanište i brodogradilište u XV, XVI i XVII veku [Belgrade as a Port and Shipyard in the 15th, 16th and 17th Century]', *Godišnjak Muzeja grada Beograda* [Yearbook of Belgrade City Museum], 5 (1958), 27–54

——, 'Trgovina Persijanaca preko Dubrovnika u XVI veku [Persian Trade via Ragusa in the 16th Century]', *Zbornik Filozofskog fakulteta* [Faculty of Philosophy Proceedings], 5.1 (1960), 257–67

Kesterčanek, Frano, 'Inventar prvog beogradskog tiskara Trojana Gundulića [Inventory of the First Belgrade Printer Trojan Gundulić]', *Anali Historijskog instituta JAZU u Dubrovniku* [Annals of the Historical Institute JAZU in Ragusa], 1 (1952), 197–206

Radojčić, Đorđe, 'Četvorojevanđelje iz 1552 god. [Tetraevangelion from 1552]', *Glasnik Narodne biblioteke* [National Library Review], 1 (1940), 12–19

Samardžić, Radovan, 'Podmladak dubrovačkih trgovaca i zanatlija u XV i XVI veku [Youth of Ragusan Merchants and Artisans in 15th and 16th Century]', *Zbornik studentskih stručnih radova* [Proceedings of Student's Professional Papers], 1 (1948), 64–78

——, 'Dubrovčani u Beogradu [Ragusans in Belgrade]', *Godišnjak Muzeja grada Beograda* [Yearbook of Belgrade City Museum], 2 (1955), 47–94

——, 'Dubrovčani u Beogradu u XVI i XVII veku [Ragusans in Belgrade in 16th and 17th Century]', in *Istorija Beograda* [History of Belgrade], ed. by Vasa Čubrilović, 3 vols (Belgrade: Prosveta, 1974), I, pp. 425–61

——, *Veliki vek Dubrovnika* [The Great Century of Ragusa] (Belgrade: Prosveta, 1983)

Tadić, Jorjo, 'O društvenoj strukturi Dalmacije i Dubrovnika u vreme renesanse [About Social Structure of Dalmatia and Ragusa during Renaissance]', *Zgodovinski časopis* [Historical Review], 6–7 (1952/1953), 552–65

Vojnović, Lujo, *Istorija Dubrovačke Republike* [History of the Republic of Ragusa] (Belgrade: Ars Libri, 2005)

Zore, Luko, 'Dubrovčanin Trojan Gundulić, prosvetitelj srpski [Ragusan Trojan Gundulić, Serbian Enlightener]', *Srđ*, 19 (1902), 895–99

MARGRIET HOOGVLIET

The Spiritual Road

European Networks and Pilgrim Travels from Northern France and the Low Countries to Rome, Venice, and Santiago (Late Fifteenth–Early Sixteenth Century)

For Elies Hagedoorn:

BFF and courageous globetrotter.

From as early as the ninth and tenth centuries, the areas we now call northern France and Belgian Flanders were emerging as important production centres of high-quality woollen cloth, which was exported throughout Europe and even across the Mediterranean to North Africa and the Middle East.[1] Inversely, Flemish and French merchants imported spices, pigments, precious gemstones, gold, silver, and silk from *Outremer*, on the eastern shores of the Mediterranean, often with Italian and Jewish merchants acting as intermediaries and investors. As a consequence, the north-western part of Europe became an important hub of the international — and even

---

1 Munro, 'Medieval Woollens', pp. 181–227; Wickham, *Framing the Early Middle Ages*, pp. 41–46, 674–804; Bautier, 'Les foires de Champagne'.

Margriet Hoogvliet earned her PhD *cum laude* in 1999 with the thesis *Pictura et Scriptura* (Brepols, 2007): a study of text–image relations in maps of the world from the twelfth to the early seventeenth century. Since 2009 she has been working as a postdoctoral researcher at the University of Groningen, alternating with positions at other Dutch universities, Leeds University, and the Université de Tours. Margriet Hoogvliet is a specialist in the field of biblical and religious reading cultures of lay people living and working in the towns of late medieval France. Her research is concerned with social, material, and spatial aspects of the dissemination and reception of religious texts in French.

Networking Europe and New Communities of Interpretation (1400–1600), ed. by Margriet Hoogvliet, Manuel F. Fernández Chaves, *and* Rafael M. Pérez García, New Communities of Interpretation, 4 (Turnhout: Brepols, 2023), pp. 215–248
BREPOLS PUBLISHERS 10.1484/M.NCI-EB.5.134316

intercontinental — travel and transportation networks in the late Middle Ages.

In spite of oft-repeated historical commonplaces about the decline of Roman long-distance travel routes during the Middle Ages,[2] until roughly the end of the sixteenth century, people were most likely much more mobile than they would be in later centuries.[3] Centuries-old pathways, Roman roads, and newly created medieval trade routes were intensively used for the transportation of merchandise, merchants, funds, and workers: over land and along rivers, as well as over sea, and in volumes that according to some estimations were only surpassed after the construction of railways in the nineteenth century.[4] Great overland travel routes to and from the Low Countries included the *Via francigena* (coming from the north, crossing the Alps via cities such as Basel, Besançon, or Lyon, and then continuing on to Rome)[5] and *le train de Flandres* (via Troyes southwards along the Seine, through the Rhône valley to the Mediterranean ports of Marseille, Arles, and Montpellier/Lattes).[6] Traditionally, navigation on the waters of the Mediterranean, the Atlantic Ocean, and the North Sea took place mainly along the coastlines. After improved rigging and navigation techniques (such as the astrolabe, the magnetic compass, marine charts, and mathematical tables for triangulation [*toletas de marteloio*]) were introduced, starting in the late twelfth and early thirteenth centuries, direct crossings over open sea — including travels outside the Mediterranean basin such as explorations along the Atlantic coast as far south

---

2 Guillerme, 'Chemins, routes, autoroutes', p. 120.
3 Scott, 'Travel and Communications', pp. 165–86, esp. pp. 170–72.
4 For long-distance travel routes from Late Antiquity and the early medieval period, see: Nelles and Salzberg, eds, *Connected Mobilities*; Sutner, ed., *Landhandelsrouten*; McCormick, *Origins of the European Economy*, pp. 501–22, 548–64, 670–95; Horden and Purcell, *The Corrupting Sea*, pp. 123–72. For a positive evaluation of the medieval road system and transportation equipment, see: Baumgärtner, Ben-Aryeh, and Kogman-Appel, eds, *Maps and Travel in the Middle Ages*; Corbiau, Van den Abeele, and Yante, eds, *La route au Moyen Âge*; Szabó, ed., *Die Welt der europäischen Strassen*; Hubert, 'Les routes du Moyen Âge'; Derville, 'La première révolution'; Bautier, *Sur l'histoire économique de la France médiévale*; Livet, *Histoire des routes et des transports en Europe*; Chiesi, Paolozzi, and Ciresi, eds, *Il Medioevo in viaggio*; Legassie, *The Medieval Invention of Travel*. However, Berings, 'Transport and Communication in the Middle Ages', suggests that long-distance travel was for most medieval people a once-in-a-lifetime experience. Mainly based on sixteenth- to eighteenth-century sources and with a critique of the commonplace that traditional societies would have been largely immobile: Roche, *Humeurs vagabondes*, pp. 187–357.
5 Stopani, *La Via Francigena*, pp. 83–91.
6 Gascon, *Grand commerce et vie urbaine au XVIe siècle*, pp. 156–59. In the early sixteenth century, the Italian traveller Antonio de Beatis noted the impressive size of the transport carts in northern Europe: 'Infinite numbers of [carriages] come and go all the time, as it is their custom to transport everything in four wheeled carts, some of which are such that they can carry more goods than four of our Lombardy ones; they are drawn by numerous powerful horses', Hale, ed., *The Travel Journal of Antonio de Beatis*, p. 78.

as sub-Saharan Africa, and to the north, circumnavigating the Iberian Peninsula to the Flemish towns near the shores of the North Sea — became more and more frequent.[7]

During the Middle Ages, pilgrims took advantage of these existing travel networks, which were otherwise used for the transportation of merchandise, finance, and merchants. Next to this, as we will see below, there was a specially dedicated infrastructure of hospitals offering free lodging and meals to poor pilgrims. Those pilgrims who were wealthy enough to afford the expenses generally stayed in the same taverns and guesthouses as those frequented by merchants on a business trip.

As mentioned in the introduction to this volume, road networks and travel itineraries can be considered the 'hardware' of social networks, for they are the tangible materialization of connections between people over long distances that facilitated the transport of people, goods, funds, practices, and ideas, including religious knowledge. Roads and routes are a core point of interest of *la médiologie*, a philosophical approach to culture originally developed by the French philosopher Régis Debray. In the words of Céline Perol, *la médiologie* is also practised by those historians 'qui s'intéressent aux méthodes de transmission et de transports et à leur impact sur les mentalités et les comportements de notre société' (interested in the methods of transmission and transportation and in their impact on the mentalities and behaviours of our society).[8] Debray himself underlined in the 1996 special issue of the *Cahiers de médiologie* dedicated to roads and itineraries that:

> La route n'est pas une anecdote, une excursion pittoresque à reléguer dans les bas-côtés du savoir. Elle donne directement, et de plain-pied, sur le bipède humain en pleine action.[9]

> (The road is not anecdotal, a picturesque excursion that should be relegated to the lower levels of human knowledge. It gives a direct and unfiltered access to two-legged humans in full action.)

Building further on Debray's thoughts on roads and transmission, this article will approach roads, routes, itineraries, market squares, and ports from a cultural and philosophical perspective, considering them as networks

---

7 There is an abundance of popularizing literature on 'medieval discoveries'; for well-documented scholarly publications about ships and navigation, see: Villain-Gandossi, 'La révolution nautique médiévale'; Unger, 'Ships and Sailing Routes'; Gertwagen, 'Nautical Technology'; Balard, *La Méditerranée médiévale*, pp. 44–60; Ash, 'Navigation Techniques and Practice in the Renaissance'; Pujades i Bataller, *Les cartes portolanes*; and Pryor, *Geography, Technology, and War*, pp. 87–101, 135–64.
8 Perol, 'Cheminement médiéval: l'homme, l'historien et la route', p. 92. See also: Dagognet, ed., *Qu'est-ce qu'une route?*
9 Debray, 'Rhapsodie sur la route', p. 17.

and hubs facilitating connections among people, sometimes over enormous distances, and transporting not only goods, but also religious texts, ideas, practices, and knowledge.

First-hand experiences of medieval travel and routes can be found in pilgrims' accounts.[10] These texts have often been studied to analyse European pilgrims' perceptions of people living in the Middle East, whereas the European parts of their itineraries have received far less attention. These accounts, however, are highly informative about trans-European travel networks and about the instrumentality of these networks in the transport and dissemination of religious knowledge. In this paper I will analyse three late fifteenth- to early sixteenth-century pilgrims' accounts written by pilgrims originating in the southern Low Countries and northern France.

1 Jean de Tournai's pilgrimage from Valenciennes to Jerusalem (1488–1489) as described in the single surviving handwritten copy of his original account.[11] Jean left his hometown Valenciennes (then situated in the Habsburg Low Countries) in 1488 in order to travel to Jerusalem, the Holy Land, and to Santiago de Compostela. In this paper, I will focus on the part of his account that covers his itinerary from Valenciennes to Rome and Venice.

2 Jehan de Zeilbeke's pilgrimage from Comines (Komen) in the Habsburg Low Countries to Santiago de Compostela, as recounted in his autograph manuscript *Le livre des Voeiages de messire Jehan de Zeilbeke à Rome, à Saint-Jacques en Galice, à Jérusalem* (1499–1513).[12] In this

---

10 For pilgrims' accounts from France and the Low Countries (including the three texts discussed here), see: Yeager, 'Medieval Pilgrimage as Heterotopia'; Germain-De Franceschi, *D'encre et de poussière*; Chareyron, *Les pèlerins de Jérusalem au Moyen Âge*; Van Herwaarden, 'Late-Medieval Religion and Expression of Faith'; Van Schaïk, '"Wer weite Reisen macht..."'; and Richard, *Les récits de voyages et de pèlerinages*. For pilgrims and pilgrimages in general, see: Webb, *Pilgrims and Pilgrimage in the Medieval West*; Webb, *Medieval European Pilgrimage*; and Yarrow, 'Pilgrimage'. Just before publication of this article, I learned about two other pilgrim accounts in Middle French from this area: an anonymous pilgrim (1419) and Georges Lengherand from Mons (1485-1486); see: Rager, 'Deux récits de pèlerinage'.

11 Valenciennes, Bibliothèque municipale, MS 493. Modern edition: Jean de Tournai, *Le récit des voyages et pèlerinages*. The manuscript text has also been transcribed by Blanchet-Broekaert and can be found online: http://lodel.irevues.inist.fr/saintjacquesinfo/index.php?id=1566. For a translation into modern French, see: Blanchet-Broekaert, ed., *Le voyage de Jean de Tournai*. More information and bibliography on the Digiberichte website: https://digiberichte.de/travel/?ID=34&FID=347&N=F&suchen1=Jean%20de%20Tournay&Vollname=Jean_de_Tournay.

12 One manuscript (autograph): Douai, Bibliothèque municipale, MS 793 (all transcriptions are mine). For a translation of part of Jehan de Zeilbeke's travel accounts into modern French, see: Desmarets, 'Jehan de Zeilbeke (1511)'. More information and bibliography on the Digiberichte website: https://digiberichte.de/travel/?ID=41&FID=429&N=NL&suchen1=Jan%20Taccoen%20van%20Zillebeke&Vollname=Jan_Taccoen_van_Zillebeke.

'home made' book, Jehan reports his pilgrimages, based on his travel notes in Middle Dutch, which he translated himself into French and copied with his own hand. Jehan's home in Comines, west of Lille, was situated in a predominantly Middle Dutch-speaking area. In his manuscript, Jehan wrote that he left his home four times for a pilgrimage: in 1499 (= 1500)[13] (Jerusalem, failed); in 1508 (= 1509) (Jerusalem, failed); 1511 (= 1512) (Santiago de Compostela, successful); and in 1513 (= 1514) (Jerusalem, successful). I will focus here on Jean's 1512 pilgrimage to Santiago de Compostela.

3   The pilgrimage account written by Pierre Mesenge, priest and canon in Rouen, who travelled to the Holy Land together with five clerics (three from Rouen and two from Lisieux), five merchants (four from Rouen and one from Caen), two noblemen, and their two servants, starting in April 1508.[14]

Before examining the three pilgrims' accounts in detail, a few words about the cultural and linguistic characteristics of the part of north-western Europe they came from are in order. Flanders (Vlaanderen) now refers to the Standard Dutch (Flemish)-speaking part of Belgium, but in the late Middle Ages it was a diffuse entity, both politically, culturally, and linguistically speaking. In this period, Flanders was formally a fief of the kings of France, but in reality most of it was in the hands of the dukes of Burgundy, and, from 1482, the house of Habsburg. A large part of present-day northern France was part of the Burgundian (later the Habsburg and Spanish) Low Countries. This region was only conquered in the seventeenth century by Louis XIV, with some areas being conquered even later: Aire-sur-la-Lys (Ariën aan de Leie), for instance, became part of France as late as 1713.

Flanders, Artois, Picardy, and the northern part of Normandy (approximately the area between Antwerp-Bruges and Paris-Beauvais-Rouen) also represented a coherent entity unto itself: the highly urbanized part of north-western Europe that was deeply involved in the production, trade, and finance of woollen cloth. The towns were strongly interconnected through commercial exchanges formalized in a Hanse trade network, and

---

13 In the later Middle Ages, in France and the Low Countries the year started at Easter (stilus Gallicus; stile de France); hence, for dates between 1 January and the (changeable) date of Easter, the year as found in the sources has to be augmented by one to arrive at the modern year.
14 At least six manuscripts of Pierre Mesenge's text survive. I have used here Amiens, Bibliothèque municipale, MS Lescalopier 99 (all transcriptions are mine). The other manuscripts known to me are: Amiens, Bibliothèque municipale, MS Lescalopier 98; Bryn Mawr, College Library, MS 13; Rouen, Bibliothèque municipale, MSS 1118 and 1119; and Private collection, location unknown. More information and bibliography on the Digiberichte website: https://digiberichte.de/travel/?ID=40&FID=367&N=F&suchen1=Pierre%20Mesenge&Vollname=Pierre_Mesenge.

the inhabitants moved freely throughout the area for trade and production work.[15]

The linguistic situation was different, too, with a sharp linguistic border demarcating Romance and Germanic languages often being absent. The dominant variety of French in this area was Picard French, and this was used as a mother tongue or as a second language in predominantly Middle Dutch-speaking towns such as Ghent, Bruges, and Antwerp.[16] Middle Dutch was the dominant mother tongue in the northern areas, but Middle Dutch-speaking communities were present in almost all primarily French- or Picard-speaking towns, most notably in Paris and Rouen. Contextual data show that speakers of both vernacular languages were in many cases prepared to learn the other language and, if necessary, they would switch linguistic codes in a pragmatic way (albeit probably more frequently from Middle Dutch to French/Picard than the other way around).[17]

In the following, I will analyse the three pilgrims' accounts presented above for the evidence they give about travel itineraries originating in north-western Europe and going to Rome and Venice (Jean de Tournai), northern Spain (Jehan de Zeilbeke), and Venice (Pierre Mesenge). These accounts give highly relevant and rarely studied information about travel networks and the existence of transnational social and commercial networks. The written accounts and other memorabilia from pilgrimages, as well as the pilgrims themselves, served to disseminate religious knowledge and religious practices among other lay people back home. I will analyse the three pilgrims' accounts according to three main themes: first, the information they provide about medieval travel and travel networks; secondly, the historical eyewitness accounts the texts contain of trans-European social and commercial networks; and, finally, the question of how pilgrimages, pilgrims as authors, and their accounts were instrumental in the dissemination of religious knowledge, as well as the sharing of religious knowledge over long distances.

---

15 Carolus-Barré, 'Les XVII villes'; Rubin, *Cities of Strangers*.
16 Lusignan, *Essai d'histoire sociolinguistique*.
17 Hoogvliet, '*Mez puy que je le enten, je suy conten*'; Hoogvliet, 'Middle Dutch Religious Reading Cultures'.

Networks for Travel and Transport

Jean de Tournai

Jean de Tournai left his home in Valenciennes (Valencijn) on Monday, 25 February 1488 (Map 10.1).[18] Valenciennes is now situated in northern France, but at the time of Jean's pilgrimage the town was part of the Habsburg Low Countries. Jean started his pilgrimage on horseback and was accompanied to the nearby town of Mons (Bergen) by his brother Monseigneur Jean de Tournai, who was abbot of St John's Abbey in Valenciennes, and several other local friends and relatives. After Brussels, Jean went to Antwerp, where he stayed for seven days. Apparently, this week was filled with social events in the company of merchants from the towns of Valenciennes, Lille (Rijsel), Antwerp, Cologne, and Aachen. On Wednesday, 5 March, after a festive goodbye lunch at an inn called *Den Engel*,[19] accompanied by good wine (possibly a reference to the Last Supper), Jean left Antwerp accompanied by several merchants from Cologne and Aachen. The group first went northwards towards 's-Hertogenbosch and Ravenstein, passing by Nijmegen on their way to Cleves and Cologne. They probably made this detour to the north in order to follow the river Rhine and to avoid the French kingdom, which was perilous for foreign travellers due to the unstable political situation and the internal wars between opposing rival factions of varying alliances: on his way back from Santiago de Compostela, Jean walked overland through France to Valenciennes, and in order to avoid heavy taxing, imprisonment, or even worse punishment, was urged to remove the red pilgrim's cross from his clothes, because this might lead people to believe that he was English. Originating from the Habsburg Low Countries, Jean had to pretend to be a poor pilgrim from Tournai, a town near Valenciennes that was a French exclave until 1521.[20]

From Cologne to Mainz Jean travelled aboard a river barge, 'because of the war', taking his horse with him. Since Mainz is upstream from Cologne, against the current of the river Rhine, the boat was towed by horses:

> [L]esdict batteaux allant dudict Couloigne jusques a Mayence vont tousjours contremont la riviere du Rhyn laquelle est très fort rade et convient que a force de chevaulx lesdictz batteaux soient tirés amont et par tout aussy long que ladicte riviere dure. [...] Et lesdictz chevaulx

---

18 Jean wrote 1487 in his account, but since the year started at Easter in that period, this is 1488 according to the modern calculation.
19 Den Engel is still in business on the Grote Markt in Antwerp.
20 Jean de Tournai, *Le récit des voyages et pèlerinages*, p. 332.

> quy tirent les batteaux sont fort beaux et valent bien la plupart de XXX a XL florins d'or.[21]

>> (Going from Cologne to Mainz, the said barges are always going upstream over the river Rhine, which has a very strong current, and by the force of the horses said barges are towed upstream all the way along the river. [...] And said horses towing the barges are very beautiful and most of them are worth thirty to forty gold florins.)

Jean's description suggests that there must have been a well-organized, regular travel and transport connection by riverboat between Cologne and Mainz.

Travel in the Empire was not without danger either, and in his account Jean advised his readers and potential pilgrims to buy safe-conducts:

> Pour la doubte desdictz gens de guerre ou aultres rustres, on prent en plusieurs lieux saulfconduit, c'est ascavoir en aulcuns lieux un signe, lequel est signé tant sur cyre comme sur papier, et le plupart se vous estes a cheval, vous aurés un homme a cheval, et se vous estes a pied ung a pied, et portant comme ung messagier une boitte à son chappeau; et ira ou chevaulcera tousjours devant vous; et parmy tout vous y yrez tousjours seurement et trouverés tousjours les chevaulx tous sellés et les hommes tous pretz esdictes maisons soit a pied ou a cheval pour en aller avec vous ou l'on vous donra ledict saulfconduyt.[22]

>> (Because of the danger of said soldiers and other bandits, one takes a safe-conduct at several places, which is a document signed on paper and in wax in that particular location. And if you are on horseback you will generally have a man on horseback and if you are walking, one on foot, wearing a small box on his hat like a messenger, and he will always go before you wherever you ride with your horse. You will always travel safely and in said houses where people sell safe-conducts you will always find saddled horses and the men ready to go with you, either on foot or on horseback.)

Jean's account shows that there must have been a well-functioning interregional transport system that allowed for fast and safe travel. Despite these provisions, in Worms Jean discovered that he was being followed by two robbers. He deceived the two men by telling them that he intended to travel via Basel, while instead travelling eastwards to Landeck at the foot of the Alps. From there, Jean probably followed the Roman *Via Claudia Augusta* over the Alps to the Po valley. Still on horseback, Jean travelled via Verona and Bologna to Florence, where he sold his horse because it

---

21 Jean de Tournai, *Le récit des voyages et pèlerinages*, p. 25.
22 Jean de Tournai, *Le récit des voyages et pèlerinages*, p. 27.

THE SPIRITUAL ROAD   223

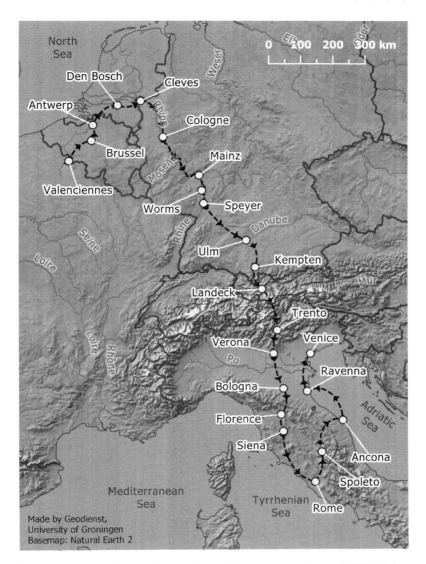

Map 10.1. Jean de Tournai's itinerary from Valenciennes to Venice (1488–1489): Valenciennes – Brussels – Antwerp – 's-Hertogenbosch – Cleves – Cologne – on board a river barge up the river Rhine to Mainz – Worms – Speyer – Ulm – Kempten – Landeck [probably taking the old Roman *Via Claudia Augusta*] – Trento – Verona – Bologna – Florence – Siena – Rome – Spoleto – Ancona – over sea to Cesenatico – Ravenna – Venice. Credit: Geodienst, University of Groningen.

was tired and 'pource que audict païs les despens des chevaulx y sont fort grandz' (because in this country the expenses for horses are very high).[23] This change of means of transport also entailed a change of Jean's identity into a real pilgrim, as testified by the pilgrim's bag and stick that he would be carrying from then on.

After his visit to Rome, having obtained permission for his pilgrimage to the Holy Land from the Pope in person, Jean continued his travels on foot and in the company of several men who were like him heading to Venice: *sire* Guillaume and a man called Hoteyn, both from the region of Tournai and also on a pilgrimage to the Holy Land. In this group were also a certain Hugues, goldsmith from Amiens; *maître* Martin, a German lute player; and a hatter from Tournai, all of whom lived in Venice.[24] The group intended to take a boat from Ancona to Venice, but due to the stormy weather they had to find shelter in the harbour of Cesenatico. From there Jean walked via Ravenna to Chioggia to take the ferry to Venice in the lagoon on 5 May 1488, after approximately ten weeks of travel, socializing, and sightseeing.

Jehan de Zeilbeke

Jehan de Zeilbeke made use mostly of the oversea shipping network in order to travel from Flanders to the Iberian Peninsula (Map 10.2). In his account, we find that in the nearby Flemish harbour town of Nieuwpoort on the shores of the North Sea 'il y auoit vng bateu de lx tonneulx prest pour aller audit st Jaque atout de pellerins. Je fis mon comparch auec le patron nomme Simon Jughebrant' (there was a ship of 60 tonnes full of pilgrims ready to sail to said Santiago. I made a deal with the ship's master named Simon Jughebrant).[25]

This was probably not a medieval cargo ship of the cog type, which could have been between 200 and 1000 tonnes, or an even larger carrack (up to 1800 tonnes), but must have instead been a much smaller and faster type of boat.[26] Jehan's remarks suggest that this ship was at least partially equipped to accommodate pilgrims, because he was able to rent one of the small huts ('une chambrette'). Likewise, in the account of his 1514 pilgrimage to Jerusalem, he recounts that he went to Vlissingen in

---

23 Jean de Tournai, *Le récit des voyages et pèlerinages*, p. 37.
24 Jean de Tournai, *Le récit des voyages et pèlerinages*, pp. 79–80.
25 Douai, Bibliothèque municipale, MS 793, fol. 31ᵛ; Desmarets, 'Jehan de Zeilbeke (1511)', p. 199.
26 Villain-Gandossi, 'La révolution nautique médiévale'; Flatman, *Ships and Shipping in Medieval Manuscripts*, pp. 91–95; Hutchinson, *Medieval Ships and Shipping*; Gardiner and Unger, ed., *Cogs, Caravels and Galleons*; Lane, *Venetian Ships and Shipbuilders*, pp. 1–53; Unger, *The Ship in the Medieval Economy 600–1600*, pp. 119–200.

THE SPIRITUAL ROAD 225

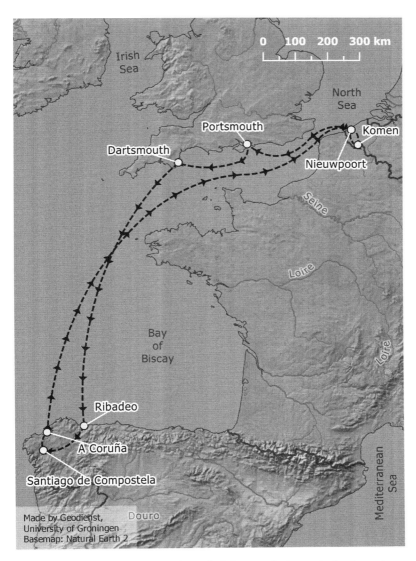

Map 10.2. The itinerary of Jehan de Zeilbeke's 1512 pilgrimage to Santiago de Compostela: Comines (Komen) — Nieuwpoort — Portsmouth — Dartsmouth — Ribadeo (*Rimerres*) — Santiago de Compostela — A Coruña — Nieuwpoort — Comines. Credit: Geodienst, University of Groningen.

Zeeland in order to wait for the pilgrims' boat from Antwerp ('le nauire dez pellerins qui deuoit partir de Anuers').[27] The traffic of pilgrims' ships from the Low Countries to the Iberian Peninsula and the Holy Land must have been quite frequent, because on the way between Vlissingen and Lisbon he saw a shipwreck that was identified by the mariners as a pilgrims' ship: 'Nous veymez vng debout dun mast droit amont atout le nauire et les marins nous dient que cestoit vne navire de peilgrins qui cuidoient aller a saint jaques et tout estoit noyet' (We saw the top of a mast straight ahead of our ship and the mariners told us that it was a ship of pilgrims who thought they were going to Santiago; they all drowned).[28] However, the ship with which Jehan travelled was not easily recognizable as a pilgrim's ship, because on the way back from A Coruña to Nieuwpoort, it was stopped by two Spanish war vessels, on the lookout for French ships:

> En retournant sur le mer il vient sur nous deulx bataulx de guerre en la mer despaeinge et quant ilz nous oient encloz ilz demandrent quj nous estions quant ils oyerent que estions de flandres et estionz peilrins de saint jaques ilz nous dirent bien vegnant et dieu vous conduise nous somes vous amis mais ilz demandreont apres des bataulx de franche.[29]

> (During our return trip, two war ships came to us in the Spanish sea and when they had closed us in, they asked who we were and when they heard that we were from Flanders and that we were pilgrims returning from Santiago, they welcomed us and said: 'May God guide you, we are your friends'. They were searching for French ships.)

The ease with which Jehan travelled is striking — oversea, but also overland — which suggests, again, that long-distance travel must have been well organized. He indicates that he walked from the coastal town Ribadeo to Santiago in three days. The distance is 165 kilometres and although his claim appears somewhat exaggerated, Jehan does not indicate that he had any trouble finding his way and, consequently, there must have been a functioning road network. For the return trip from Santiago to the ship that was waiting in A Coruña for the pilgrims, a distance of sixty-five kilometres, Jehan took a horse that apparently could be rented and returned in another place ('Il y a de saint jaques a la coulongne une

---

27 Douai, Bibliothèque municipale, MS 793, fol. 35ʳ; Desmarets, 'Jehan de Zeilbeke (1511)', p. 214.
28 Douai, Bibliothèque municipale, MS 793, fol. 35ʳ; Desmarets, 'Jehan de Zeilbeke (1511)', p. 214.
29 Douai, Bibliothèque municipale, MS 793, fol. 34ᵛ; Desmarets, 'Jehan de Zeilbeke (1511)', p. 213.

jornee de cheval'),[30] another indication of a well-equipped road and travel network.

Lodging at an inn or guesthouse in Santiago de Compostela was apparently easily obtained by Jehan de Zeilbeke, who was fortunate enough to be able to cover the expenses. Since it was a jubilee year and there was a great influx of pilgrims, less wealthy pilgrims had to stay in people's homes, and the poor pilgrims were offered a bed in the hospital:

> Et fumez logis as trois coulons deuant lhomme sauage et y fumez bien traitiet car lostesse [...] estoit de flandres [...] mais pour ce quil estoit la lan de grace il y auoit tant de pellerins quon ne pouoit aucun logir il faloit loger sur les borgois et gens de mestier et pourez gens alloynt logier a lospitael.[31]

> (And we were lodged in The Three Doves in front of The Wild Man and we were well treated there because the hostess was from Flanders. [...] But because it was then the Holy Year and there were so many pilgrims who could not find lodging, they had to sleep in the houses of bourgeois and artisans, while poor people were lodged in the hospital.)

The hospital was the Real Hospital, financed by the royal couple Ferdinand and Isabella.[32] Jehan admired it greatly, and his account contains a lengthy description of its facilities: 'Et quel ospitael est vne merueileuse chose [...] car je croy quil nia point de pareil de biaulte de grandeur et de ricesse' (And the hospital was an extraordinary place [...] because I think that there is none equal in beauty, grandeur, and riches).[33]

Pierre Mesenge

Pierre Mesenge and his company, composed of merchants, clerics, and aristocrats, travelled on horseback from Rouen via Orléans to Lyons in eleven days, over almost 600 kilometres (Map 10.3). The most obvious itinerary would have been to follow the river Loire from Orléans upstream to Moulins and to cross the hills and valleys of the Massif Central near

---

30 Douai, Bibliothèque municipale, MS 793, fol. 34ʳ; Desmarets, 'Jehan de Zeilbeke (1511)', p. 213.
31 Douai, Bibliothèque municipale, MS 793, fol. 32ʳ; Desmarets, 'Jehan de Zeilbeke (1511)', p. 202. See also: Portela Silva, *Historia de la ciudad de Santiago de Compostela*, p. 183.
32 Portela Silva, *Historia de la ciudad de Santiago de Compostela*, pp. 104–08.
33 Douai, Bibliothèque municipale, MS 793, fol. 32ʳ; Desmarets, 'Jehan de Zeilbeke (1511)', p. 202.

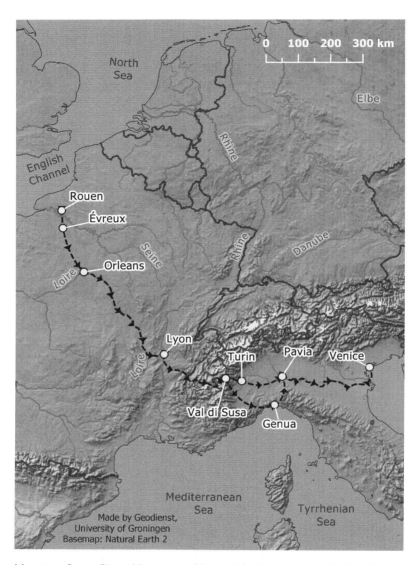

Map 10.3. Canon Pierre Mesenge and his party's itinerary to Venice (1508): Rouen — Évreux — Orléans — probably using a part of the *Via Agrippa* to Lyon — the *Via francigena* to Val di Susa — Turin or Genoa — Pavia — aboard a river barge over the river Po to Venice. Credit: Geodienst, University of Groningen.

Roanne to Lyon, possibly taking the ancient *Via Agrippa*.[34] While this part of the pilgrimage apparently passed quickly and without any major obstacles, rumour had it that the passage through the Alps was much more perilous:

> Et pour ce qui'il estoit bruyt que en Daulphine et en Savoye avoit grant nombre de gens de guerre et adventuriers qui suyvoient larmee du Roy qui alloit a Gennes et destroussoient les marchans et autres gens quilz trouvoient sur le chemin il y en eut aucuns en nostre compaignye qui firent quelque difficulte de passer oultre. Touteffoiz nous confians en dieu deliberasmes tous ensemble de passer quelque danger quil y peust avoir.[35]

> (And because there was a rumour that in the Dauphiné and Savoie there were a great number of men of arms and adventurers who followed the army of the King [Louis XII, King of France] on his way to Genoa and who robbed merchants and other people they found on the road, some in our party protested against crossing the Alps. Nevertheless, having confidence in God, we decided all together to travel to the other side whatever danger there might be.)

The group of men crossed the Alps taking the *Via francigena* and, apparently, they encountered no particular troubles on the way. Once they arrived in Pavia, some of the pilgrims left their horses there in the care of locals, or they sold them.[36] This seems to have been a well-functioning system, because the agreements were kept and the horses were retrieved in good condition during the return trip later that year:

> Ledit jour de dymenche qui fut xiiij^e jour dudit moys de de novembre environ sept heures de soir nous allasmes dormir en une barque qui nous porta toute la nuyt a Padoue ou nous arrivasmes le lundi xv^e jour dudit moys a sept heures au matin. Et apres desiuner nous louasmes des chevaulx pour nous porter jusques a Pavye ou nous avions laisse nos chevaulx lesquelz nous allasmes recueillir. Et de la a layde de dieu nous en retournasmes en France chacun en sa maison. Et fusmes de retour en ceste ville de Rouen le vingtieme jour de decembre en lan dessusdit.[37]

---

34 This itinerary is described in the *Guide des chemins de France* written by Charles Estiennes and first published in 1553. Quoted in: Imberdis, 'Les routes médiévales', p. 413. See also: Berlioz and Rossiaud, 'La route des merveilles'.
35 Amiens, Bibliothèque municipale, MS Lescalopier 99, fol. 4^r.
36 'Et la aucuns de nous vendrent leurs chevaulx et les autres les laisserent en garde jusques au retour' (And there [in Pavia] some of us sold their horses and the others left them guarded there until our return). Amiens, Bibliothèque municipale, MS Lescalopier 99, fol. 4^v.
37 Amiens, Bibliothèque municipale, MS Lescalopier 99, fol. 96^r.

230   MARGRIET HOOGVLIET

(On said Sunday that was the fourteenth day of said month of November, around seven in the evening, we went to sleep on board a river barge that took us during the night to Padua, where we arrived on Monday the fifteenth day of said month at seven in the morning. And after breakfast we rented horses to carry us to Pavia where we had left our horses, and which we went to retrieve. And from there, with the help of God, we returned to France, each one of us to his home. And we were back in this town of Rouen the twentieth day of December in the above-mentioned year [1508].)

Making an educated guess, the return journey from Pavia to Rouen must have taken the pilgrims about thirty days on horseback, covering a distance of a little over 1000 kilometres. The casual way this last stretch of the pilgrimage is evoked, or rather omitted, in Pierre's account, reveals that in the early sixteenth century, long-distance overland travel was well organized: in spite of the ever-present danger of robbers and pillaging soldiers, the roads must have been well marked, as there is no mention at all of going astray, and there appears to have been an orderly infrastructure for renting horses and buying the provisions for their care. This is not necessarily surprising, because these overland infrastructures sustained large-scale and long-distance networks of connected people.

Social and Commercial Networks

Apart from giving details on roads and travel networks, the three pilgrims' accounts are very informative about the nature of the social, commercial, and courtly networks that connected people, even when they were physically separated by vast distances. I will first discuss smaller networks, such as family members, friends, the aristocratic court, and the *natio*. Secondly, I will turn to larger, internationally operating commercial networks connecting merchants.

Jean de Tournai from Valenciennes reported that he had family members living and travelling elsewhere in Europe: his cousin Jean de Rains lived in Antwerp, and another cousin, Jossequin Pouchin, was based in Venice. The latter had been in Antwerp during the previous Lent, and on that occasion Jean had given him two gold *florins* to be returned to him in Venice, possibly as a form of international money transfer.[38] Similarly, Jehan de Zeilbeke mentions almost casually in the account of his 1514 pilgrimage to Jerusalem that one of his sons, Wulfard, was living in Santiago de Compostela at the time.[39] Since Jehan gives no details, it

---

38 Jean de Tournai, *Le récit des voyages et pèlerinages*, pp. 20, 86.
39 Desmarets, 'Jehan de Zeilbeke (1511)', p. 214.

cannot be established if Wulfard was living there for business, or if he had entered a religious order.

The pilgrims also made use of their social networks of friends and acquaintances. In Rome, Jean de Tournai addressed the bishop of Tournai, who had previously been deacon of the collegiate church Notre-Dame de la Salle (later Saint-Géry) in Valenciennes. Jean had known him as a boy in Valenciennes and he now asked the bishop to help him approach the Pope:

> Cedict jour je présentay l'aultre lettre de recommandation a monseigneur l'evesque de Tournay, lequel s'appelloit de surnom Monissart, natif de la ville de Montz en Haynaut, et estoit doyen de l'eglise Nostre Dame de la Salle en Vallentiennes. [...] Auquel evesque de ma josnesse j'avois en grande cognoissance, et ce adcause que j'avois par plusieurs annees chanté a touttes les heures du jour la ou il avoit esté présent; lequel seigneur madicte lettre présentée, me recognut tresbien et me fit fort grand chiere.[40]

> (On that day I presented the other letter of recommendation to *Monseigneur* the Bishop of Tournai, whose surname was Monissart, native of the town of Mons in Hainaut and who had been dean of the church Notre-Dame de la Salle in Valenciennes. [...] I had known the bishop very well during my youth, because I used to sing the Hours in his presence. After having been presented with my letter, said lord recognized me very well and received me with joy.)

The medieval *nationes* — although during the Middle Ages very loosely defined, with a meaning that frequently changed over time and varied according to circumstance — were another point of convergence for people who had a certain feeling of shared origin or culture.[41] For instance, once he arrived in Venice, Jean de Tournai asked for an inn called the White Lion, owned by a married couple born in Ghent:[42]

---

40 Jean de Tournai, *Le récit des voyages et pèlerinages*, pp. 42–43.
41 The etymological origin of *natio* is the Latin *nasci*, 'to be born'. The term is a geographical reference to one's place of birth and does not necessary imply genetic or ethnic belonging. For a critical discussion of the medieval use of *nationes*, see: Kahl, 'Einige Beobachtungen zum Sprachgebrauch von *natio*'; Reynolds, *Kingdoms and communities in Western Europe*; Geary, *The Myth of Nations*; and Breuilly, 'Changes in the Political Uses of the Nation'. The evidence from the pilgrims' accounts strongly disqualifies statements such as 'Nevertheless, in many cases at least, terms like *populus* and *natio* were clearly deployed to signify communities understood simultaneously as political and ethnic unities', Scales and Zimmer, 'Introduction', p. 7.
42 Located in San Bartolomeo, owned and staffed by people from Flanders; see: Van Gelder, *Trading Places*, pp. 105–06. In the sixteenth century, an *albergo del Leon bianco* was located in the Ca' da Mosto situated on the Canal Grande near the Rialto; see: Schülz, 'Ca' da Mosto', esp. p. 87 n. 8.

> Moy venu audict Venize, j'arrivay en la place sainct Marc, je demanday aprés le Lyon Blanc et on m'y adrescha. Moy venu a l'hostel, mon hoste s'appelloit Jacop et estoit natif de la ville de Gand au païs de Flandres, et sa femme pareillement, lesquelz me reçuprent bien gracieusement.[43]
>
> (Coming to said Venice, I arrived at Saint Mark's square. I asked for the White Lion and they brought me there. Arriving at the inn, my host was named Jacop and he was born in the town of Ghent, in the land of Flanders, as was his wife, and they received me kindly.)

Jacop and his wife were almost certainly primarily speakers of Middle Dutch (Flemish). Coming from Ghent, they also would have had knowledge of French and Picard. Jean de Tournai, although francophone, had a predilection for these hosts who were born in Flemish-speaking Flanders, and he was informed beforehand that this inn was an appropriate choice for lodging.

Curiously, Pierre Mesenge and his company asked for exactly the same lodging, because in their perception it was the usual assembly place of the French: 'Et nous allasmes loger au Lyon blanc ou les francoys logent communement ou nous trouvasmes dautres pelerins dont nous fusmes tresjoyeux' (And we went to stay in the White Lion where the French stay together and where we found other pilgrims, to our great joy).[44]

A few lines further down in his text, however, Pierre testifies that his group definition based on geographical origin was in reality quite variable: 'Apres disner nous pelerins francoys, brebencons, lorrains et flammens assemblasmes a Saint Marc pour deliberer si nous prendrions la nave ou la gallee pour faire nostre voyage' (After dinner we, French, Brabantian, Lorrainian, and Flemish pilgrims, assembled at Saint Mark's to discuss if we should take a ship or a galley for our voyage).[45] It turns out that for Pierre Mesenge 'we' did not necessarily refer to 'subjects of the king of France', but could include 'people coming from a larger geographical area in north-western Europe'. It is also interesting to note that the discussions in Saint Mark's Cathedral were performed unproblematically by speakers of different languages: French, Flemish, and possibly also German.

As discussed above, in Santiago, Jehan de Zeilbeke also apparently had no problem finding the inn The Three Doves. The inn was owned by a Flemish woman who treated him well, possibly because of their shared culture and language. It was customary practice to lodge people according to their *natio*, because Jehan de Zeilbeke notes that poor pilgrims were lodged in this way in the Hospital Real in Santiago: 'Chacun quj veult la logier est logie selon son estaet et chacun nachion en son quartier homes et

---

43 Jean de Tournai, *Le récit des voyages et pèlerinages*, p. 86.
44 Amiens, Bibliothèque municipale, MS Lescalopier 99, fol. 4ᵛ.
45 Amiens, Bibliothèque municipale, MS Lescalopier 99, fol. 4ᵛ.

femmez chacun parluj' (Everyone who wishes to stay there will be lodged according to his social class, and every *natio* has its own quarter, men and women separated).[46] The grouping of pilgrims in Santiago de Compostela according to their *natio* was not always applied very strictly, because Jean de Tournai from Valenciennes in the Habsburg Low Countries stayed in an inn with the sign of the *Escu de France* — typically referring to a heraldic shield with three French royal lilies — where he met two men from Picardie in France.[47]

Political and courtly relations were yet other types of social networks co-shaping the pilgrims' itineraries. Some men from Pierre Mesenge's party diverted from the Alps to Genoa to see the French king, Louis XII, who was there with his army in order to suppress the town's revolt and to defend it against the emperor:[48]

> Le mardi xxvij^e jour dudit moys davril nous allasmes diner a Viliane et apres disner aucuns de nostre compaignye prindrent le chemin de Thurin pour aller tout droit a Pavye et les autres sen allerent par Gennes ou estoit le Roy. Et la sen retournerent audit lieu de Pavye ou ils arriverent le deuxieme jour de may.[49]

> (On Tuesday the 27th day of said month of April we had dinner in Avigliana and after dinner some men of our group took the road to Turin to go straight to Pavia and the others went to Genoa, where the King was. And from there they returned to said town of Pavia where they arrived the second day of May.)

Next to social networks of family, friends, and courtly relations, which nevertheless could stretch out over vast distances as we have seen, the pilgrims also made use of long-distance commercial networks. These varied from itineraries used for trade and transportation to internationally operating trading firms and banks. Some of these late medieval multinationals were called *compagnie*.[50] Merchants' networks and *compagnie* had an important facilitating function in Jean de Tournai's pilgrimage. After the banquets with a group of business relations in Antwerp, Jean was accompanied by two merchants from Cologne to their hometown. Upon arrival, they

---

46 Douai, Bibliothèque municipale, MS 793, fol. 32^r; Desmarets, 'Jehan de Zeilbeke (1511)', p. 202.
47 Jean de Tournai, *Le récit des voyages et pèlerinages*, p. 322.
48 A contemporary account with spectacular miniatures can be found in Jean Marot's *Voiage de Gênes* (Paris, BnF, MS fr. 5091).
49 Amiens, Bibliothèque municipale, MS Lescalopier 99, fol. 4^v.
50 For the phenomenon of the international trading and banking *compagnia*, see: Gelderblom, *Cities of Commerce*, pp. 84–86; Pinto, *Economie urbane ed etica economica*, pp. 115–16; Hunt, *Medieval Super-Companies*; and Parker, 'Entrepreneurs, Families, and Companies', pp. 202–07.

showed him the town and arranged for a convivial dinner in the house of an important family member of theirs, Jacob van Bulle, one of Cologne's aldermen.[51] Another of Jean de Tournai's business relations from Antwerp, Cornille Van Bomberg, apparently kept a lodging in Venice, managed by a Flemish servant who lived there on a more permanent basis. Jean was invited to stay there, but he declined the offer:

> Le serviteur de Cornille van Bomberg demorant en la ville d'Anvers lequel s'appelloit Guillaume Mol, me vint bienveigner et me dit que ma chambre estoit appointié et que son maistre Cornille luy avoit rescript qu'il me fist ottel comme a sa propre personne et que je ne paierois riens de nulz despens, car son maistre luy avoit commendé par lettres qu'il luy avoit rescript. Neantmoins, je m'excusay et ossy je le remerciay, et demoray à ladicte hostellerie du Lion Blanc.[52]

> (The servant of Cornille Van Bomberg who was in the town of Antwerp, whose name was Guillaume Mol, came to welcome me and informed me that my room was ready and that his master Cornille had written him that he should prepare the house as he would have done for him and that I would not have to pay any of the expenses, because his master had ordered it in the letters that he had written. Nevertheless, I excused myself, thanking him, and stayed at the said inn of the White Lion.)

It is noteworthy here that even before the establishment of state-regulated international postal services, communication by letter over long distances was already well organized.[53] It is also striking that it was natural for all those involved to expect a servant to be able to read letters with instructions.

Through his business activities, Jean de Tournai was apparently connected to a wider international trade and finance network operating on a pan-European scale: the *compagnie des Mousquerons*. Mousqueron most likely refers to an international firm in which Alexandre and Jean Mousqueron, or Moscheroni, from Bruges, participated,[54] and which apparently also ran a banking branch in Rome:

> Le vendredy au matin le XIe d'apvril aprés Pasques *anno Domini* mil IIII^c. IV^{xx} et VIII, je m'en vins en Camp de Flours a tout plusieurs

---

51 Jean de Tournai, *Le récit des voyages et pèlerinages*, pp. 24–25.
52 Jean de Tournai, *Le récit des voyages et pèlerinages*, pp. 86–87.
53 Allan, *Post and Courier Service*, pp. 1–21; Caizzi, *Dalla posta dei Re alla posta di tutti*; Contamine, 'Introduction', esp. pp. 14–18; Doumerc, 'Par Dieu écrivez plus souvent!'; Infelise, 'From Merchants' Letters to Handwritten Political *Avvisi*'; Infelise, 'La circolazione dell'informazione commerciale'; and Kittler, 'Caught between Business, War and Politics'.
54 Blanchet-Broekaert, ed., *Le voyage de Jean de Tournai*, p. 61.

lettres, entre lesquelles j'en avois deux de grand recommandation: l'une adreschante a Pierrequin Sellenbien au banc des Mousquerons, laquelle je presentay audict Pierrequin, et fus fort bien recupt audict bancq et y fus logés tout autant comme je fus audict Romme.[55]

> (Friday morning the 11th of April after Easter, the divine year 1488, I arrived at the Campo de'Fiori with several letters, among which I had several with very important recommendations: one addressed to Pierrequin Sellenbien at the bank of the Mousquerons, which I presented to said Pierrequin. And I was very well received at said bank and I stayed there as long as I was in said Rome.)

Once he had arrived in Venice, another member of the *compaignie des Mousquerons* came to meet Jean de Tournai: 'Aprés me vint bienveigner Jehan Marchecler, natif de Tournay, adcause des lettres que j'avois raporté de Romme, car il estoit de la compaignie des Mousquerons' (And then Jehan Marchecler, born in Tournai, came to greet me because of the letters that I had brought with me from Rome, and he was of the *compaignie des Mousquerons*).[56] Jean de Tournai's business activities had apparently given him strong connections to the *compagnie* of the Mousquerons, and Jean made use of their facilities for travel, lodging, and communication. It is even possible that Jean used their bank for international money withdrawals, because it does not seem likely that he would have carried heavy and cumbersome cash with him for his expenses during his entire pilgrimage.

In a similar vein, Jehan de Zeilbeke recommended that his readers place approximately 900 *livres* in a commercial bank, in Bruges or elsewhere, five to six months before leaving on a pilgrimage, because it was safer to travel with letters of credit than with cash. The letters could be exchanged in Rome, Venice, or elsewhere.[57] In this manner, the financial services that were originally created for international business were also used by pilgrims.

---

55 Jean de Tournai, *Le récit des voyages et pèlerinages*, p. 42.
56 Jean de Tournai, *Le récit des voyages et pèlerinages*, p. 86. There must have been a community of merchants from northern Europe in Venice, which was linked to international merchants' networks: 'My estant audict Venize, touttes les festes et dimences allois disner et souper avec les marchantz de par deça, entre lesquelz Jan de Grove, serviteur a Cornille van Bomberg, Gautier de Bruges, messiere Raisot, serviteur de Piet Dick et a aultres, Jehan Sars dudict Bruges, Jehan Marchaller'. (During my stay in Venice, on feast days and on Sundays I had dinner with the merchants from the north, among whom Jan de Grove, servant to Cornille van Bomberg, Gautier de Bruges, *messire* Raisot, servant to Piet Dick and others, Jehan Sars from said Bruges, Jehan Marchaller). Jean de Tournai, *Le récit des voyages et pèlerinages*, pp. 103–04.
57 Desmarets, 'Jehan de Zeilbeke (1511)', p. 218.

As observed above, the pilgrims shared a significant amount of infrastructure with internationally operating merchants: roads, river barges, provisions for horses, and inns. The two worlds usually operated together unproblematically, but the situation could be quite different aboard seafaring ships. Apparently, many of these ships were used for pilgrimage and commerce simultaneously; the combination of both interests regularly caused conflicts, as can be inferred from Pierre Mesenge's description, recounting a case in point. On the return trip from the Holy Land, his ship remained in Corfu for four days:

> De ceste longue demeure les pelerins murmurent fort contre le patron pour quoy il fist lever les anchres ledit jour de samedi xxx^e et penultime jour dudit moys doctobres. Et si fismes voille environ huit heures de matin. Ce quil fist seullement pour contenter les pelerins car apres que nous eusmes nage deux lieus ou environ il fist regecter les anchres en la mer et demeurasmes la tout le jour et le lendemain qui fut dymenche derrenier jour dudit moys durant lequel temps on apporta en la nave plusieurs marchandises qui estoient demoureess derriere, de quoy se sourdit grant debat entre les pelerins et ledit patron.[58]

> (Because of this long stop the pilgrims protested strongly against the ship's master, leading him to have the anchors lifted on said day, Saturday, 30th day of said month of October, and we were under sail around eight in the morning. Which he only did to please the pilgrims, because after having sailed approximately two miles, he ordered the anchors be thrown out in the sea again and we stayed there all day and the following day, which was Sunday the last day of said month. During this time, they brought several pieces of merchandise that were left behind on the quay, and because of which a major dispute arose between the pilgrims and said ship's master.)

Due to the possible conflict between pilgrimage and commerce, Jehan de Zeilbeke gave the following revealing advice to future pilgrims on the last folios of his manuscript:

> Et le patron trompe les pelerins il lez mainent la ou il veulent pour lez marchans faire leur marchandise on dist que cest le naue dez pelerins mes che est mieulx le nauire des marchans dieu doint que vous peult bien aller.[59]

---

58 Amiens, Bibliothèque municipale, MS Lescalopier 99, fol. 94^v.
59 Douai, Bibliothèque municipale, MS 793, fol. 72^r; Desmarets, 'Jehan de Zeilbeke (1511)', p. 230.

(And the ships' masters cheat the pilgrims. They bring them where they want, so that the merchants can do their business. They say that it is the pilgrims' boat, but it is better to call it the merchants' boat. May God provide that you will travel well.)

Authoring a Pilgrim's Account and the Dissemination of Religious Knowledge

Late medieval pilgrims made use of internationally operating networks, both travel infrastructure and social networks, and in doing so, the pilgrims themselves and their accounts became a part of these networks as well. As discussed in this volume's introductory chapter about social network theory, one of the particularities of social networks is that they enable the transportation of objects, ideas, and — most importantly for my argument here — information, in this case religious knowledge. The texts of the pilgrims' accounts can be considered to be connected hubs in a transnationally operating information network, because they communicate to the readers information about pilgrimages to faraway places, about Christian morality and practices, and about sacred places.

Although the three pilgrim's accounts discussed here were never printed, the texts and their materiality show that they did actually find readers and that the information they contain was shared with wider audiences. Jehan de Zeilbeke's text only survives as an autograph manuscript, but he explicitly addressed future readers, most notably in the last part of his account, where he gives detailed advice on how to prepare for a pilgrimage and what to expect during the journey.[60] An inscription on the first folio of the manuscript also indicates that Jehan's account was intended for other readers: 'Memoire pour auertir touz pelerinz qui veullent aller a Rome pour prendre leur chemin comme nous lauez' (Account to advise all pilgrims who want to go to Rome to follow the same itinerary as we did).[61] Jean de Tournai's original text is now lost, but the single surviving manuscript reveals that it was copied at least once by a later scribe.[62] As indicated above, canon Pierre Mesenge's account was copied at least six times, which shows that it was disseminated relatively broadly. He, too, gives practical information to future pilgrims:

> Les choses qui leur estoient necessaires lesquelles jay voullu mettre par escript affin que ceulx qui vouldront faire ledit voyage soyent aduertiz

---

60 Desmarets, 'Jehan de Zeilbeke (1511)', pp. 217–30.
61 Douai, Bibliothèque municipale, MS 793, fol. 1ʳ.
62 Blanchet-Broekaert, ed., *Le voyage de Jean de Tournai*, pp. 29–30.

et instruictz de faire prouvsion de tout ce quil leur sera besoing tant en la mer que en la terre.[63]

> (The things that were necessary and that I wanted to put into writing so that those who would like to make said voyage will be informed and instructed to provision everything that they will need on sea and on land.)

Jehan de Zeilbeke and Jean de Tournai were both lay people who composed a religious text intended both for other lay people and for clerics. Their accounts were in part recorded while travelling, giving them a strong flavour of first-hand experience. Jehan de Zeilbeke gives the following comment on the gestation of his account: 'Et moy qui suy flamen et en faisant mon voyage le mis tout en flamen. Et moy aprez mon venue lay translate de flamen en franchoys qui mestoit paine et rompement de teste' (And me, being Flemish, noted everything during my pilgrimage in Flemish. And after my return I translated it from Flemish into French, which was very hard to do and gave me headaches).[64] Jean de Tournai tells his readers that he spent the endless days aboard the galley to the Holy Land occupied with drafting his account:

> Je m'en allois desjuner et puis je passoys le tampz à escripre au mieulx que je pooys, tout che que je veois pour ledict jour. En aprés nous alliesmes disner, aprés disner escripre, aussy dire mes heures, passer le tampz autour des gallios.[65]

> (I usually had breakfast and afterwards used my time to put into writing as well as I could everything that I saw during that day. Later we would have lunch, followed by writing, praying the Hours, and hanging out with the rowers.)

Jehan de Zeilbeke and Jean de Tournai were both laymen who were capable of drafting a book-length account of their pilgrimages. They must have carried paper, pen, and ink with them during their entire journey, allowing them to note their experiences as they travelled. The two laymen taking up their pens and writing about a religious subject promotes them to authoritative voices in these matters.

The transfer of religious knowledge through pilgrim's accounts to wider audiences operates at three different levels. First, the accounts communicate practical information about pilgrimages to their clerical and lay readers: knowledge of roads and itineraries, and advice on how to negotiate, how to prepare, what to expect, and what to avoid. By giving the readers an

---

63 Amiens, Bibliothèque municipale, MS Lescalopier 99, fol. 7ʳ.
64 Douai, Bibliothèque municipale, MS 793, fol. 65ᵛ.
65 Jean de Tournai, *Le récit des voyages et pèlerinages*, p. 117.

exciting narrative of a successful pilgrimage to the holy sites in Jerusalem, the readers were also incited to follow the author's example.

Secondly, the textual information given about holy places and religious practices — not only in Jerusalem, but also those encountered in Europe — provides the readers with first-hand knowledge about these places' material characteristics and religious importance, as well as religious practices. Jean de Tournai in particular gives detailed information about the relics and sacred sites he encountered during his journey: for instance, the relics of the Three Kings, the Thousand Virgins, and the head of Saint Ursula, and other relics in Cologne.[66] In Bologna he notes that the position of the priests in Italy during Mass is different from what he knew at home: with their faces turned towards the participants, instead of turning their backs to them.[67] Jean's descriptions of the seven major churches of Rome, their relics and indulgences, as well as other sacred sites and religious practices in that city, are particularly elaborate and very informative for the reader.[68]

Jean de Tournai experienced a spiritual transformation when he approached Rome:

> Je m'en vins disner à ladicte hostellerie et aprés mon repas prins, je vendis a mon hoste mes houseaux; et puis je prins ma bougette et mondict hoste m'alla querir ung baston. Et lors que je percupz ce baston, je me commencay ung peu a ratendrir, et adonc Jesu
> Crist quy jamais n'oublie ses serviteurs ne me laissa, et me vint en memoire qu'il estoit le jour de vendredy sainct; et comme Nostre Seigneur en cedict jour avoit pour nous reçut la mort et passion et qu'il estoit grande heure que je fasse penitence.[69]

> (I had lunch in my hotel and after my meal, I sold my riding boots to my host, and I took my pilgrim's bag and my host found a stick for me. When I saw the stick, I started to become a little emotional. And Jesus Christ, who never forgets his servants, did not leave me. I remembered that it was Good Friday and how our Lord on that day had received death and suffered the Passion, and that it was about time for me to do penance.)

Pierre Mesenge, although a canon, actually wrote a more factual account than the two lay pilgrims studied here, but he, too, informs his readers about the spiritual experience of his participation in a procession in Venice, before departing from there to the Holy Land:

---

66 Jean de Tournai, *Le récit des voyages et pèlerinages*, pp. 23–25.
67 Jean de Tournai, *Le récit des voyages et pèlerinages*, p. 37.
68 Jean de Tournai, *Le récit des voyages et pèlerinages*, pp. 46–83.
69 Jean de Tournai, *Le récit des voyages et pèlerinages*, p. 38. For spiritual transformation during pilgrimages, see: Locker, 'The Secret Language of Movement'.

A la quelle procession toutes les eglises de la ville tant de religion que parochialles assistent qui est la plus singuliere et magniffique chose que jaye jamais veue. Et ne croy point que en toute la crestiente se face procession si sollempnelle ne si deuote.[70]

> (In which procession all the city's churches participate, both those of convents and parishes, which is the most singular and magnificent thing that I have ever seen. And I do not think that in all Christianity there is another procession that is comparable in solemnity and devotion.)

By recounting the spiritual aspects of pilgrimages and their own participation in religious exercises, as well as the accounts of their confessions and prayers during their travels, the pilgrims depict themselves as exemplary men of virtue, inviting their readers to follow their examples, either by entering upon a pilgrimage or imitating them in devout behaviour.

A third function of the pilgrim's accounts is to provide the readers with enough vivid details so that they can perform a virtual pilgrimage by simply reading the text, or by listening to someone else reading aloud from the text.[71] First-hand knowledge of sacred sites in Jerusalem, Compostela, Rome, and sacred places encountered elsewhere in Europe, journeyed with the pilgrims through the international travel network to readers at home. Those who could not embark upon a real pilgrimage because of their situation, for instance because they were restrained by religious vows, a lack of sufficient funding, or the demands of family and business, could use a pilgrim's account as a starting point for a virtual pilgrimage, in which the descriptions would make the devotional exercises more vivid and would allow the reader to imagine himself or herself travelling with the narrator.

Conclusion

Medieval travel networks such as roads, rivers, and seafaring routes were important infrastructure which not only connected merchants and internationally operating companies, but also facilitated the movement of pilgrims. These travel resources, enabling the extraordinary mobility of medieval people, also allowed them to create social networks stretching over the whole European continent and even beyond. With the mobility of merchants and pilgrims, religious knowledge was transferred over equally large distances. Pilgrims and their accounts, such as the three late fifteenth-

---

70 Amiens, Bibliothèque municipale, MS Lescalopier 99, fol. 8ᵛ.
71 Beebe, *Pilgrim and Preacher*; on virtual pilgrimage, see pp. 178–201, but mainly described as a phenomenon that occurred in relation to the Observant movement and the increasing enclosure of nuns.

and early sixteenth-century texts studied here, were connected hubs in these social networks and, as a consequence, they were instrumental in the transfer of practical knowledge, and above all of religious knowledge and practices over thousands of kilometres. The pilgrims, both lay and religious, were on the move and connected human beings. They created an authoritative voice in the accounts of their pilgrimages. In their accounts, the authors shaped their own identities as humble, yet religiously exemplary pilgrims. At the same time, they directly influenced the circulation of religious knowledge among their lay and religious audiences, thus creating a community of readers of their own.

Works Cited

Manuscripts and Archival Sources

Amiens, Bibliothèque municipale, MS Lescalopier 98
———, MS Lescalopier 99
Bryn Mawr, College Library, MS 13
Douai, Bibliothèque municipale, MS 793
Paris, Bibliothèque nationale de France, MS fr. 5091
Private collection, location unknown
Rouen, Bibliothèque municipale, MS 1118
———, MS 1119
Valenciennes, Bibliothèque municipale, MS 493

Primary Sources

Blanchet-Broekaert, Fanny, ed., *Le voyage de Jean de Tournai. De Valenciennes à Rome, Jérusalem et Compostelle (1488–1489)* (Cahors: La Louve, 2012)
———, Transcription du manuscrit de Jean de Tournai <http://lodel.irevues.inist.fr/saintjacquesinfo/index.php?id=1566> [accessed 7 January 2022]
Hale, J. R., ed., *The Travel Journal of Antonio de Beatis: Germany, Switzerland, the Low Countries, France and Italy, 1517–1518* (London: The Hakluyt Society, 1979)
Jean de Tournai, *Le récit des voyages et pèlerinages, 1488–1489*, ed. by Béatrice Dansette and Marie-Adélaïde Nielen (Paris: CNRS Éditions, 2017)

Secondary Studies

Allan, John B., *Post and Courier Service in the Diplomacy of Early Modern Europe* (The Hague: Nijhoff, 1972)
Ash, Eric H., 'Navigation Techniques and Practice in the Renaissance', in *The History of Cartography*, III: *Cartography in the European Renaissance*, ed. by David Woodward (Chicago: University of Chicago Press, 2007), pp. 509–27
Balard, Michel, *La Méditerranée médiévale* (Paris: Picard, 2006) <10.3917/pica.balar.2006.01> [accessed 16 February 2023]
Baumgärtner, Ingrid, Debby Nirit Ben-Aryeh, Katrin Kogman-Appel, eds, *Maps and Travel in the Middle Ages and the Early Modern Period: Knowledge, Imagination, and Visual Culture* (Berlin: De Gruyter, 2019)
Bautier, Robert-Henri, 'Les foires de Champagne. Recherches sur une évolution historique', *La Foire: Recueils de la Société Jean Bodin*, 5 (1953), 97–147
———, *Sur l'histoire économique de la France médiévale: la route, le fleuve, la foire* (Aldershot: Variorum, 1991)

Beebe, Kathryne, *Pilgrim and Preacher: The Audiences and Observant Spirituality of Friar Felix Fabri (1437/8–1502)* (Oxford: Oxford University Press, 2014)

Berings, Geert, 'Transport and Communication in the Middle Ages', in *Kommunikation und Alltag in Spätmittelalter und früher Neuzeit*, ed. by Helmut Hundsbichler (Vienna: Österreichischen Akademie der Wissenschaften, 1992), pp. 47–73

Berlioz, Jacques, and Jacques Rossiaud, 'La route des merveilles. De Valenciennes en Avignon et de Lyon à Paris, à la fin du XIIIe siècle', *Le Monde alpin et rhodanien. Revue régionale d'ethnologie, Le Monde alpin et rhodanien*, 28.4 (2000), 7–52

Breuilly, John, 'Changes in the Political Uses of the Nation: Continuity or Discontinuity?', in *Power and the Nation in European History*, ed. by Len Scales and Olivier Zimmer (Cambridge: Cambridge University Press, 2009), pp. 67–101

Caizzi, Bruno, *Dalla posta dei Re alla posta di tutti: territoirio e comunicaioni in italia dal XVI secolo all'unita* (Milan: Franco Angeli 1993)

Carolus-Barré, Louis, 'Les XVII villes. Une hanse vouée au grand commerce de la draperie', *Comptes-rendus des séances de l'Académie des Inscriptions et Belles-Lettres*, 109.1 (1965), 20–30

Chareyron, Nicole, *Les pèlerins de Jérusalem au Moyen Âge. L'aventure du Saint Voyage d'après les journaux et mémoires* (Paris: Imago, 2000)

Chiesi, Benedetta, Beatrice Paolozzi, and Ilaria Ciresi, eds, *Il Medioevo in viaggio* (Florence: Giunti, 2015)

Contamine, Philippe, 'Introduction', in *La circulation des Nouvelles au Moyen Âge. XXIVe Congrès de la S.H.M.E.S. (Avignon, juin 1993)* (Rome: École française de Rome, 1994), pp. 9–24

Corbiau, Marie-Hélène, Baudouin Van den Abeele, and Jean-Marie Yante, eds, *La route au Moyen Âge. Réalités et représentations* (Turnhout: Brepols 2021)

Dagognet, François, ed., *Qu'est-ce qu'une route? Les cahiers de médiologie*, 2 (1996)

Debray, Régis, 'Rhapsodie sur la route', *Qu'est-ce qu'une route? Les cahiers de médiologie*, 2 (1996), 5–17

Derville, Alain, 'La première révolution des transports commerciaux (1000–1300)', *Les transports au Moyen Âge, Annales de Bretagne et des pays de l'Ouest*, 85.2 (1978), 181–207

Desmarets, Jean-Sébastien, 'Jehan de Zeilbeke (1511)', in *Récits de Pèlerins de Compostelle. Neuf pèlerins racontent leur voyage à Compostelle (1414–1531)*, ed. by Denise Péricard-Méa (Cahors: La Louve, 2011), pp. 193–230

Doumerc, Bernard, 'Par Dieu écrivez plus souvent! La lettre d'affaires à Venise à la fin du Moyen Âge', in *La circulation des Nouvelles au Moyen Âge. XXIVe Congrès de la S.H.M.E.S. (Avignon, juin 1993)* (Rome: École française de Rome, 1994), pp. 99–109

Flatman, Joe, *Ships and Shipping in Medieval Manuscripts* (London: British Library, 2009)

Gardiner Robert, and Richard W. Unger, eds, *Cogs, Caravels and Galleons* (London: Conway Maritime Press, 1994)

Gascon, Richard, *Grand commerce et vie urbaine au XVIe siècle. Lyon et ses marchands* (Paris: Mouton, 1971)

Geary, Patrick, *The Myth of Nations: The Medieval Origins of Europe* (Princeton: Princeton University Press, 2002)

Gelder, Maartje van, *Trading Places: The Netherlandish Merchants in Early Modern Venice* (Leiden: Brill, 2009)

Gelderblom, Oscar, *Cities of Commerce: The Institutional Foundations of International Trade in the Low Countries, 1250–1650* (Princeton: Princeton University Press, 2013)

Germain-De Franceschi, Anne-Sophie, *D'encre et de poussière: l'écriture du pèlerinage à l'épreuve de l'intimité du manuscrit. Récits manuscrits de pèlerinages rédigés en français pendant la renaissance et la contre-réforme, 1500–1620* (Paris: Champion, 2009)

Gertwagen, Ruthy, 'Nautical Technology', in *A Companion to Mediterranean History*, ed. by Peregrine Horden and Sharon Kinoshita (Chichester: Blackwell, 2014), pp. 154–69

Guillerme, André, 'Chemins, routes, autoroutes', *Qu'est-ce qu'une route? Cahiers de médiologie*, 2 (1996), 117–29

Herwaarden, Jan van, 'Late-Medieval Religion and Expression of Faith: Pilgrimages to Jerusalem and the Cult of the Passion and the Way of the Cross', in *Between Saint James and Erasmus: Studies in Late-Medieval Religious Life: Devotion and Pilgrimages in the Netherlands*, ed. by Jan van Herwaarden (Leiden: Brill, 2003), pp. 36–58

Hoogvliet, Margriet, 'Middle Dutch Religious Reading Cultures in Late Medieval France', *Queeste: Journal of Medieval Literature in the Low Countries*, 22 (2015), 29–46

——, '*Mez puy que je le enten, je suy conten*: French-Middle Dutch Bilingualism in the Towns of the Southern Low Countries and Northern France (c. 1400– c. 1550)', in *Mittelalterliche Stadtsprachen*, ed. by Maria Selig and Susanne Ehrich (Regensburg: Schnell & Steiner, 2016), pp. 43–59

Horden, Peregrine, and Nicholas Purcell, *The Corrupting Sea: A Study of Mediterranean History* (Oxford: Blackwell, 2000)

Hubert, Jean, 'Les routes du Moyen Âge', in *Les routes de France depuis les origines jusqu'à nos jours*, ed. by Guy Michaud (Paris: ADPF, 1959), pp. 25–49

Hunt, Edwin S., *Medieval Super-Companies: A Study of the Peruzzi Company of Florence* (Cambridge: Cambridge University Press, 1996)

Hutchinson, Gillian, *Medieval Ships and Shipping* (London: Leicester University Press, 1994)

Imberdis, F., 'Les routes médiévales: mythes et réalités historiques', *Annales d'Histoire Sociale*, 4 (1939), 411–16

Infelise, Mario, 'From Merchants' Letters to Handwritten Political *Avvisi*: Notes on the Origins of Public Information', in *Cultural Exchange in Early Modern Europe*, III: *Correspondence and Cultural Exchange in Europe, 1400–1700*, ed. by Francisco Bethencourt and Florike Egmond (Cambridge: Cambridge University Press, 2007), pp. 33–52

———, 'La circolazione dell'informazione commerciale', in *Il Rinascimento italiano e l'Europa*, IV: *Commerio e cultural mercantile*, ed. by Franco Franceschi, Richard A. Goldthwaite, and Reinhold C. Mueller (Treviso: Fondazione Cassamarca, 2007), pp. 499–522

Kahl, Hans-Dietrich, 'Einige Beobachtungen zum Sprachgebrauch von *natio* im mittelalterlichen Latein mit Ausblicken auf das neuhochdeutsschen Fremdwort "Nation"', in *Aspekte der Nationenbildung im Mittelalter. Ergebnisse der Marburger Rundgespräche 1972–1975*, ed. by Helmut Beumann and Werner Schröder (Sigmaringen: Thorbecke, 1978), pp. 63–108

Kittler, Juraj, 'Caught between Business, War and Politics: Late Medieval Roots of the Early Modern European News Networks', *Mediterranean Historical Review*, 33.2 (2018), 199–222

Lane, Frederic Chapin, *Venetian Ships and Shipbuilders of the Renaissance* (Baltimore: Johns Hopkins University Press, 1992)

Legassie, Shayne Aaron, *The Medieval Invention of Travel* (Chicago: University of Chicago Press, 2017)

Livet, Georges, *Histoire des routes et des transports en Europe. Des chemins de Saint-Jacques à l'âge d'or des diligences* (Strasbourg: Presses Universitaires, 2003)

Locker, Martin, 'The Secret Language of Movement: Interior Encounters with Space and Transition during Medieval Pilgrimage', in *Place and Space in the Medieval World*, ed. by Meg Boulton, Jane Hawkes, and Heidi Stoner (New York: Routledge, 2018), pp. 1–11

Lusignan, Serge, *Essai d'histoire sociolinguistique: le français picard au Moyen Âge* (Paris: Classiques Garnier, 2012)

McCormick, Michael, *Origins of the European Economy: Communications and Commerce, A.D. 300–900* (Cambridge: Cambridge University Press, 2001)

Munro, John H., 'Medieval Woollens: Textiles, Textile Technology and Industrial Organisation, c. 800–1500', in *The Cambridge History of Western Textiles*, ed. by David Jenkins (Cambridge: Cambridge University Press, 2003), pp. 181–227

Nelles, Paul, and Rosa Salzberg, eds, *Connected Mobilities in the Early Modern World: The Practice and Experience of Movement* (Amsterdam: Amsterdam University Press, 2023)

Parker, Charles H., 'Entrepreneurs, Families, and Companies', in *The Cambridge World History*, VI: *The Construction of a Global World, 1400–1800*, ed. by Jerry H. Bentley, Sanjay Subrahmanyam, and Merry Wiesner-Hanks (Cambridge: Cambridge University Press, 2015) pp. 190–212

Perol, Céline, 'Cheminement médiéval: l'homme, l'historien et la route', in *L'historien en quête d'espaces*, ed. by Jean-Luc Fray and Céline Perol (Clermont-Ferrand: Presses Universitaires Blaise Pascal, 2004), pp. 92–107

Pinto, Giuliano, *Economie urbane ed etica economica nell'Italia medievale* (Rome: Laterza, 2005)

Portela Silva, Ermelinda, *Historia de la ciudad de Santiago de Compostela* (Concello de Santiago: Universidade de Santiago de Compostela, 2003)

Pryor, John H., *Geography, Technology, and War: Studies in the Maritime History of the Mediterranean, 649–1571* (Cambridge: Cambridge University Press, 1988)

Pujades i Bataller, Ramón J., *Les cartes portolanes: la representació medieval d'una mar solcada* (Barcelona: Inst. Cartogràfic de Catalunya, 2007)

Rager, Cléo, 'Deux récits de pèlerinage du XVe siècle conservés à la Bibliothèque municipale de Lille', *Le carnet de recherches AGRELITA Project ERC Advanced Grant*, 6 February 2023, <https://agrelita.hypotheses.org/2606> [accessed 16 February 2023]

Reynolds, Susan, *Kingdoms and Communities in Western Europe, 900–1300* (Oxford: Clarendon Press, 1997)

Richard, Jean, *Les récits de voyages et de pèlerinages* (Brepols: Turnhout, 1981)

Roche, Daniel, *Humeurs vagabondes: de la circulation des hommes et de l'utilité des voyages* (Paris: Fayard, 2003)

Rubin, Miri, *Cities of Strangers: Making Lives in Medieval Europe* (Cambridge: Cambridge University Press, 2020)

Scales, Len, and Olivier Zimmer, 'Introduction', in *Power and the Nation in European History*, ed. by Len Scales and Olivier Zimmer (Cambridge: Cambridge University Press, 2009), pp. 1–29

Schaïk, Remi van, '"Wer weite Reisen macht…". Niederländische Palästinareisen und Palästinareiseberichte aus dem fünfzehnten Jahrhundert', in *Non Nova, sed Nove. Mélanges de civilisation médiévale dédiés à Willem Noomen*, ed. by Martin Gosman and Jaap van Os (Groningen: Bouma's Boekhuis, 1984), pp. 211–24

Schülz, Juergen, 'Ca' da Mosto', in *Medieval and Renaissance Venice*, ed. by Ellen E. Kittell and Thomas F. Madden (Urbana: University of Illinois Press, 1999)

Scott, Hamish, 'Travel and Communications', in *The Oxford Handbook of Early Modern European History, 1350–1750*, I: *Peoples and Place*, ed. by Hamish Scott (Oxford: Oxford University Press, 2015), pp. 165–86

Stopani, Renato, *La Via Francigena. Una strada europea nell'Italia del medioevo* (Florence: Le lettere, 1988)

Sutner, Philipp A., ed., *Landhandelsrouten: Adern des Waren- und Ideenaustauschs (500 v.–1500 n. Chr.)* (Vienna: Mandelbaum, 2022)

Szabó, Thomas, ed., *Die Welt der europäischen Strassen. Von der Antike bis in die Frühe Neuzeit* (Cologne: Böhlau, 2009)

Unger, Richard W., *The Ship in the Medieval Economy 600–1600* (London: Croom Helm Press, 1980)

——, 'Ships and Sailing Routes in Maritime Trade Around Europe, 1300–1600', in *The Routledge Handbook of Maritime Trade around Europe 1300–1600*, ed. by Wim Blockmans, M. M. Krom, and Justyna Wubs-Mrozewicz (Abingdon: Routledge, 2017), pp. 17–34

Villain-Gandossi, Christiane, 'La révolution nautique médiévale (XIIIe–XVe siècles)', in *The Sea in History. The Medieval World; La mer dans l'histoire. Le moyen âge*, ed. by Michel Balard (Woodbridge: Boydell, 2017), pp. 70–89
Webb, Diana, *Pilgrims and Pilgrimage in the Medieval West* (London: Tauris, 2001)
——, *Medieval European Pilgrimage, c. 700–c. 1500* (Basingstoke: Palgrave, 2002)
Wickham, Chris, *Framing the Early Middle Ages: Europe and the Mediterranean 400–800* (Oxford: Oxford University Press, 2005)
Yarrow, Simon, 'Pilgrimage', in *The Routledge History of Medieval Christianity: 1050–1500*, ed. by Robert N. Swanson (Abingdon: Routledge, 2015), pp. 159–71
Yeager, Suzanne M., 'Medieval Pilgrimage as Heterotopia: The Pilgrim as Maritime Adventurer and Aspiring Crusader in Saewulf's Relatio de situ Jerusalem', *Journal of Medieval and Early Modern Studies*, 50.2 (2020), 233–68

Online Resources

Digiberichte website:
https://digiberichte.de/travel/?ID=34&FID=347&N=F&suchen1=Jean%20de%20Tournay&Vollname=Jean_de_Tournay [accessed 16 February 2023]
Digiberichte website:
https://digiberichte.de/travel/?ID=41&FID=429&N=NL&suchen1=Jan%20Taccoen%20van%20Zillebeke&Vollname=Jan_Taccoen_van_Zillebeke [accessed 16 February 2023]
Digiberichte website:
https://digiberichte.de/travel/?ID=40&FID=367&N=F&suchen1=Pierre%20Mesenge&Vollname=Pierre_Mesenge [accessed 16 February 2023]